CHINA IN TRANSITION

CHINESE PUBLIC PENSIONS ANALYZED BY OLG MODELS

CHINA IN TRANSITION

Additional books in this series can be found on Nova's website under the Series tab.

Additional e-books in this series can be found on Nova's website under the e-book tab.

CHINA IN TRANSITION

CHINESE PUBLIC PENSIONS ANALYZED BY OLG MODELS

ZAIGUI YANG
China Institute for Actuarial Science,
Central University of Finance and Economics
Beijing, China

New York

Copyright © 2015 by Nova Science Publishers, Inc.

All rights reserved. No part of this book may be reproduced, stored in a retrieval system or transmitted in any form or by any means: electronic, electrostatic, magnetic, tape, mechanical photocopying, recording or otherwise without the written permission of the Publisher.

We have partnered with Copyright Clearance Center to make it easy for you to obtain permissions to reuse content from this publication. Simply navigate to this publication's page on Nova's website and locate the "Get Permission" button below the title description. This button is linked directly to the title's permission page on copyright.com. Alternatively, you can visit copyright.com and search by title, ISBN, or ISSN.

For further questions about using the service on copyright.com, please contact:
Copyright Clearance Center
Phone: +1-(978) 750-8400   Fax: +1-(978) 750-4470   E-mail: info@copyright.com.

NOTICE TO THE READER

The Publisher has taken reasonable care in the preparation of this book, but makes no expressed or implied warranty of any kind and assumes no responsibility for any errors or omissions. No liability is assumed for incidental or consequential damages in connection with or arising out of information contained in this book. The Publisher shall not be liable for any special, consequential, or exemplary damages resulting, in whole or in part, from the readers' use of, or reliance upon, this material. Any parts of this book based on government reports are so indicated and copyright is claimed for those parts to the extent applicable to compilations of such works.

Independent verification should be sought for any data, advice or recommendations contained in this book. In addition, no responsibility is assumed by the publisher for any injury and/or damage to persons or property arising from any methods, products, instructions, ideas or otherwise contained in this publication.

This publication is designed to provide accurate and authoritative information with regard to the subject matter covered herein. It is sold with the clear understanding that the Publisher is not engaged in rendering legal or any other professional services. If legal or any other expert assistance is required, the services of a competent person should be sought. FROM A DECLARATION OF PARTICIPANTS JOINTLY ADOPTED BY A COMMITTEE OF THE AMERICAN BAR ASSOCIATION AND A COMMITTEE OF PUBLISHERS.

Additional color graphics may be available in the e-book version of this book.

Library of Congress Cataloging-in-Publication Data

Chinese public pensions analyzed by OLG models / editor, Zaigui Yang.
    pages cm. -- (China in transition)
 Includes index.
 ISBN 978-1-63463-979-8 (hardcover)
 1. Pensions--China. 2. Retirement income--Government policy--China. I. Yang, Zaigui.
 HD7230.C466 2015
 331.25'20951--dc23
 2014050111

Published by Nova Science Publishers, Inc. † New York

Contents

Preface		vii
Acknowledgments		xi
I. Urban Pension, Exogenous Model, Contribution Rate		1
Chapter 1	Basic OLG Model for Urban Public Pension	3
Chapter 2	Lifetime Uncertainty and Urban Pension Contribution Rates	19
Chapter 3	Altruistic Motives, Life Expectancy and Urban Public Pension	31
II. Urban Pension, Endogenous Growth Model		43
Chapter 4	Urban Public Pension, Human Capital and Endogenous Growth	45
Chapter 5	Urban Public Pension, Exogenous Fertility and Endogenous Growth	57
Chapter 6	Urban Public Pension, Endogenous Fertility and Economic Growth	67
III. Urban Pension, Exogenous Model, Replacement Rate		79
Chapter 7	Optimal Replacement Rate of Urban Pension under Population Aging	81
Chapter 8	Altruistic Motives, Life Expectancy and Urban Pension Replacement Rates	95
IV. Rural Pension, Exogenous Model		109
Chapter 9	Basic OLG Model for Rural Public Pension	111
Chapter 10	Gift Motive and Rural Public Pension	127
V. Rural Pension, Endogenous Growth Model		139
Chapter 11	Rural Public Pension, Human Capital and Endogenous Growth	141
Chapter 12	Rural Public Pension, Uncertain Lifetime and Endogenous Growth	155

VI. Extensive Discussions on Public Pension in China — 167

Chapter 13   Urban Public Pension with Capital Taxation   169

Chapter 14   Urban Public Pension, VAT and Endogenous Growth   179

Chapter 15   Fertility Linked Pension Systems and Endogenous Growth   191

References   205

Index   209

PREFACE

China has been reforming its public pension system since the middle of 1980s. The Chinese State Council published a series of documents regarding the urban public pension system: the *Decision on Reform of Pension System for Enterprise Employees* (State Council Document 33 in 1991), *Circular on Deepening the Reform of Pension System for Enterprise Employees* (State Council Document 6 in 1995), *Decision on Establishing a Unified Basic Pension System for Enterprise Employees* (State Council Document 26 in 1997), *Decision on Improving the Basic Pension System for Enterprise Employees* (State Council Document 38 in 2005), and *Decision on Reform of Pension System for Government and Public Institution Employees* (State Council Document 2 in 2015). The last one was published in January 2015.

The regulations of the State Council Document 2 in 2015 are almost the same as that of the State Council Document 38 in 2005. It is called system combination, the Pension System for Government and Public Institution Employees has been merged into the Pension System for Enterprise Employees. The former covered 39 million participants and the later 412 million participants in January 2015. Thereby, the Pension System for Enterprise Employees can represent the urban public pension system.

Regarding the rural public pension system, the central government published the *Guidelines on New-Type Rural Public Pension Trials* (State Council Document 32 in 2009), and *Opinions on Establishing Unified Basic Pension System for Urban and Rural Residents* (State Council Document 8 in 2014). By the State Council Document 8 in 2014, the public pension for non-employed urban residents was merged into the new-type rural public pension. The former covered 23 million participants and the later 460 million by the end of 2012. Obviously, the coverage and influence of the later is far greater than that of the former. Furthermore, to solve the existing problems in the rural public pension system are of great importance for rural and non-employed urban residents. Hence regarding the rural and non-employed urban residents, this book still focuses on the rural public pension.

China promulgated its first Social Insurance Law in October 2010. The Chinese State Council also published the Guidelines on Developing Public Pension for Non-Employed Urban Residents Trials (State Council Document 18 in 2011) in June 2011, which as mentioned above was merged into the new-type rural public pension system. Among the important documents mentioned above, the State Council Documents 26 in 1997, State Council Document 38 in 2005, and State Council Document 8 in 2014 are three milestones in the road of Chinese public pension system development.

By employing exogenous and endogenous growth overlapping generations (OLG) models, this book investigates the urban and rural public pension systems in China, respectively. It is composed of three blocks. Block one, including three parts, analyzes the urban public pension system. Block two, including two parts, explores the rural public pension system. Block three, including one part, discusses some possible public pension systems.

Part one uses exogenous OLG model to examine contribution rate in the urban public pension system, which is made up three chapters. Chapter 1 introduces a basic exogenous OLG model for the urban public pension system to examine the effects of the pension policy variables. Chapters 2 – 3 expand the analysis framework by introducing lifetime uncertainty and bequest motive into the exogenous OLG model, respectively.

Part two examines the urban public pension system by employing endogenous growth OLG model, which is also made up three chapters. Chapter 4 develops an endogenous growth model fitting for the public pension system for urban enterprise employees. Chapter 5 assumes that fertility is exogenous variable because the viewpoint, the Chinese special population policy make individuals cannot choose their number of children, is comparatively strong. Chapter 6 adopts the correct assumption that individuals can choose their number of children, and utilizes the principle that physical capital must receive the same rate of return when allocated to either sector of production.

Part three uses exogenous OLG model to examine replacement rate in the urban public pension system, which is made up two chapters. Chapter 7 employs a model with uncertain lifetime to examine the effects of the benefit replacement rates, life expectancy and population growth rate on the capital-labor ratio, pension benefits, etc, and looks for the optimal social pool benefit replacement rate. Introducing altruistic motives into the last chapter's OLG model, Chapter 8 examines the effects of the individual account benefit replacement rate and social pool benefit replacement rate in the urban public pension system.

Part four examines the rural public pension system by utilizing exogenous OLG model, which is composed of two chapters. Chapter 9 develops a basic exogenous OLG model for the rural public pension system, and Chapter 10 introduces gift motive into the basic model to examine the effects of the policy variables.

Part five examines the rural public pension system by employing endogenous growth OLG model, which is made up two chapters. Taking human capital into account, Chapter 11 examines the effect of the rural public pension system on economic growth and population size. Introducing uncertain lifetime, Chapter 12 examines the effects of the life expectancy, individual contribution rate, village subsidy rate, local government allowance rate and basic benefit rate on the labor income growth rate, population growth rate, etc.

Part six discusses possibilities of some other public pension systems. Pension revenue in general relies on labor income taxation. Is it possible to collect pension revenue with capital income taxation? It will be explored in Chapter 13. We discuss a public pension system financed by value added tax in Chapter 14. And finally, we investigate fertility linked public pension systems for developing and developed countries in Chapter 15. Some chapters are revised versions of the papers published in journals such as Insurance Mathematics and Economics, Optimization, Asia-Pacific Journal of Risk and Insurance, and so on.

This book has the following distinctive features. Firstly, instead of pay-as-you-go or fully funded public pension systems, this book uses OLG models to examine the Chinese partially funded systems combined social pool account and individual accounts. Each chapter includes the author's original research. Secondly, it investigates the public pension systems in a way of following proper sequence and making steady progress. Such a way is convenient for readers to deepen their understanding and recognition in analyses on the Chinese public pension systems with OLG model.

The book fits for scholars outside China who are interested in the Chinese public pension systems, researchers of China who want to investigate the Chinese public pension systems with OLG model and hope to write papers in English, doctorial students, master degree students and senior undergraduate students. Firstly, this book can help scholars outside China to promote their research on the Chinese public pension systems. Secondly, it had been prevailing for economists in developed countries to study public pension systems by employing OLG model since 1970s. But the model is still strange for most Chinese scholars. This book can help them to utilize the model, describe their research in English and express in comparative normal presentation. Thirdly, this book can provide references for doctorial students, master degree students and senior undergraduate students to learn how to use OLG models to study Chinese public pensions.

Finally, it can open a door to the world outside China, show the state of research on public pension systems with OLG mode in China, and promote exchange and talk for the Chinese and foreign academic circles.

Zaigui Yang
China Institute for Actuarial Science,
Central University of Finance and Economics
Beijing, China
January 2015
yangzaigui@hotmail.com

ACKNOWLEDGMENTS

Financial support from the Program for New Century Excellent Talents in Universities of China Ministry of Education (NCET-11-0755) and the Beijing Philosophy and Social Science Programming Project (11JGB089) is gratefully acknowledged.

I. Urban Pension, Exogenous Model, Contribution Rate

Chapter 1

BASIC OLG MODEL FOR URBAN PUBLIC PENSION[1]

ABSTRACT

The Chinese economic growth rate was not lower than 10% from 2003 to 2007, the inflation rate was high, the total investment in fixed assets over-fast and the economy was so called over-warm. Under these circumstance, this chapter employs an OLG model to investigate the urban public pension system in China. We examine the effects of the pension contribution rates and population growth rate on the capital-labor ratio, social pool benefits, individual account principal, consumption and utility, and seek the optimal firm contribution rate. Raising the individual contribution rate only increases the individual account principal. Raising the firm contribution rate increases the social pool benefits, whereas decreases the capital-labor ratio, individual account principal, working-period consumption, retirement-period consumption and utility. A fall in the population growth rate increases the capital-labor ratio, individual account principal, working-period consumption and utility, whereas decreases the social pool benefits and retirement-period consumption. The optimal firm contribution rate falls with the population growth rate. It will do more good than harm to raise the individual contribution rate, reduce the firm contribution rate and control the population growth rate.

Keywords: urban public pension; firm contribution rate; overlapping generations model

1. INTRODUCTION

China reformed its public pension system for urban enterprise employees, which represents the urban public pension system, by publishing the *State Council Decision on Establishing a Unified Basic Pension System for Enterprise Employees* (Chinese State Council Document 26 in 1997). The central government published the *State Council Decision on Improving the Basic Pension System for Enterprise Employees* (Chinese State Council Document 38 in 2005) to improve the public pension system. The government establishes an individual account for each employee and a social pool for all employees and retirees. Each firm contributes 20% of its payroll to the social pool, while each employee contributes 8% of

---

[1] This chapter is the original version of the paper, Optimal Contribution Rate of Public Pension in China within an OLG Model, published in International Journal of Sociology Study, Vol. 2 Issue 1, 2014: 26-32.

her/his wage to her/his individual account. The social pool fund is used to pay the retirees in current period as pay-as-you-go (PAYG) pension benefits, while the accumulation in an individual account is used to pay the individual herself/himself when she/he retires in the next period as fully funded pension benefits. Each retiree receives funded pension benefits from her/his individual account and PAYG pension benefits from the social pool. Such a public pension system is called a partially funded pension system.

A main goal of the Chinese State Council Document 38 in 2005 is to make the individual accounts have full real assets and pull off the social pool balance between revenue and payment. In the last fifteen years, the social pool overdrew the individual accounts because the former was short of paying PAYG pension benefits. Hence, the individual accounts had not full real asset accumulation as designed. Obviously, the new public pension system has not only effect on the social pool and individual accounts, but also on investment and consumption. In most years from the beginning of Chinese reform and opening door policy to the beginning of international financial crisis, China's investment in fixed assets was over-fast. In the first ten years of this century, the Chinese economy grew very rapid. Particularly from 2003 to 2007, the economic growth rate was not lower than 10%, the inflation rate was also high, the total investment in fixed assets in the whole country was over-fast and the economy was so called over-warm.

In addition, the population growth rate has been falling because mainly of the Chinese special population policy. The government in general requires each couple to give birth not more than one time. In some special cases, a couple was eligible to give birth to two or more children. The social pool in urban public pension belongs to intergenerational transfers with PAYG type. Thus, a fall in the population growth rate must have effect on the pension contribution rate to the social pool, which is the firm contribution rate.

The above effects can be examined by overlapping generations (OLG) model. Some of the literature investigating public pension with OLG model studied PAYG pension system (e.g., Pecchenino and Pollard, 2002; Groezen et al., 2003). Some studies analyzed fully funded pension system (e.g., Abel, 1987a). Some investigated both PAYG and fully funded pension systems (e.g., Altig and Davis, 1993; Zhang et al., 2001). This chapter will explore China's partially funded public pension system. Samuelson (1975) studied the optimum social security in a life-cycle growth model. It is possible to adjust the capital-labor ratio to the modified golden rule level to maximize social welfare by controlling the social security taxes. The approach to find the optimal social security taxes is to equate the rate of interest to the growth rate of economy in a decentralized economy without considering technological progress. Blanchard and Fischer (1989) elaborated the principle of social optimum. That is, a social planner maximizes social welfare by rationally allocating social resources.

This chapter employs Blanchard and Fischer's (1989) OLG model, but using specialized utility and production functions, to investigate the partially funded public pension in China. We examine the effects of the pension contribution rates and population growth rate on the capital-labor ratio, social pool benefits, individual account principal, consumption and utility, and look for the optimal firm contribution rate. It is interesting to find that raising the firm contribution rate increases the social pool benefits, whereas decreases the consumption of retirees, and the optimal firm contribution rate should decrease rationally with the population growth rate. In the above literature, pensions are financed only by wage taxes. However, in most of the countries that have public pension systems, the governments levy pension taxes

2. THE MODEL

This model introduces a partially funded public pension system to replace that in Blanchard and Fischer (1989). A closed economy is composed of numerous individuals and firms, and a government. The generation born at the beginning of period t is called generation t. The population grows at the rate of $n = (N_t/N_{t-1}) - 1$, where N_t is the population size of generation t.

2.1. Individuals

Individuals live for two periods: working period and retirement period. Each individual earns wage by supplying inelastically one unit of labor, makes pension contributions, consumes part of her or his income, and saves the remainder of the income during her or his working period. In the retirement period, she or he consumes her or his savings with accrued interest, funded pension benefits and PAYG pension benefits.

Each individual derives utility from the working-period consumption c_{1t} and retirement-period consumption c_{2t+1}. The utility is described by an additively separable logarithmic function. Note that the logarithmic utility function guarantees interior solutions for life-cycle consumption[2]. By choosing consumption and savings, each individual maximizes the utility:

$$\max_{\{c_{1t}, c_{2t+1}, s_t\}} U_t = \ln c_{1t} + \theta \ln c_{2t+1}, \tag{1}$$

s.t.
$$c_{1t} = (1-\tau)w_t - s_t, \tag{2}$$

$$c_{2t+1} = (1 + r_{t+1})s_t + (1 + r_{t+1})I_t + P_{t+1}, \tag{3}$$

where $\theta \in (0,1)$ denotes the individual discount factor, w_t the wage, τ the individual contribution rate, s_t the savings, r_{t+1} the interest rate, I_t the individual account principal per worker, and P_{t+1} PAYG pension benefits.

---

[2] There is no borrowing in the model. China is only able to provide a basic public pension. It is impossible to implement very high individual pension contributions. Hence, any nonnegativity constraint on private savings will not be binding. Abel (1987b, footnote 13), Wigger (1999, endnote 8) and Zhang et al. (2001, p.489) gave analogous explanations.

Substituting equations (2) and (3) into equation (1), and letting the partial derivative of equation (1) with respect to s_t be zero gives the first-order condition for the utility maximization:

$$-c_{2t+1} + \theta(1+r_{t+1})c_{1t} = 0. \qquad (4)$$

This familiar expression implies that the utility loss from reducing one unit of working-period consumption is equal to the utility gain from increasing $(1+r_{t+1})$ units of retirement-period consumption.

2.2. Firms

Firms produce a homogenous commodity in competitive markets. The production is described by Cobb-Douglas function $Y_t = AK_t^\alpha N_t^{1-\alpha}$ or $y_t = Ak_t^\alpha$, where Y_t denotes the output in period t, K_t the capital stock, $\alpha \in (0,1)$ the capital share of income, A the productivity, $k_t = K_t/N_t$ the capital-labor ratio, and y_t the output-labor ratio.

Firms make pension contributions at the rate of $\eta \in (0,1)$ on their payroll. According to the product distribution, one can get that $AK_t^\alpha N_t^{1-\alpha} = r_t K_t + (1+\eta)w_t N_t$. Firms act competitively, renting capital to the point where the marginal product of capital is equal to its rental rate, and hiring labor to the point where the marginal product of labor is equal to $(1+\eta)w_t$:

$$r_t = \alpha A k_t^{\alpha-1}, \qquad (5)$$

$$w_t = \frac{(1-\alpha)Ak_t^\alpha}{1+\eta}. \qquad (6)$$

2.3. The Government

The social pool fund is used to pay the retirees in current period as PAYG pension benefits: $P_t N_{t-1} = \eta w_t N_t$, or

$$P_t = (1+n)\eta w_t. \qquad (7)$$

The accumulation in an individual account is used to pay the individual when she or he retires in the next period as funded pension benefits: $(1+r_{t+1})\tau w_t = (1+r_{t+1})I_t$, or

$$I_t = \tau w_t. \tag{8}$$

2.4. Dynamic Equilibrium

The savings and individual account principal of workers in period t generate the capital stock in period $t + 1$[3]:

$$s_t + I_t = (1+n)k_{t+1}. \tag{9}$$

Given the initial condition k_0 and the values of parameters τ and η, a competitive equilibrium for the economy is a sequence as $\{c_{1t}, c_{2t+1}, w_t, r_{t+1}, s_t, I_t, P_t, k_{t+1}\}_{t=0}^{\infty}$ that satisfies equations (1) - (9) for all t.

Substituting equations (2), (3) and (5) - (9) into equation (4) gives a dynamic equilibrium system described by the following difference equation:

$$-(1+n)\left[k_{t+1}\left(1+\alpha A k_{t+1}^{\alpha-1}\right)+\frac{\eta}{1+\eta}(1-\alpha)A k_{t+1}^{\alpha}\right]$$
$$+\theta\left(1+\alpha A k_{t+1}^{\alpha-1}\right)\left(\frac{1}{1+\eta}(1-\alpha)A k_t^{\alpha}-(1+n)k_{t+1}\right)=0 \tag{10}$$

Assume that there is unique, stable and nonoscillatory steady state equilibrium (see, e.g., Blanchard and Fischer, 1989, p. 96). In order to find the stability condition, we linearize the dynamic system around the steady state (k). Some manipulation gives

$$i(k_{t+1}-k)+j(k_t-k)=0, \tag{11}$$

where

$$i = -(1+\theta)(1+n)(1+\alpha^2 A k^{\alpha-1})-(1+n)\frac{\eta}{1+\eta}\alpha(1-\alpha)Ak^{\alpha-1}-\frac{\theta\alpha}{1+\eta}(1-\alpha)^2 A^2 k^{2\alpha-2},$$

$$j = \theta(1+\alpha A k^{\alpha-1})\frac{1}{1+\eta}\alpha(1-\alpha)Ak^{\alpha-1} > 0$$

---

[3] See Blanchard and Fischer (1989, p.94) or Barro and Sala-I-Martin (2004, p.193) for details.

The assumption that the equilibrium is unique, stable and nonoscillatory is equivalent to $0 < \frac{k_{t+1}-k}{k_t - k} = -\frac{j}{i} < 1$. Therefore, the stability condition is

$$i + j < 0.$$

3. COMPARATIVE STATICS

Totally differentiating equation (10) around the steady state gives

$$(i+j)dk + md\eta + \beta dn = 0, \qquad (12)$$

where

$$m = -\frac{1-\alpha}{(1+\eta)^2} Ak^\alpha \left[(1+n) + \theta(1+\alpha Ak^{\alpha-1})\right] < 0,$$

$$\beta = -(1+\theta)k(1+\alpha Ak^{\alpha-1}) - \frac{\eta}{1+\eta}(1-\alpha)Ak^\alpha < 0.$$

3.1. Effect of Individual Contribution Rate

Using equation (12) gives

$$\frac{\partial k}{\partial \tau} = 0.$$

In the steady state, the PAYG pension benefits, individual account principal, working-period consumption and retirement-period consumption can be written as

$$P = (1+n)\frac{\eta}{1+\eta}(1-\alpha)Ak^\alpha, \qquad (13)$$

$$I = \frac{\tau}{1+\eta}(1-\alpha)Ak^\alpha, \qquad (14)$$

$$c_1 = \frac{1}{1+\eta}(1-\alpha)Ak^\alpha - (1+n)k, \qquad (15)$$

$$c_2 = (1+n)\left(k(1+\alpha Ak^{\alpha-1}) + \eta\frac{1-\alpha}{1+\eta}Ak^\alpha\right). \qquad (16)$$

Differentiating P, I, c_1, c_2 and U with respect to τ gives

$$\frac{\partial P}{\partial \tau} = 0,$$

$$\frac{\partial I}{\partial \tau} = \frac{1}{1+\eta}(1-\alpha)Ak^\alpha > 0,$$

$$\frac{\partial c_1}{\partial \tau} = 0,$$

$$\frac{\partial c_2}{\partial \tau} = 0,$$

$$\frac{\partial U}{\partial \tau} = 0.$$

Raising the individual contribution rate induces the increase in the individual account principal, while it has no effect on the capital-labor ratio, social pool benefits, working-period consumption, retirement-period consumption and utility.

From equation (14), one can get that raising the individual contribution rate increases the individual account principal. Because the individual savings are crowded out by one-for-one when the individual account principal (the mandatory savings) increases, the individual contribution rate has no effect on the capital-labor ratio, furthermore, no effect on the social pool benefits by virtue of equation (13). Similarly, it has no effect on the working-period consumption, retirement-period consumption and utility.

3.2. Effect of Firm Contribution Rate

Using equation (12) gives

$$\frac{\partial k}{\partial \eta} = -\frac{m}{i+j} < 0.$$

Differentiating P, I, c_1, c_2 and U with respect to η gives

$$\frac{\partial P}{\partial \eta} = \frac{(1+n)(1-\alpha)Ak^\alpha}{-(i+j)(1+\eta)^2}\left[\begin{array}{c}(1+\theta)(1+n)(1+\alpha^2 Ak^{\alpha-1}) \\ +\theta\alpha(1-\alpha)Ak^{\alpha-1}\left(\dfrac{1-\alpha}{1+\eta}Ak^{\alpha-1}-(1+\alpha Ak^{\alpha-1})\right)\end{array}\right] > 0$$

if $\dfrac{1-\alpha}{1+\eta}Ak^{\alpha-1} > (1+\alpha Ak^{\alpha-1})$ or $w > (1+r)k$,

$$\frac{\partial I}{\partial \eta} = \tau\frac{(1-\alpha)Ak^\alpha}{(i+j)(1+\eta)^2}\left[\begin{array}{c}(1+\theta)(1+n)(1+\alpha^2 Ak^{\alpha-1}) \\ +\dfrac{(1-\alpha)^2}{1+\eta}A^2 k^{2\alpha-2}\theta\alpha + (1+n)\alpha(1-\alpha)Ak^{\alpha-1}\end{array}\right] < 0,$$

$$\frac{\partial c_1}{\partial \eta} = \frac{-(1-\alpha)Ak^\alpha}{(i+j)(1+\eta)^2}\left[(1+n)(n-\alpha Ak^{\alpha-1}) + \theta\alpha(1-\alpha)Ak^{\alpha-1}\left(1+n-\frac{1-\alpha}{1+\eta}Ak^{\alpha-1}\right)\right] < 0$$

if $r > n$ and $w > (1+r)k$,

$$\frac{\partial c_2}{\partial \eta} = \frac{(1+n)(1-\alpha)Ak^\alpha}{-(i+j)(1+\eta)^2}\left[\begin{array}{c}\theta(n-\alpha Ak^{\alpha-1})(1+\alpha^2 Ak^{\alpha-1}) \\ +\theta\alpha(1-\alpha)Ak^{\alpha-1}\left(\dfrac{1-\alpha}{1+\eta}Ak^{\alpha-1}-(1+\alpha Ak^{\alpha-1})\right)\end{array}\right] > 0$$

if $r < n$ and $w > (1+r)k$,

$$\frac{\partial U}{\partial \eta} = \frac{n-\alpha Ak^{\alpha-1}}{-(i+j)}\frac{(1-\alpha)Ak^\alpha}{(1+\eta)^2 c_1}\left[(1+n)\left(1+\theta\frac{1+\alpha^2 Ak^{\alpha-1}}{1+\alpha Ak^{\alpha-1}}\right) + \theta\alpha\frac{(1-\alpha)Ak^{\alpha-1}}{1+\alpha Ak^{\alpha-1}}\frac{1-\alpha}{1+\eta}Ak^{\alpha-1}\right],$$

$\dfrac{\partial U}{\partial \eta} < 0$ if $r > n$, $\dfrac{\partial U}{\partial \eta} > 0$ if $r < n$.

  Raising the firm contribution rate decreases the capital-labor ratio and individual account principal, increases the social pool benefits if the wage is more than the capital-labor ratio with accrued interest, decreases the working-period consumption if the interest rate is higher than the population growth rate and the wage is more than the capital-labor ratio with accrued interest, increases the retirement-period consumption if the interest rate is lower than the population growth rate and the wage is more than the capital-labor ratio with accrued interest, decreases the utility if the interest rate is higher than the population growth rate and vice versa.

  A rise in the firm contribution rate decreases the wage, further decreases the savings and individual account principal, hence the capital-labor ratio falls. A rise in the firm contribution rate directly increases the social pool benefits; while it decreases the wage, which indirectly decreases the social pool benefits. The former dominates the later and increases the social pool benefits if the wage is more than the capital-labor ratio with accrued interest. The working-period consumption decreases because the wage and capital-labor ratio fall. A fall in the capital-labor ratio increases the interest rate, together with the rise in the social pool benefits increases the retirement-period consumption if the interest rate is lower than the population growth rate. The utility decreases since the working-period consumption falls when the interest rate is higher than the population growth rate, and increases since the retirement-period consumption rises when the interest rate is lower than the population growth rate.

3.3. Effect of Population Growth Rate

Using equation (12) gives

$$\frac{\partial k}{\partial n} = -\frac{\beta}{i+j} < 0.$$

Differentiating P, I, c_1, c_2 and U with respect to n gives

$$\frac{\partial P}{\partial n} = \frac{\eta(1-\alpha)Ak^\alpha}{-(i+j)(1+\eta)}\left\{(1+n)(1+\theta)(1-\alpha)+\theta\frac{1-\alpha}{1+\eta}\alpha Ak^{\alpha-1}\left[(1-\alpha)Ak^{\alpha-1}-(1+\alpha Ak^{\alpha-1})\right]\right\} > 0$$

if $w > (1+r)k$,

$$\frac{\partial I}{\partial n} = \tau\frac{1-\alpha}{1+\eta}\alpha Ak^{\alpha-1}\frac{\partial k}{\partial n} < 0,$$

$$\frac{\partial c_1}{\partial n} = \frac{-(1-\alpha)Ak^\alpha}{(i+j)(1+\eta)}\left[(1-\alpha)\eta(1+n)-\alpha(1+\alpha Ak^{\alpha-1})-\alpha(1-\alpha)\left(\theta+\frac{\eta}{1+\eta}\right)Ak^{\alpha-1}\right] < 0,^{4}$$

$$\frac{\partial c_2}{\partial n} = \frac{\theta}{i+j}\frac{1-\alpha}{1+\eta}Ak^\alpha\left\{\begin{array}{l}\alpha\left[(1+\alpha Ak^{\alpha-1})-(1-\alpha)Ak^{\alpha-1}\right]\cdot\left[(1+\alpha Ak^{\alpha-1})+\eta\frac{1-\alpha}{1+\eta}Ak^{\alpha-1}\right]\\ -\eta(1+n)(1-\alpha)\end{array}\right\} > 0$$

if $w > (1+r)k$,

$$\frac{\partial U}{\partial n} = \frac{-\theta(1-\alpha)Ak^\alpha}{c_2(i+j)(1+\eta)}\left\{\begin{array}{l}\eta(1-\alpha)(1+n)(1+\theta+\alpha Ak^{\alpha-1})-\alpha(1+\theta)(1+\alpha Ak^{\alpha-1})^2\\ -\alpha\eta\frac{1-\alpha}{1+\eta}Ak^{\alpha-1}\left[(1+\theta)(1+\alpha Ak^{\alpha-1})-\theta(1-\alpha)Ak^{\alpha-1}\right]\end{array}\right\} < 0.^{5}$$

A fall in the population growth rate increases the capital-labor ratio, individual account principal, working-period consumption and utility; decreases the social pool benefits and

---

[4] $\alpha, \eta \in (0,1)$, hence $(1-\alpha)\eta(1+n)$ is in the magnitude of 10^{-2}, $\alpha(1+\alpha Ak^{\alpha-1}) = \alpha(1+r)$ higher than the magnitude.
[5] $\alpha, \eta, \theta \in (0,1)$, hence $\eta(1-\alpha)(1+n)(1+\theta+\alpha Ak^{\alpha-1})$ is in the magnitude of 10^{-2}, $\alpha(1+\theta)(1+\alpha Ak^{\alpha-1})^2$ higher than the magnitude. Analogously, the magnitude of $(1+\theta)(1+\alpha Ak^{\alpha-1})$ is higher than that of $\theta(1-\alpha)Ak^{\alpha-1}$.

retirement-period consumption if the wage is more than the capital-labor ratio with accrued interest.

A fall in the population growth rate increases the density of capital, which increases the wage and further the individual account principal. The working-period consumption increases since the effects of the rise in the wage and the fall in the population growth rate dominate that of the rise in the capital-labor ratio. The social pool benefits decrease because the effect of the fall in the population growth rate dominates that of the rise in the wage if the wage is more than the capital-labor ratio with accrued interest. Under the same condition, the retirement-period consumption decreases since the effects of the falls in the population growth rate and social pool benefits dominate that of the rise in the capital-labor ratio. The utility increases because the effect of the rise in the working-period consumption dominates that of the fall in the retirement-period consumption.

4. NUMERICAL EXPERIMENT

About half effects of the firm contribution rate and population growth rate depend on certain conditions. The effects are ambiguous if the conditions are not satisfied. Hence, we check the effects by simulations below.

4.1. Parameter Calibration

Assume that the individual discount factor per year is 0.98, which is similar to that found by Auerbach and Kotlikoff (1987) and used by Pecchenino and Pollard (2002). Hence, the individual discount factor per period (26 years[6]) is $\theta = 0.98^{26}$.

There are several calibers for population statistics in China. Since the public pension system for urban enterprise employees is different from that for rural residents, and only the former is studied in this chapter, so the caliber of "Urban Population" is selected. The population growth rate in the period from 1978 to 2004 is computed to be $n \approx 2.148$ according to the "Population and Its Composition" in China Statistical Yearbook.

The capital share of income is usually to be estimated as 0.3 in developed countries (e.g., Zhang et al., 2001; Pecchenino and Pollard, 2002). The labor in China is comparatively cheaper. Hence, the labor share of income is lower, while the capital share of income is higher than that in developed countries. Thereby, it is proper to assume that α in China is 0.35. Since the technological progress is not reflected in this model and what we want to see here is how the endogenous variables change relatively with the exogenous variables, the constant A can be normalized as 1. The above values are benchmark values of the parameters.

---

[6] Assume a period length in this model to be 26 years because the length in the literature on OLG model is usually in the interval of 25 -30 years.

4.2. Simulation on Firm Contribution Rate

At first, let the firm contribution rate be 18%. Substituting the above parameter values into equation (10) in the steady state and calculating repeatedly with different k until the sum of the two items becomes 0, one can get the capital-labor ratio, $k \approx 0.0120$. Substituting the values of the relative parameters and k into equations (13) - (16) and (1) gives the social pool benefits, individual account principal, working-period consumption, retirement-period consumption and utility. Then, let the firm contribution rate be 20% and 22%, respectively. Repeating the above procedure yields the result shown in Table 1.

Table 1. Effect of firm contribution rate

η	18%	20%	22%
k	0.0120	0.0115	0.0110
P	0.0664	0.0714	0.0760
I	0.0094	0.0091	0.0088
c_1	0.0794	0.0773	0.0753
c_2	0.3383	0.3379	0.3375
U	-3.1746	-3.2020	-3.2291

It is shown that raising the firm contribution rate decreases the capital-labor ratio, increases the social pool benefits, and decreases the individual account principal, working-period consumption, retirement-period consumption and utility. Comparing with the result in the comparative statics gives the only difference is that the effect on the retirement-period consumption. The reason is that the condition, $r < n$, in the comparative statics cannot be satisfied in the simulation.

4.3. Simulation on Population Growth Rate

Analogous to the approach to estimate the population growth rate in the period from 1978 to 2004, the population growth rate in the period from 1979 to 2005 is estimated as 2.039. Extrapolating one year and predicting simply gives the rate in the period from 1980 to 2006, 1.931. Simulating with the benchmark parameter values and the estimated population growth rates yields the result shown in Table 2.

Table 2. Effect of population growth rate

n	2.148	2.039	1.931
k	0.0115	0.0121	0.0128
P	0.0714	0.0702	0.0619
I	0.0091	0.0092	0.0094
c_1	0.0773	0.0788	0.0803
c_2	0.3379	0.3339	0.3299
U	-3.2020	-3.1900	-3.1777

A fall in the population growth rate induces the rise in the capital-labor ratio, the fall in the social pool benefits, the rises in the individual account principal and working-period consumption, the fall in the retirement-period consumption, and the rise in the utility. The simulation gives the same results as the comparative statics.

5. SOCIAL OPTIMUM

Since the firm contribution rate, a policy variable, has effect on the capital-labor ratio, it is possible to find the optimal firm contribution rate to maximize social welfare. The social welfare function is defined as the sum of lifetime utilities of all current and future generations[7]:

$$W = \theta \ln c_{20} + \sum_{i=0}^{\infty} \rho^i \left(\ln c_{1i} + \theta \ln c_{2i+1} \right). \tag{17}$$

where $\rho \in (0,1)$ denotes the social discount factor, which reflects the preference of social planner. The resource constraint is

$$k_i + Ak_i^\alpha = (1+n)k_{i+1} + c_{1i} + c_{2i}/(1+n). \tag{18}$$

The initial condition is that k_0 is given, and the terminal condition is $k_\infty = 0$.

The social planner maximizes the social welfare subject to the resource constraint, initial condition and terminal condition. Appendix A gives the first-order conditions for the social welfare maximization problem:

$$\theta(1+n)c_1^* = \rho c_2^*, \tag{19}$$

$$1 + \alpha A(k^*)^{\alpha-1} = \frac{1+n}{\rho} \quad \text{or} \quad k^* = \left(\frac{1+n-\rho}{\rho \alpha A} \right)^{\frac{1}{\alpha-1}}, \tag{20}$$

where the superscript * denotes the optimal steady state values of variables. The capital-labor ratio satisfying equation (20) is at the modified golden rule level, which means that the social welfare reaches the maximum.

In order to maximize the social welfare of the decentralized economy in steady state, we control the policy variable to adjust the capital-labor ratio of the decentralized economy in steady state to the modified golden rule level, namely, $k = k^*$. Substituting equation (20) into equation (10) and rearranging gives

---

[7] Blanchard and Fischer (1989) and Groezen et al. (2003) also use an analogous social welfare function.

$$\eta^* = \frac{\theta(1-\alpha)(1+n-\rho)-\rho\alpha(1+n)(1+\theta)}{\rho(1-\alpha)(1+n-\rho)+\rho\alpha(1+n)(1+\theta)}. \tag{21}$$

The optimal firm contribution rate depends on the individual discount factor θ, social discount factor ρ, capital share of income α, and population growth rate n.

How will the optimal firm contribution rate be affected when the population growth rate falls? The sign of the partial derivative of η^* with respect to n is proved to be undetermined. This implies that the effect of the population growth rate on the optimal firm contribution rate is ambiguous, which can be examined by simulating.

It is necessary to estimate the social discount factor at first, which indicates how much the government weights different generations in its social welfare calculations. Hence, it should be estimated according to the government's regulations. Based on the Chinese State Council Document 38 in 2005, one can get that the optimal firm contribution rate decided by the government is 20%. Substituting the relative benchmark values in Table 1 into equation (21) and calculating repeatedly until the difference between the two sides becomes 0, one can get that $\rho \approx 0.4257395$.

Table 3. Optimal firm contribution rates under different population growth rates

n	2.148	2.039	1.931
η^*	20.00%	19.66%	19.30%

Substituting the population growth rate, 2.039, and the benchmark values of θ and α and the estimated ρ into equation (21) gives the optimal firm contribution rate, 19.66%. Analogously, when the population growth rate falls to 1.931, the optimal firm contribution rate becomes 19.30%. The result is shown in Table 3.

The optimal firm contribution rate falls along with the population growth rate. This result is contradictory to general image. A fall in the population growth rate increases the capital-labor ratio, furthermore raises the wage. When the effect of the increase in the two variables dominates that of the fall in the population growth rate, the income in retirement-period will rise. The social optimum needs to retain the optimal retirement-period consumption. Hence, the optimal firm contribution rate has to be adjusted to fall with the population growth rate.

CONCLUSION

Employing the basic OLG model with general equilibrium, this chapter studies the partially funded public pension system for urban enterprise employees in China. It examines the effects of the individual contribution rate, firm contribution rate and population growth rate on the capital-labor ratio, social pool benefits, individual account principal, consumption and utility, and finds the optimal firm contribution rate.

Adopting logarithmic utility function and Cobb-Douglas production function, we use the data in China such as the urban population, capital share of income, public pension policy variables, etc. to simulate the effects of the exogenous variables on the endogenous variables and the change in the optimal firm contribution rate when the population growth rate falls.

The main results are as follows. Raising the individual contribution rate increases the individual account principal, while has no effect on the capital-labor ratio, social pool benefits, consumption and utility. Raising the firm contribution rate increases the social pool benefits, whereas decreases the capital-labor ratio, individual account principal, working-period consumption, retirement-period consumption and utility. A fall in the population growth rate induces the rises in the capital-labor ratio, individual account principal, working-period consumption and utility, whereas the falls in the social pool benefits and retirement-period consumption.

The optimal firm contribution rate depends on the individual discount factor, social discount factor, capital share of income and population growth rate. It should decrease along with the population growth rate.

The above results include the following policy implications: (a) In order to decrease the capital-labor ratio to restrain the over-fast growth of capital assets investment in China in most years from the beginning of Chinese reform and opening door policy to the beginning of international financial crisis in 2008, it is necessary to raise the firm contribution rate or properly relax the Chinese special population policy. (b) To increase the social pool benefits, it is necessary to raise the firm contribution rate or properly relax the special population policy. (c) To increase the individual account principal, it is necessary to raise the individual contribution rate or reduce the firm contribution rate or control the population growth rate. (d) To increase the consumption of workers, it is necessary to reduce the firm contribution rate or control the population growth rate. (e) To increase the consumption of retirees, it is necessary to reduce the firm contribution rate or properly relax the special population policy. (f) To raise the utility level, it is necessary to reduce the firm contribution rate or control the population growth rate.

Integrating the above six aims, it will do more good than harm to raise the individual contribution rate, reduce the firm contribution rate and control the population growth rate. The following two results are interesting.

Firstly, raising the firm contribution rate increases the social pool benefits, whereas decreases the consumption of retirees. If the median aim is to increase the social pool benefits and the ultimate aim is to increase the retirement-period consumption and utility, then raising the firm contribution rate can realize the median aim but runs counter to the ultimate aim. Secondly, the optimal firm contribution rate should decrease rationally with the population growth rate.

This is derived from the social welfare maximization and widely different from general image. Both of them strengthen the implication of reducing properly the firm contribution rate.

APPENDIX A

The Lagrange function for the social welfare maximization problem is

$$L = \cdots$$
$$+ \rho^{t-1}(\ln c_{1t-1} + \theta \ln c_{2t}) + \lambda_{t-1}\left[k_{t-1} + Ak_{t-1}^{\alpha} - (1+n)k_t - c_{1t-1} - \frac{c_{2t-1}}{1+n}\right]$$
$$+ \rho^{t}(\ln c_{1t} + \theta \ln c_{2t+1}) + \lambda_{t}\left[k_{t} + Ak_{t}^{\alpha} - (1+n)k_{t+1} - c_{1t} - \frac{c_{2t}}{1+n}\right]$$
$$+ \rho^{t+1}(\ln c_{1t+1} + \theta \ln c_{2t+2}) + \lambda_{t+1}\left[k_{t+1} + Ak_{t+1}^{\alpha} - (1+n)k_{t+2} - c_{1t+1} - \frac{c_{2t+1}}{1+n}\right]$$
$$+ \cdots$$

where λ_t is the Lagrange multiplier for the resource constraint in period t. Differentiating L with respect to c_{1t}, c_{2t} and k_{t+1}, and letting the derivatives be zero gives:

$$\rho^t / c_{1t} - \lambda_t = 0, \tag{A1}$$

$$\rho^{t-1}\theta / c_{2t} - \lambda_t / (1+n) = 0, \tag{A2}$$

$$-\lambda_t(1+n) + \lambda_{t+1}(1 + \alpha Ak_{t+1}^{\alpha-1}) = 0. \tag{A3}$$

Rearranging equations (A1) - (A3) at the optimal steady state (k^*, c_1^*, c_2^*) yields equations (19) and (20).

Chapter 2

LIFETIME UNCERTAINTY AND URBAN PENSION CONTRIBUTION RATES

ABSTRACT

Impacted by the international financial crisis beginning in 2008, China's economic growth rate has fallen evidently in recent years. The central government has been attaching importance to the economic growth as well as the economy quality and efficiency. Population aging was very rapid in China because of fallen population growth rate and risen longevity. Introducing lifetime uncertainty into the model of the last chapter, we examine the effects of the contribution rates of urban public pension system, life expectancy and population growth rate on the capital-labor ratio, per capita consumption and pension benefits, and look for the optimal contribution rate. Raising the individual contribution rate only increases the pension benefits. Raising the firm contribution rate decreases the capital-labor ratio and per capita consumption, while increases the pension benefits. A rise in the life expectancy increases the capital-labor ratio, per capita consumption and pension benefits. A fall in the population growth rate increases the capital-labor ratio and per capita consumption, while decreases the pension benefits. The optimal firm contribution rate rises under the joint case of risen life expectancy and fallen population growth rate. It has more advantages than disadvantages to raise the individual contribution rate, reduce the firm contribution rate, improve the living and medical conditions, and moderately relax the special population policy.

Keywords: urban public pension; contribution rate; population aging

1. INTRODUCTION

In the last chapter, we establish a basic OLG model to investigate the public pension system for urban enterprise employees without considering individual's uncertain lifetime. In fact, individuals are always confronted with death probability. Especially, old persons are in face of high mortality. Therefore, we introduce lifetime uncertainty into the model of the last chapter to study the effect of population aging on the Chinese economy and public pension system. The Chinese State Council Document 38 in 2005, *State Council Decision on Improving the Basic Pension System for Enterprise Employees*, introduces a new public pension system for urban enterprise employees in China. One of the main goals of this document is to make individual accounts have full real assets and pull off balance between revenue and payment of the social pool account.

It is worth studying the effects of the public pension system in the real situations of China in the era of post-crisis of international finance. Firstly, impacted by the international financial crisis, the Chinese economic growth has fallen evidently in recent years. The GDP in 2011 was 9.3% higher than that in the last year, and the rate in both 2012 and 2013 was 7.7%. The economic growth rate has fallen below 10%, but the annual growth rate from 2003 to 2007 was not less than 10%. Hence, the Chinese government put the economic growth in more important position. Secondly, the pension benefit level of enterprise retirees was evidently lower than that of government agency retirees. The central government has been raising the pension benefit level of enterprise retirees for ten years, and announced to continue raising the level. Finally, the population growth rate has been falling mainly because of China's special population policy, and the population life expectancy rising stem from improved living and medical conditions. It is predicted that the Chinese population aging peak will occur in 2030s.

Pecchenino and Pollard (1997, 2002), Abel (1987), Sheshinski and Weiss (1981), Zhang et al. (2001) used overlapping generations (OLG) models to study the relationship between life expectancy, population growth rate and public pension systems. In their models, pensions are financed only by wage taxes, which are usually lump-sum taxes. However, in most of the countries that have public pension systems, governments levy pension taxes on each employee's wage and on each enterprise's payroll using a proportional taxation schedule. So does the Chinese government. Samuelson (1975) studied the optimum social security in a life-cycle growth model. By controlling the social security taxes, Samuelson adjusted capital-labor ratio to the modified golden rule level to maximize social welfare. The approach to find the optimal social security taxes is to equate the interest rate in the decentralized economy to the growth rate of economy. Blanchard and Fischer (1989) elaborated the principle of social optimum. That is, a social planner maximizes social welfare by rationally allocating social resources.

This chapter adopts an OLG model with lifetime uncertainty to investigate the public pension system for urban enterprise employees in China. It examines the effects of the pension contribution rates, life expectancy and population growth rate on the capital-labor ratio, per capita consumption and pension benefits. With the data in China Statistical Yearbook, we simulate the intensities of the effects. By comparing the decentralized economy with the social optimum, we look for the optimal contribution rate that has effect on the capital-labor ratio. We also simulate the effects of the risen life expectancy and fallen population growth rate on the optimal contribution rate and estimate the optimal contribution rate during the period of population aging peak.

2. THE MODEL

A closed economy is composed of numerous individuals and firms and a government. The generation born at the beginning of period t is called generation t. The population grows at rate $n = (N_t/N_{t-1}) - 1$, where N_t is the population size of generation t.

2.1. Individuals

Each individual survives to the end of his/her working period certainly, but survives in retirement period with probability, $p \in (0, 1]$. In the working period, each individual earns wage by supplying inelastically one unit of labor and makes pension contributions. It is possible for him/her to inherit some unintentional bequests from his/her parent. He/she consumes part of his/her income and saves the remainder. If he/she survives in the retirement period, then he/she consumes his/her savings with accrued interest, funded pension benefits and PAYG pension benefits. If he/she dies at the beginning of the retirement period, then his/her savings with accrued interest and funded pension benefits are inherited equally by his/her children as unintentional bequests. Each individual derives utility from his/her working-period consumption c_{1t} and possible retirement-period consumption c_{2t+1}. The utility is described by an additively separable logarithmic function. Each individual maximizes her/his own utility by choosing lifetime consumption and savings, thus solves the following maximization problem:

$$\max_{\{c_{1t},c_{2t+1},s_t\}} U_t = \ln c_{1t} + \theta p \ln c_{2t+1}, \tag{1}$$

s.t.
$$c_{1t} = (1-p)b_t + (1-\tau)w_t - s_t, \tag{2}$$

$$c_{2t+1} = (1+r_{t+1})s_t + I_{t+1} + P_{t+1}, \tag{3}$$

$$(1+n)b_{t+1} = (1+r_{t+1})s_t + I_{t+1}, \tag{4}$$

where $\theta \in (0,1)$ denotes the individual discount factor, τ the individual contribution rate, w_t the wage, s_t the savings, r_{t+1} the interest rate, I_{t+1} the individual account benefits, P_{t+1} the social pool benefits, and b_{t+1} the unintentional bequests inherited by each children.

Substituting equations (2) - (4) into equation (1), and letting the partial derivative of equation (1) with respect to s_t be zero gives the first-order condition for the utility maximization:

$$c_{2t+1} = \theta p(1+r_{t+1})c_{1t}. \tag{5}$$

This expression implies that the utility loss from reducing one unit of working-period consumption is equal to the utility gain from increasing $(1+r_{t+1})$ units of possible retirement-period consumption.

2.2. Firms

Firms produce a homogenous commodity in competitive markets. The production is described by Cobb-Douglas function $Y_t = AK_t^\alpha N_t^{1-\alpha}$ or $y_t = Ak_t^\alpha$, where Y_t is the output in period t, K_t the capital stock, $\alpha \in (0,1)$ the capital share of income, A the productivity, $k_t = K_t/N_t$ the capital-labor ratio, and y_t the output-labor ratio.

Firms make pension contributions at rate $\eta \in (0,1)$ on their payroll. According to the product distribution, one can get that $AK_t^\alpha N_t^{1-\alpha} = r_t K_t + (1+\eta)w_t N_t$. Based on Euler's theorem, the interest rate is equal to the marginal product of capital, and $(1+\eta)w_t$ equals the marginal product of labor, $(1-\alpha)Ak_t^\alpha$:

$$r_t = \alpha A k_t^{\alpha-1}, \tag{6}$$

$$w_t = (1-\alpha)Ak_t^\alpha /(1+\eta). \tag{7}$$

2.3. The Government

The social pool fund is paid to the retirees in current period as PAYG pension benefits: $pN_{t-1}P_t = \eta w_t N_t$ or

$$P_t = (1+n)\eta w_t / p. \tag{8}$$

The accumulation in individual account is used to pay the individual when he/she retires in the next period as funded pension benefits:

$$I_{t+1} = (1+r_{t+1})\tau w_t. \tag{9}$$

2.4. Dynamic Equilibrium System

The savings and individual pension contributions in period t generate the capital stock in period $t + 1$ (See Blanchard and Fischer, 1989; or Barro and Sala-I-Martin, 2004):

$$s_t + \tau w_t = (1+n)k_{t+1}. \tag{10}$$

Given the initial condition k_0 and values of the parameters τ and η, a competitive equilibrium for the economy is a sequence as $\{c_{1t}, c_{2t+1}, s_t, w_t, r_{t+1}, B_{t+1}, P_t, b_t, k_{t+1}\}_{t=0}^{\infty}$ that satisfies equations (1) - (10) for all t.

Substituting equations (2) - (4) and (6) - (10) into equation (5) gives a dynamic equilibrium system described by the following difference equation:

$$(1+n)\left[(k_{t+1} + \alpha A k_{t+1}^{\alpha}) + \frac{\eta}{p}\frac{1-\alpha}{1+\eta} A k_{t+1}^{\alpha}\right] =$$
$$\theta p(1 + \alpha A k_{t+1}^{\alpha-1})\left[(1-p)(k_t + \alpha A k_t^{\alpha}) + \frac{1-\alpha}{1+\eta} A k_t^{\alpha} - (1+n)k_{t+1}\right]. \quad (11)$$

Assume that there is unique, stable and nonoscillatory steady state equilibrium. To find the stability condition, we linearize the dynamic system around the steady state (k). Some manipulation gives

$$i(k_{t+1} - k) + j(k_t - k) = 0,$$

where

$$i = (1+n)\left[(1 + \alpha^2 A k^{\alpha-1}) + \frac{\eta}{p}\left(\frac{1-\alpha}{1+\eta}\right)\alpha A k^{\alpha-1} + \theta p(1 + \alpha A k^{\alpha-1})\right]$$
$$+ \theta p(1-\alpha)\alpha A k^{\alpha-2}\left[(1-p)(k + \alpha A k^{\alpha}) + \frac{1-\alpha}{1+\eta} A k^{\alpha} - (1+n)k\right],$$

$$j = -\theta p(1 + \alpha A k^{\alpha-1})\left[(1-p)(1 + \alpha^2 A k^{\alpha-1}) + \frac{1-\alpha}{1+\eta}\alpha A k^{\alpha-1}\right] < 0.$$

The assumption that the equilibrium is unique, stable and nonoscillatory is equivalent to $0 < \frac{k_{t+1} - k}{k_t - k} = -\frac{j}{i} < 1$. Therefore, the stability condition is

$$i + j > 0.$$

3. EFFECTS OF EXOGENOUS VARIABLES

Define per capita consumption in period t as $c_t \equiv \frac{N_t c_{1t} + p N_{t-1} c_{2t}}{N_t + N_{t-1}}$, and pension benefits as $B_t \equiv I_t + p P_t$. When the dynamic system converges to its steady state, the per capita consumption and pension benefits become

$$c = (Ak^\alpha - nk)(1+n)/(2+n), \quad (12)$$

$$B = [\tau(1+\alpha Ak^{\alpha-1}) + (1+n)\eta](1-\alpha)Ak^\alpha/(1+\eta). \quad (13)$$

Partially differentiating k, c and B with respect to τ, η, p and n can give the effects of the individual contribution rate, firm contribution rate, life expectancy and population growth rate on the capital-labor ratio, per capita consumption and pension benefits. The dynamic equilibrium system tells us that the individual contribution rate has no effect on the capital-labor ratio since the individual contribution rate does not appear in the dynamic equilibrium system. That is because the mandatory savings (the individual pension contributions) crowd out the voluntary savings by one-for-one. The expressions of B and c indicate that the individual contribution rate has positive effect on the pension benefits, but has no effect on the per capita consumption. It can be shown that some of the partial derivatives of k, c and B with respect to η, p and n are ambiguous, which are dependent on the relevant parameters. Hence, we first estimate the parameter values and then examine the effects by simulating.

3.1. Parameter Calibration

According to the Chinese State Council Document 38 in 2005, the firm contribution rate $\eta = 20\%$, and the individual contribution rate $\tau = 8\%$. Assume one period length is 30 years since the length is usually in the interval of 25 - 30 years in the literature on OLG model. Similar with Pecchenino and Pollard (2002), the individual discount factor per year is 0.98. Hence, the individual discount factor per period is $\theta = 0.98^{30}$.

The capital share of income is usually 0.3 in developed countries. The labor in China is comparatively cheaper, thus the labor share of income is lower, while the capital share of income is higher than that in developed countries. Hence, we assume that α in China could be 0.35. What we want to see here is how the endogenous variables change with the exogenous variables, the constant A can be normalized as 1.

The survival probability in retirement period is estimated by the life expectancy. According to National Bureau of Statistics of China (2012), the life expectancy of Chinese people in 2010 is 74.83 years old. Since one period length is 30 years, the life-span from birth to the end of working-period is 60 years (Even if childhood period is omitted in the model, it must be taken into account when we practically compute the life-span). The life-span from birth to the end of retirement period is 90 years. The concept of life expectancy gives $(1 - p) \times 60 + p \times 90 = 74.83$, hence, $p \approx 49.43\%$. Although the choice of period length is arbitrary, it has to obey the following rule: Three times of the period length should be longer than or equal to the life expectancy to ensure that $p \leq 1$.

There are several calibers for population statistics in China. Since the public pension system for urban enterprise employees is different from that for rural residents, and only the former is studied in this chapter, so the caliber of "Urban Population" is selected. The population growth rate during the period 1981 - 2011 is computed to be $n \approx 2.425$ according to the "Population and Its Composition" in China Statistical Yearbook, which has in fact reflected immigration from the rural areas. The above calibrated values are baseline values.

3.2. Effect of Firm Contribution Rate

Utilizing the baseline parameter values but raising the firm contribution rate from 16% to 20% and 22%, respectively, we simulate how k, c and B change along with η. The result is shown in Table 1. A rise in the firm contribution rate induces the decrease in the capital-labor ratio and per capita consumption, and the increase in the pension benefits. It is easy to calculate the arc elasticity of the three endogenous variables with respect to the firm contribution rate.

3.3. Effect of Life Expectancy

Risen life expectancy implies risen survival probability in retirement period. According to National Bureau of Statistics of China (2012), the life expectancies in 1990, 2000 and 2010 are 68.55, 71.40 and 74.83 years old, respectively. Use Excel to add a trend line on the curve of the life expectancy, which is (life expectancy) = 5.543·ln (ordinal number) + 68.28, R^2 of the trend line is 0.959. By the trend line, we forecast the life expectancies in 2020 and 2030, which are 75.96 and 77.20 years old, respectively. The corresponding survival probabilities in retirement period are 53.21% and 57.33%, respectively. Simulating with the forecasted survival probabilities and the baseline parameter values gives the result shown in Table 2. Risen life expectancy increases the capital-labor ratio, per capita consumption and pension benefits.

Table 1. Effect of firm contribution rate

η	16%	20%	24%	Elasticity with respect to η
k	0.0055	0.0049	0.0043	-61%
c	0.1151	0.1108	0.1070	-18%
B	0.1317	0.1392	0.1455	25%

Table 2. Effect of life expectancy

p	49.43%	53.20%	57.33%	Elasticity with respect to p
k	0.0049	0.0054	0.0060	136%
c	0.1108	0.1143	0.1176	40%
B	0.1392	0.1393	0.1395	1%

3.4. Effect of Population Growth Rate

According to National Bureau of Statistics of China (1989), the sample of urban population from 2000 to 2011 can give a trend line, (population) = 2085· (ordinal number) + 43856, R^2 of the trend line is 0.999. According to the trend line, we forecast the population in 2031 and 2036, and yield the population growth rates during 2001 - 2031 and 2006 - 2036, which are 1.301 and 1.076, respectively. Simulating with the forecasted population growth rates and the baseline parameter values gives the result shown in Table 3. A fall in the population growth rate increases the capital-labor ratio and per capita consumption, and decreases the pension benefits.

3.5. Intensities of the Effects

Comparing the elasticity of k, c and B with respect to η, p and n shown in Tables 1 - 3 gives the intensities of the effects. The effects of the life expectancy on the capital-labor ratio and per capita consumption are stronger than that of the population growth rate, which in turn stronger than that of the firm contribution rate. The effect of the population growth rate on the pension benefits is stronger than that of the firm contribution rate, which in turn stronger than that of the life expectancy.

4. OPTIMAL FIRM CONTRIBUTION RATE

4.1. Social Welfare Maximization

Since the firm contribution rate as a policy variable has effect on the capital-labor ratio, it is possible to find the optimal firm contribution rate to maximize social welfare. The social welfare function is defined as the sum of the lifetime utilities of all current and future generations (Blanchard and Fischer, 1989; and Groezen et al., 2003; also use an analogous social welfare function):

$$W = \theta p \ln c_{20} + \sum_{i=0}^{\infty} \rho^i \left(\ln c_{1i} + \theta p \ln c_{2i+1} \right), \tag{14}$$

Table 3. Effect of population growth rate

n	2.425	1.301	1.076	Elasticity with respect to n
k	0.0049	0.0093	0.0111	-101%
c	0.1108	0.1272	0.1314	-22%
B	0.1392	0.1186	0.1140	26%

where $\rho \in (0,1)$ is the social discount factor, which reflects the preference of social planner. The resource constraint is

$$k_i + Ak_i^\alpha = (1+n)k_{i+1} + c_{1i} + pc_{2i}/(1+n). \tag{15}$$

The initial condition is that k_0 is given, and the terminal condition is $k_\infty = 0$.

The social planner maximizes the social welfare subject to the resource constraint, initial condition and terminal condition. The first-order conditions for the social welfare maximization problem are:

$$\theta(1+n)c_1^* = \rho c_2^*, \tag{16}$$

$$1 + \alpha A(k^*)^{\alpha-1} = \frac{1+n}{\rho} \text{ or } k^* = \left(\frac{1+n-\rho}{\rho \alpha A}\right)^{\frac{1}{\alpha-1}}, \tag{17}$$

where the superscript * denotes the optimal steady state values of variables. The capital-labor ratio satisfying equation (17) is at the modified golden rule level, which means that the social welfare achieves the maximum.

In order to make the steady state of the market economy to reach the optimal steady state, we control the firm contribution rate to adjust the capital-labor ratio in the steady state of the market economy to the modified golden rule level, namely, $k = k^*$. Substituting equation (17) into equation (11) and rearranging gives

$$\eta^* = \frac{\theta p^2(1-\alpha)(1+n-\rho) - \alpha p \rho(1+n)(1+\theta p) + \alpha \theta p^2(1-p)(1+n)}{\rho(1-\alpha)(1+n-\rho) + \alpha p \rho(1+n)(1+\theta p) - \alpha \theta p^2(1-p)(1+n)}. \tag{18}$$

The optimal firm contribution rate depends on the individual discount factor θ, social discount factor ρ, capital share of income α, survival probability in retirement period p, and population growth rate n.

The effects of the risen life expectancy and fallen population growth rate on the optimal firm contribution rate can be obtained by partially differentiating η^* with respective to p and n. The signs of the partial derivatives are dependent on the relevant parameters. We also check the effects of the life expectancy and population growth rate on the optimal firm contribution rate by simulating. It is necessary to estimate the social discount factor at first, which indicates how much the government weights different generations in its social welfare calculations. Hence, it should be estimated according to the government's regulations. Based on the Chinese State Council Document 38 in 2005, the optimal firm contribution rate adopted by the government is 20%. Substituting it and the relevant parameter baseline values into equation (18) and calculating repeatedly until the equation holds, one can get that $\rho \approx 0.2816$.

4.2. Risen Life Expectancy

Simulating with the forecasted survival probabilities and the relevant baseline parameter values gives the result shown in Table 4. The optimal firm contribution rate rises with the life expectancy.

Table 4. η^* under different life expectancies

p	53.20%	57.33%	Elasticity with respect to p
η^*	23.64%	27.65%	209%

Table 5. η^* under different population growth rates

n	1.301	1.076	Elasticity with respect to n
η^*	18.99%	18.64%	9.8%

Table 6. η^* under risen life expectancy and fallen population growth rate

p	n	η^*
53.20%	1.301	22.52%
53.20%	1.076	22.12%
57.33%	1.301	26.38%
57.33%	1.076	25.94%

4.3. Fallen Population Growth Rate

Simulating with the forecasted population growth rates and the baseline parameter values gives the result shown in Table 5. The optimal firm contribution rate falls with the population growth rate.

4.4. Risen Life Expectancy and Fallen Population Growth Rate

The parameters, ρ, θ and α, are at baseline values. Simulating four combinations of the forecasted life expectancies and population growth rates, respectively, gives the result shown in Table 6. The optimal firm contribution rate rises under the joint case of risen life expectancy and fallen population growth rate because it is much more sensitive to the life expectancy than to the population growth rate. It is around 26% in 2030s.

CONCLUSION

Employing the OLG model with lifetime uncertainty, this chapter investigates the public pension system for urban enterprise employees in China. We examine the effects of the contribution rates, life expectancy and population growth rate on the capital-labor ratio, per capita consumption and pension benefits and the effect intensities. By adjusting the firm contribution rate to make the capital-labor ratio to reach the modified golden rule level, we also find the optimal firm contribution rate. Utilizing the data in China Statistical Yearbook, we simulate the optimal firm contribution rate in 2030s when the population aging peak occurs.

The results are as follows: Raising the individual contribution rate only increases the pension benefits. Raising the firm contribution rate decreases the capital-labor ratio and per capita consumption, while increases the pension benefits. A rise in the life expectancy increases the capital-labor ratio, per capita consumption and pension benefits. A fall in the population growth rate increases the capital-labor ratio and per capita consumption, while decreases the pension benefits. The effects of the life expectancy on the capital-labor ratio and per capita consumption are stronger than that of the population growth rate, which in turn stronger than that of the firm contribution rate. The effect of the population growth rate on the pension benefits is stronger than that of the firm contribution rate, which in turn stronger than that of the life expectancy.

The optimal firm contribution rate depends on the individual discount factor, social discount factor, capital share of income, life expectancy and population growth rate. It rises with the life expectancy, while falls with the population growth rate. It is much more sensitive to the life expectancy than to the population growth rate. It rises under the joint case of risen life expectancy and fallen population growth rate. The optimal firm contribution rate when the population aging peak appears in 2030s is around 26% if the trend of the life expectancy and population growth rate does not change.

For recovery from financial crisis and keeping a stable, healthy and sustainable economic growth, China needs to increase investment and consumption. It is also necessary to take some measures to increase the pension benefit level of enterprise retirees. In order to increase the investment, it is necessary to reduce the firm contribution rate, improve the living and medical conditions or control the population growth rate. To increase the consumption, it is necessary to reduce the firm contribution rate, improve the living and medical conditions or control the population growth rate. To increase the pension benefits, it is necessary to raise the individual contribution rate and firm contribution rate, improve the living and medical conditions or properly relax the population policy.

Integrating the above economic goals and the effects and the effect intensities, it has more advantages than disadvantages to raise the individual contribution rate, reduce the firm contribution rate, improve the living and medical conditions, and moderately relax the special population policy. The positive effects of reducing the firm contribution rate and a rise in life expectancy on the capital-labor ratio and per capita consumption can adequately dominate the negative effects of a rise in population growth rate. The positive effects of a rise in population growth rate and life expectancy on the pension benefits can offset the negative effect of reducing the firm contribution rate; in addition, raise the individual contribution rate can also increase the pension benefits. China announced a new population policy in 2013, a couple with husband or wife is sole child in his or her own family before they get married is eligible to give birth to two children. It is expected to raise the population growth rate in the future, hence the optimal firm contribution rate while the population aging peak will not be as high as 26%. The suggestion for population policy is different from that in Chapter 1 because of two reasons. One is that the economic goals in the two chapters are different, and the other is that investigated historical periods are different. In Chapter 1, we consider the issue to restrain the over-fast growth of capital assets investment in China in most years from the beginning of Chinese reform and opening door policy to the beginning of international financial crisis in 2008. In this chapter, the issue is to recover from the international financial crisis and promote economic growth in the era of post-crisis of international finance. In addition, this chapter includes the element of population aging peak, whereas the last chapter does not.

Chapter 3

ALTRUISTIC MOTIVES, LIFE EXPECTANCY AND URBAN PUBLIC PENSION

ABSTRACT

China's investment was over-fast in most years from the beginning of reform and opening door policy to the beginning of international financial crisis. This chapter employs an overlapping generations model with altruistic motives and lifetime uncertainty to investigate the public pension system for urban enterprise employees in China. We examine the effects of the individual contribution rate, firm contribution rate, life expectancy and population growth rate on the capital-labor ratio, individual account benefits, social pool benefits, working-period consumption, retirement-period consumption and utility, and find the optimal firm contribution rate. According to the economic goals and the effects of the exogenous variables on the endogenous variables and that of the life expectancy and population growth rate on the optimal firm contribution rate, it will do more good than harm to raise the individual contribution rate, reduce the firm contribution rate and control the population growth rate. The optimal firm contribution rate decreases under the joint case of risen life expectancy and fallen population growth rate when altruistic motives are taken into account.

Keywords: urban public pension; contribution rate; altruistic motives; lifetime uncertainty

1. INTRODUCTION

In this chapter, we introduce a new element into the previous model. People are altruistic through bequests or gifts. We did not consider individuals' altruistic motives in Chapters 1 and 2. But in real life, individuals are in general altruistic to their family members. For example, the young when they get married or buy house can get material support from their parents. The old when they pass away usually leave bequests to their children. Such kind of behavior is generally a custom for Chinese people. Thereby, we should take the behavior tradition into the previous model.

As mentioned by Chapter 1, the Chinese State Council Document 38 in 2005, *State Council Decision on Improving the Basic Pension System for Enterprise Employees* introduces a partially funded public pension system for urban enterprises. It is necessary to study the effects within the following real situations: First, Chinese people are altruistic displaied through bequests or gifts. Second, their life expectancy has risen because of improved living and medical conditions. Third, China's investment was over-fast in most years from the beginning of reform and opening door policy to the beginning of international financial crisis. Particularly, the Chinese economy was over-warm from 2003 to 2007. Final, the population growth rate fell in the last three decades because of the Chinese special population policy before 2013. In general, the government required each couple to give birth not more than one time. In some special cases, e.g., both wife and husband are only child in their respective families before they get married, peasant couples that produce only one child and it is a girl, couples who are from the minority nationalities with population below one million persons, etc., the couples are eligible to give birth to two or more children. There are some ways for rural residents to become urban residents, e.g., graduated college students get jobs in urban areas; military officers transfer to civilian works in urban areas; urbanization makes corresponding rural residents become urban residents; etc.

Some literature used OLG model with altruistic motive and lifetime uncertainty to study public pension or social security. Sheshinski and Weiss (1981) examined the annuity aspect of social security within the framework of an OLG model, in which the duration of life was assumed to be uncertain. Abel (1987a) solved the consumption and portfolio decision problem of a consumer who lives for either one period or two periods and who can hold his wealth in the form of riskless bonds and actuarially fair annuities. Abel (1989) demonstrated the effect of a lump-sum tax on debt neutrality in an OLG model with lifetime uncertainty. There is not any production sector in these models. Fuster (2000) studied how the lack of an annuities market affects savings behavior and intergenerational transfers in a dynastic OLG economy. It was found that the answer to this question depends crucially on altruism. Zhang et al. (2001) examined how mortality decline affects long-run steady state growth by assuming actuarially fair annuity markets in an OLG model with uncertain lifetime and social security.

Samuelson (1975) studied the optimum social security in a life-cycle growth model by equating the interest rate in the decentralized economy to the growth rate of economy. Blanchard and Fischer (1989) elaborated the principle of social optimum. A social planner maximizes social welfare by rationally allocating social resources. Babu et al. (1997) get a tax path that would result in Pareto efficient allocations by equating the market equilibrium solution with the social planner's solution. This approach is an application of the principle of Samuelson (1975), and can be used to derive the optimal pension contribution rate in China's partially funded public pension system. The above literature provides helpful framework and approach for this chapter.

Employing an OLG model with altruistic motive and uncertain lifetime, this chapter investigates the public pension system for urban enterprise employees in China. We examine the effects of the pension contribution rates, life expectancy and population growth rate on the capital-labor ratio, pension benefits, consumption and utility. By comparing the market equilibrium solution with the social optimum solution, we also look for the optimal contribution rate. Instead of only individuals make pension contributions in the literature; both individuals and firms make contributions in this model.

2. THE MODEL

This chapter introduces a production sector into Abel's (1987a) two-period OLG model with lifetime uncertainty and replaces the fully funded public pension system in it with China's partially funded one. A closed economy is composed of numerous individuals and firms and a government. Each individual survives to the end of her working period certainly, but survives in retirement period with probability $p \in (0,1]$. The generation born at the beginning of period t is called generation t. The population grows at the rate of $n = N_t/N_{t-1} - 1$, where N_t is the population size of generation t.

2.1. Individuals

In the working period, each individual earns wage by supplying inelastically one unit of labor and makes pension contributions. He or she gets bequests or gifts from his or her parent, consumes part of the income and saves the remainder. If he or she survives in the retirement period, he or she distributes his or her savings with accrued interest, individual account benefits and social pool benefits between his or her consumption and the gifts to his or her children. If he or she dies at the beginning of the retirement period, the savings with accrued interest and individual account benefits are inherited equally by his or her children as bequests.

Each individual derives utility from her working-period consumption c_{1t}, possible retirement-period consumption c_{2t+1}, bequests b_{t+1}^D or gifts b_{t+1}^S. The utility is described by an additively separable logarithmic function. Thus, the utility maximization problem is as follows:

$$Max_{\{s_t, c_{2t+1}\}} U_t = \ln c_{1t} + \theta p \ln c_{2t+1} + \delta(1-p)\ln b_{t+1}^D + \delta p \ln b_{t+1}^S, \tag{1}$$

s.t.
$$c_{1t} = [(1-p)b_t^D + pb_t^S]/(1+n) + (1-\tau)w_t - s_t, \tag{2}$$

$$c_{2t+1} + b_{t+1}^S = (1+r_{t+1})s_t + B_{t+1} + P_{t+1}, \tag{3}$$

$$b_{t+1}^D = (1+r_{t+1})s_t + B_{t+1}, \tag{4}$$

where $\theta \in (0,1)$ denotes the individual discount factor, $\delta \in (0,1)$ the altruism intensity, w_t the wage, τ the individual contribution rate, s_t the savings, r_{t+1} the interest rate, B_{t+1} the individual account benefits, and P_{t+1} the social pool benefits. Without losing generality, it is supposed that $\theta > \delta$ since there is a limit to each individual's altruism.

Substituting equations (2) - (4) into equation (1) and letting the partial derivatives of equation (1) with respect to s_t and c_{2t+1} be zero gives the first-order conditions for the utility maximization problem:

$$\delta(1+r_{t+1})\left(\frac{1-p}{b_{t+1}^D}+\frac{p}{b_{t+1}^S}\right)=\frac{1}{c_{1t}}, \tag{5}$$

$$\theta b_{t+1}^S = \delta c_{2t+1}. \tag{6}$$

Equation (5) describes the tradeoff between the marginal utility of working-period consumption and that of bequests or gifts. Equation (6) describes the tradeoff between the marginal utility of gifts and that of retirement-period consumption.

2.2. Firms

Firms produce a homogenous commodity in competitive markets. The production is described by Cobb-Douglas function $Y_t = AK_t^\alpha N_t^{1-\alpha}$ or $y_t = Ak_t^\alpha$, where Y_t is the output in period t, K_t the capital stock, $\alpha \in (0,1)$ the capital share of income, A the productivity, $k_t = K_t/N_t$ the capital-labor ratio, and y_t the output-labor ratio.

Firms make pension contributions at the rate of $\eta \in (0,1)$ on their payroll. According to the product distribution, one can get $AK_t^\alpha N_t^{1-\alpha} = r_t K_t + (1+\eta)w_t N_t$. The first-order conditions for the profit maximization problem are:

$$r_t = \alpha A k_t^{\alpha-1}, \tag{7}$$

$$w_t = \frac{(1-\alpha)Ak_t^\alpha}{1+\eta}. \tag{8}$$

2.3. The Government

The social pool fund is used to pay the retirees in current period as PAYG pension benefits: $pN_{t-1}P_t = \eta w_t N_t$, or

$$P_t = \frac{1+n}{p}\eta w_t. \tag{9}$$

The accumulation in individual account is used to pay the individual when she retires in the next period as funded pension benefits:

$$B_{t+1} = (1 + r_{t+1})\tau w_t. \tag{10}$$

2.4. Dynamic Equilibrium

The savings and individual pension contributions in period t generate the capital stock in period $t + 1$ (See Blanchard and Fischer, 1989, or Barro and Sala-I-Martin, 2004, for details):

$$s_t + \tau w_t = (1+n)k_{t+1}. \tag{11}$$

Given the initial condition k_0 and values of the parameters τ and η, a competitive equilibrium for the economy is a sequence as $\{c_{1t}, c_{2t+1}, w_t, r_{t+1}, s_t, b_{t+1}^D, b_{t+1}^S, B_{t+1}, P_t, k_{t+1}\}_{t=0}^{\infty}$ that satisfies equations (1) - (11) for all t.

Substituting equations (2) - (4) and (7) - (11) into equations (5) - (6) and rearranging gives a dynamic equilibrium system described by the following difference equation:

$$\left[k_t + Ak_t^\alpha - (1+n)k_{t+1} - \frac{p\theta}{\theta+\delta}\left(k_t + \alpha Ak_t^\alpha + \frac{\eta}{p}\frac{1-\alpha}{1+\eta}Ak_t^\alpha\right)\right] \cdot$$

$$\left[(1-p)\frac{\delta}{\theta+\delta}\left(k_{t+1} + \alpha Ak_{t+1}^\alpha + \frac{\eta}{p}\frac{1-\alpha}{1+\eta}Ak_{t+1}^\alpha\right) + p\left(k_{t+1} + \alpha Ak_{t+1}^\alpha\right)\right] \tag{12}$$

$$= \frac{1+n}{\theta+\delta}k_{t+1}\left(k_{t+1} + \alpha Ak_{t+1}^\alpha + \frac{\eta}{p}\frac{1-\alpha}{1+\eta}Ak_{t+1}^\alpha\right)$$

Assume that there is unique, stable and nonoscillatory steady state equilibrium (e.g., Blanchard and Fischer, 1989, p. 96). The stability condition refers to Appendix A.

3. EFFECTS OF EXOGENOUS VARIABLES

This section examines the effects of the contribution rates, life expectancy and population growth rate on the capital-labor ratio, pension benefits, consumption and utility. When the dynamic system converges to its steady state, the social pool benefits, individual account benefits, working-period consumption, retirement-period consumption and utility become

$$P = \frac{1+n}{p}\frac{\eta}{1+\eta}(1-\alpha)Ak^\alpha, \tag{13}$$

$$B = \tau(1 + \alpha Ak^{\alpha-1})\frac{1-\alpha}{1+\eta}Ak^\alpha, \tag{14}$$

$$c_1 = Ak^\alpha - nk - \frac{p\theta}{\theta+\delta}\left(k + \alpha Ak^\alpha + \frac{\eta}{p}\frac{1-\alpha}{1+\eta}Ak^\alpha\right), \tag{15}$$

$$c_2 = \frac{\theta}{\theta+\delta}(1+n)\left(k + \alpha Ak^\alpha + \frac{\eta}{p}\frac{1-\alpha}{1+\eta}Ak^\alpha\right), \tag{16}$$

$$U = \ln c_1 + \theta p \ln c_2 + \delta(1-p)\ln\left[(1+n)(k+\alpha Ak^\alpha)\right] + \delta p \ln(\delta c_2/\theta). \tag{17}$$

The individual contribution rate does not appear in the dynamic equilibrium system because the mandatory savings (the individual contributions) crowd out the voluntary savings by one-for-one. Hence, it has no effect on the capital-labor ratio. Consequently, raising the individual contribution rate has no effect on the social pool benefits, working-period consumption, retirement-period consumption and utility but increases the individual account benefits.

The effects of the firm contribution rate, life expectancy and population growth rate on the endogenous variables can be obtained by partially differentiating k, P, B, c_1, c_2 and U with respect to η, p and n, respectively. It can be shown that most of the partial derivatives are ambiguous, i.e., the corresponding effects are dependent on the values of relevant parameters. Hence, we calibrate the parameter values at first, and then examine the effects by simulating.

3.1. Parameter Calibration

In this model we set the length of each period as 26 years. Analogous to Pecchenino and Pollard (2002), we assume that the individual discount factor per year is 0.985, and the altruism intensity per year 0.965. Hence, the individual discount factor per period is $\theta = 0.985^{26}$, and the altruism intensity per period is $\delta = 0.965^{26}$.

The capital share of income is assumed to be 0.35. Since what we want to see is how the endogenous variables change with the exogenous variables, the constant A can be normalized as 1. The caliber of "Urban Population" is selected to compute the population growth rate. The rate is $n \approx 2.015$ during 1980 - 2006 according to the "Population and Its Composition" in China Statistical Yearbook, which has in fact reflected immigration from rural areas.

The survival probability in retirement period is estimated by the life expectancy. According to UN Secretariat (2007), the life expectancy of Chinese people in 2000 - 2005 is 72.0 years old. Since one period length is 26 years, the life-span from birth to the end of working-period is 52 years. The life-span from birth to the end of retirement period is 78 years. According to the concept of life expectancy, one can get $(1 - p) \times 52 + p \times 78 = 72.0$, which gives $p \approx 76.92\%$. Although the choice of period length is arbitrary, it has to obey the following rule: Three times of the period length should be longer than or equal to the life expectancy to ensure $p \leq 1$.

According to the Chinese State Council Document 26 in 1997 and the Chinese State Council Document 38 in 2005, the firm contribution rate is $\eta = 20\%$, and the individual contribution rate is $\tau = 8\%$. The above estimated values are baseline values of the parameters.

3.2. Effect of Firm Contribution Rate

Substituting the above baseline parameter values into equation (12) in steady state and calculating repeatedly until the equation holds, we get the capital-labor ratio, $k \approx 0.0380$. Substituting it and the baseline parameter values into equations (13) - (17) gives the values of the five endogenous variables, as shown in Table 1. Then, let the firm contribution rate be 18% and 22%, respectively, repeating the above procedure gives the result shown in Table 1. Raising the firm contribution rate induces the decrease in the capital-labor ratio, individual account benefits, working-period consumption and utility, whereas the increase in the social pool benefits and retirement-period consumption.

3.3. Effect of Life Expectancy

A rise in life expectancy implies an increase in the survival probability in retirement period. According to UN Secretariat (2007), the life expectancy of Chinese people in 2005 - 2010 is 73.0 years old, and that in 2010 - 2015 is 74.0 years old. Hence, the survival probabilities in retirement period are computed to be 80.77% and 84.62%, respectively. Simulating with the survival probabilities and the baseline parameter values gives the result shown in Table 2. A rise in the life expectancy leads to the increase in the capital-labor ratio, whereas the decrease in the social pool benefits, individual account benefits, working-period consumption, retirement-period consumption and utility.

Table 1. Effect of firm contribution rate

η	18 %	20 %	22 %
k	0.0391	0.0380	0.0370
P	0.1250	0.1352	0.1449
B	0.0550	0.0542	0.0536
c_1	0.1491	0.1476	0.1461
c_2	0.3670	0.3693	0.3714
U	-2.9625	-2.9693	-2.9763

Table 2. Effect of life expectancy

p	76.92%	80.77%	84.62%
k	0.0380	0.0383	0.0385
P	0.1352	0.1291	0.1235
B	0.05424	0.05419	0.05415
c_1	0.1476	0.1439	0.1402
c_2	0.3693	0.3665	0.3637
U	-2.9693	-3.0381	-3.1083

3.4. Effect of Population Growth Rate

The population growth rate during 1984 - 2010 can be computed according to the "Population and Its Composition" in China Statistical Yearbook, which is 1.789. In order to find the population growth rate during 1989 - 2015, we first predict the urban population in 2015. It is straightforward to predict with the TREND function in Microsoft Excel, where $R^2 \approx 0.9925$ implies a very good fitness. Comparing with the urban population in 1989 gives the population growth rate during 1989 - 2015 is 1.272. Simulating with the predicted population growth rates and the baseline parameter values gives the result shown in Table 3. A fall in the population growth rate induces the increase in the capital-labor ratio, working-period consumption and utility, whereas the decrease in the social pool benefits, individual account benefits and retirement-period consumption.

4. SOCIAL OPTIMUM

The firm contribution rate has effect on the capital-labor ratio, furthermore, effects on the other endogenous variables. Hence, controlling the firm contribution rate can adjust the capital-labor ratio in market economy to the modified golden rule level to maximize social welfare.

The social welfare is the sum of the lifetime utilities of all current and future generations (Blanchard and Fischer, 1989, and Groezen et al., 2003, also use an analogous social welfare function):

Table 3. Effect of population growth rate

n	2.015	1.789	1.272
k	0.0380	0.0435	0.0623
P	0.1352	0.1311	0.1211
B	0.0542	0.0533	0.0513
c_1	0.1476	0.1554	0.1790
c_2	0.3693	0.3644	0.3552
U	-2.9693	-2.9292	-2.8102

$$W = \theta p \ln c_{20} + \delta(1-p)\ln b_0^D + \delta p \ln b_0^S$$
$$+ \sum_{i=0}^{\infty} \rho^i \left[\ln c_{1i} + \theta p \ln c_{2i+1} + \delta(1-p)\ln b_{i+1}^D + \delta p \ln b_{i+1}^S \right], \tag{18}$$

where $\rho \in (0,1)$ denotes the social discount factor, which reflects the preference of social planner. The resource constraint is

$$k_i + Ak_i^\alpha = (1+n)k_{i+1} + c_{1i} + pc_{2i}/(1+n). \tag{19}$$

The initial condition is that k_0 is given, and the terminal condition is $k_\infty = 0$.

The social planner maximizes the social welfare subject to the resource constraint, initial condition and terminal condition. The Lagrange function is

$$L = \cdots$$
$$+ \rho^{t-1}\left[\ln c_{1t-1} + \theta p \ln c_{2t} + \delta(1-p)\ln b_t^D + \delta p \ln b_t^S\right] + \lambda_{t-1}\left[k_{t-1} + Ak_{t-1}^\alpha - (1+n)k_t - c_{1t-1} - \frac{pc_{2t-1}}{1+n}\right]$$
$$+ \rho^t\left[\ln c_{1t} + \theta p \ln c_{2t+1} + \delta(1-p)\ln b_{t+1}^D + \delta p \ln b_{t+1}^S\right] + \lambda_t\left[k_t + Ak_t^\alpha - (1+n)k_{t+1} - c_{1t} - \frac{pc_{2t}}{1+n}\right]$$
$$+ \rho^{t+1}\left[\ln c_{1t+1} + \theta p \ln c_{2t+2} + \delta(1-p)\ln b_{t+2}^D + \delta p \ln b_{t+2}^S\right] + \lambda_{t+1}\left[k_{t+1} + Ak_{t+1}^\alpha - (1+n)k_{t+2} - c_{1t+1} - \frac{pc_{2t+1}}{1+n}\right]$$
$$+ \cdots$$

where λ_t is the Lagrange multiplier for the resource constraint in period t. Let the partial derivatives $\partial L/\partial c_{1t}$, $\partial L/\partial c_{2t}$ and $\partial L/\partial k_{t+1}$ be zero, and rearranging at the steady state (k^*, c_1^*, c_2^*) gives the first-order conditions for this maximization problem:

$$\theta(1+n)c_1^* = \rho c_2^*, \tag{20}$$

$$1 + \alpha A(k^*)^{\alpha-1} = \frac{1+n}{\rho} \text{ or } k^* = \left(\frac{1+n-\rho}{\rho\alpha A}\right)^{\frac{1}{\alpha-1}}, \tag{21}$$

where the superscript * denotes the optimal steady state values of variables. The capital-labor ratio satisfying equation (21) is at the modified golden rule level.

In order to maximize the social welfare of market economy, we control the policy variable to adjust the capital-labor ratio of the market economy in steady state to the modified golden rule level, namely, $k_{t+1} = k_t = k = k^*$. Substituting equation (21) into equation (12) and rearranging gives

$$p\theta\delta(1-p)\varphi^2 + p\frac{1+n}{\rho}\left(n - \frac{1+n-\rho}{\rho\alpha}\right) + \left[p^2\theta\frac{1+n}{\rho} + (1+n) + \delta(1-p)\left(n - \frac{1+n-\rho}{\rho\alpha}\right)\right]\varphi = 0, \tag{22}$$

where $\varphi = \dfrac{1}{\theta+\delta}\left(\dfrac{1+n}{\rho} + \dfrac{\eta^*}{p}\dfrac{1-\alpha}{1+\eta^*} \cdot \dfrac{1+n-\rho}{\rho\alpha}\right)$.

The optimal firm contribution rate depends on the individual discount factor θ, social discount factor ρ, altruism intensity δ, capital share of income α, survival probability in retirement period p, and population growth rate n.

5. OPTIMAL FIRM CONTRIBUTION RATE

The effects of the life expectancy and population growth rate on the optimal firm contribution rate can be obtained by partially differentiating η^* with respect to p and n. It can be shown that the signs of the derivatives are dependent on the relevant parameter values. Hence, we check the effects by simulating.

It is necessary to estimate the social discount factor at first, which indicates how much the government weights different generations in its social welfare calculation. Hence, it should be estimated according to the government's regulations. Based on the stipulated firm contribution rate, the optimal firm contribution rate adopted by the government is 20%. Substituting the above baseline parameter values into equation (22) and calculating repeatedly until the equation holds, we get $\rho \approx 0.7422$.

Table 4. η^* under risen life expectancy

p	76.92%	80.77%	84.62%
η^*	20.00%	21.59%	22.12%

Table 5. η^* under fallen population growth rate

n	2.015	1.789	1.272
η^*	20.00%	18.12%	12.20%

Table 6. η^* under risen life expectancy and fallen population growth rate and the elasticity

p	n	η^*	elasticity η^*/p	elasticity η^*/n
80.77%	1.789	18.64%	-	-
80.77%	1.272	12.50%	-	114%
84.62%	1.789	19.06%	48%	-
84.62%	1.272	12.71%	35%	115%

5.1. Risen Life Expectancy

According to UN Secretariat (2007), the life expectancy of Chinese people in 2005 - 2010 is 73.0 years old, and that in 2010 - 2015 is 74.0 years old. Hence, the survival probabilities in retirement period are 80.77% and 84.62%, respectively. Simulating with the estimated survival probabilities and the baseline values of θ, δ, α, ρ and n gives the result shown in Table 4. A rise in the life expectancy leads to the increase in the optimal firm contribution rate.

5.2. Fallen Population Growth Rate

As computed in Section 3.4, the population growth rate from 1984 to 2010 is 1.789, and that from 1989 to 2015 is 1.272. Simulating with the population growth rates and the baseline values of θ, δ, α, ρ and p gives the result shown in Table 5. A fall in the population growth rate induces the decrease in the optimal firm contribution rate.

5.3. Risen Life Expectancy and Fallen Population Growth Rate

Simulating the four combinations of the above estimated survival probabilities and population growth rates, gives the result shown in Table 6. The optimal firm contribution rate falls under the joint case of risen life expectancy and fallen population growth rate. The reason is that the elasticity of η^* with respect to n is much higher than that to p. This implies that the optimal firm contribution rate is much more sensitive to the population growth rate than to the life expectancy.

CONCLUSION

This chapter employs the OLG model with altruistic motives and lifetime uncertainty to investigate the public pension system for urban enterprise employees in China. We examine the effects of the individual contribution rate, firm contribution rate, life expectancy and population growth rate on the capital-labor ratio, social pool benefits, individual account benefits, working-period consumption, retirement-period consumption and utility. By controlling the firm contribution rate, the policy variable that can affect the capital-labor ratio, to adjust the capital-labor ratio of market economy to the modified golden rule level, we find the optimal firm contribution rate.

The results are as follows. Raising the individual contribution rate can only increase the individual account benefits. Raising the firm contribution rate increases the social pool benefits and retirement-period consumption, whereas decreases the capital-labor ratio, individual account benefits, working-period consumption and utility. A fall in the population growth rate leads to the increase in the capital-labor ratio, working-period consumption and utility, whereas the decrease in the social pool benefits, individual account benefits and retirement-period consumption. A rise in the life expectancy induces the increase in the capital-labor ratio, whereas the decrease in the social pool benefits, individual account benefits, working-period consumption, retirement-period consumption and utility.

The optimal firm contribution rate depends on the individual discount factor, social discount factor, altruism intensity, capital share of income, survival probability in retirement period, and population growth rate. It falls with the population growth rate, whereas rises with the life expectancy. It decreases under the joint case of risen life expectancy and fallen population growth rate because it is much more sensitive to the population growth rate than to the life expectancy.

These results have some policy implications: (a) In order to control the capital-labor ratio to restrain the over-fast growth of capital assets investment in China in most years from the beginning of Chinese reform and opening door policy to the beginning of international financial crisis, it is necessary to raise the firm contribution rate or properly relax the Chinese special population policy. (b) To increase the social pool benefits, it is necessary to raise the firm contribution rate or properly relax the special population policy. (c) To increase the individual account benefits, it is necessary to raise the individual contribution rate or reduce the firm contribution rate or properly relax the special population policy. (d) To increase the consumption of workers, it is necessary to reduce the firm contribution rate or control the population growth rate. (e) To increase the consumption of retirees, it is necessary to raise the firm contribution rate or properly relax the special population policy. (f) To increase the utility level, it is necessary to reduce the firm contribution rate or control the population growth rate.

Integrating the above elements and weighting the utility more, it will do more good than harm to raise the individual contribution rate, reduce the firm contribution rate and control the population growth rate. This result is advantageous for firms to reduce heavy burden regarding social insurance. The social insurance in China includes public pension, medical, unemployment, work-related injury, and maternity insurances. Firm's contribution rates for the five items of insurance are 20%, 6%, 2%, 1%, and 1%, respectively. The total contribution rate composed of social insurance and housing security has amounted to 40% of firms' payroll. The heavy burden can be reduced if the firm contribution rate for public pension could be decreased.

APPENDIX A

To find the stability condition, we linearize the dynamic system (12) around the steady state (k). Some manipulation gives

$$i(k_{t+1} - 1) + j(k_t - 1) = 0,$$

where

$$i = -\frac{1+n}{\theta+\delta}\left(k + \alpha A k^\alpha + \frac{\eta}{p}\frac{1-\alpha}{1+\eta}A k^\alpha\right)\left\{\delta(1-p) + \frac{p\theta}{1+n}\left[\delta\frac{1-p}{\theta+\delta}\left(1+\alpha^2 A k^{\alpha-1} + \frac{\eta}{p}\frac{1-\alpha}{1+\eta}\alpha A k^{\alpha-1}\right) + p\left(1+\alpha^2 A k^{\alpha-1}\right)\right] + 1\right\}$$
$$- p\left[(1+n)(k + \alpha A k^\alpha) + (nk - A k^\alpha)(1+\alpha^2 A k^{\alpha-1})\right]\frac{1+n}{\theta+\delta}\left[k + \delta\frac{1-p}{1+n}(nk - A k^\alpha)\right]\left(1+\alpha^2 A k^{\alpha-1} + \frac{\eta}{p}\frac{1-\alpha}{1+\eta}\alpha A k^{\alpha-1}\right),$$

$$j = \left[1 + \alpha A k^{\alpha-1} - \frac{p\theta}{\theta+\delta}\left(1+\alpha^2 A k^{\alpha-1} + \frac{\eta}{p}\frac{1-\alpha}{1+\eta}\alpha A k^{\alpha-1}\right)\right] \cdot \left[\delta\frac{1-p}{\theta+\delta}\left(k + \alpha A k^\alpha + \frac{\eta}{p}\frac{1-\alpha}{1+\eta}A k^\alpha\right) + p(k + \alpha A k^\alpha)\right] > 0.$$

The assumption that the equilibrium is unique, stable and nonoscillatory is equivalent to $0 < \frac{k_{t+1} - k}{k_t - k} = -\frac{j}{i} < 1$. Thereby, the stability condition is

$$i + j < 0.$$

II. URBAN PENSION, ENDOGENOUS GROWTH MODEL

Chapter 4

URBAN PUBLIC PENSION, HUMAN CAPITAL AND ENDOGENOUS GROWTH[1]

ABSTRACT

As a developing country with low per capita GDP and over-population, China needs to keep a stable, healthy and sustainable economic growth and rationally control the population size. Employing an endogenous growth model, this chapter investigates China's public pension system for urban enterprise employees. We examine the effects of the firm contribution rate and individual contribution rate on the per capita income growth rate, population growth rate, saving rate and education expense rate. The results are as follows: Raising the firm contribution rate decreases the per capita income growth rate and saving rate, whereas increases the population growth rate and education expense rate. Raising the individual contribution rate decreases the per capita income growth rate, saving rate and education expense rate, whereas increases the population growth rate. The effect of the firm contribution rate on the per capita income growth rate is much greater than that of the individual contribution rate. The effects of the firm contribution rate on the population growth rate, saving rate and education expense rate are smaller than that of the individual contribution rate. It has more advantages than disadvantages to reduce the firm contribution rate and raise the individual contribution rate.

Keywords: urban public pension; endogenous growth; firm contribution rate; individual contribution rate

1. INTRODUCTION

China transformed its pay-as-you-go (PAYG) public pension system for urban enterprise employees to a partially funded one in 1997, and reformed the pension system again in 2005. The government establishes an individual account for each employee and a social pool account for all employees and retirees. Each firm contributes 20% of its payroll to the social pool account, while each employee contributes 8% of her/his wage to her/his individual account. The social pool fund is used to pay the current retirees as PAYG pension benefits,

---

[1] This chapter is based on the original version of the paper, Urban Public Pension and Economic Growth in China, Asia-Pacific Journal of Risk and Insurance, 2012, Vol. 6, Iss. 2, Article 4.

while the accumulation in an individual account is used to pay the individual herself/himself when she/he retires in the next period as funded pension benefits. Each retiree receives funded pension benefits from her/his individual account and PAYG pension benefits from the social pool account.

It is worth examining the effects of the public pension system on the economic growth and population in China based on the following real situations: Firstly, China as a developing country with low per capita GDP and over-population needs to keep a stable, healthy and sustainable economic growth and rationally control the population size. Secondly, household saving rate was too high in China in most years from the beginning of reform and opening door policy. The fraction of education expenses to family income has become higher and higher since the beginning of 1980s. It is necessary to decrease the saving rate and education expense ratio especially in the era of post-crisis of international finance. Thirdly, Chinese generally pay much attention to their children's human capital, zealously invest in education to their children and satisfy for their children's high human capital. Fourthly, China implemented a special population policy before 2013. In principle, the Chinese government required each couple to give birth not more than one time. In some special cases, e.g., both wife and husband are only one child in their respective families before they get married, peasant couples that produce only one child and it is a girl, couples who are from the minority nationalities with population below one million persons, and so on, the couples are eligible to give birth to two or more children. Finally, after the new public pension system implementing some years, retirees from urban enterprises will be dependent mainly on their own savings and pension benefits, not on their children' material support.

Many works studied the relationship between economic growth, population and public pension in OLG model with endogenous growth[2]. Zhang and Zhang (1995) used an endogenous growth model, in which altruism runs from children to parents, to examine the effects on fertility and output growth rates of three kinds of PAYG social security systems: a system without social security, a conventional social security system and a fully fertility-related social security system. Zhang and Zhang (1998) applied an endogenous growth model with three specifications of utility functions to analyze the effects of social security on savings, fertility and per capita income growth. With the specification that individuals only care about their own consumptions, Zhang and Zhang showed that in the presence of intergenerational transfers, higher (lower) social security taxes lead to lower (higher) fertility, lower (higher) gift ratio and higher (lower) growth. Wigger (1999a) employed a model in which parents derive utility from having children and expect support from children to study the interrelation between growth, fertility and PAYG-public pension size. It was shown that small sized public pensions stimulate per capita income growth, but further increases in public pensions reduce it. A rise in public pensions reduces fertility if they are either small or large, and stimulates fertility if they are medium sized. A common feature of these studies is to transform the capital per unit of effective labor into a constant and the production function into so-called "AK model"[3] by adopting a special type of productivity.

Zhang (1995) examined the effects of social security on the growth of per capita income and fertility in an endogenous growth model, in which agents care about their own

---

[2] The key property of the endogenous growth models is the absence of diminishing returns to capital (see, e.g., Barro and Sala-I-Martin, 2004, p.63).

[3] $Y = AK$, where Y denotes output, K capital. A is a positive constant that reflects the level of the technology (see, e.g., Barro and Sala-I-Martin, 2004, p.63).

consumption, number of children and each child's welfare. Instead of transforming the production function into "*AK* model", Zhang introduced human capital, which grows at the same rate with the physical capital per unit of labor in balanced growth equilibrium. It was shown that an unfunded program may stimulate growth by reducing fertility and increasing the ratio of human capital investment per child to per family income when bequests are positive. Zhang (2001) used the same approach to compare long-run implications for growth and fertility of four types of taxation for social security with positive bequests. Yew and Zhang (2009) investigated the optimal scale of PAYG social security in a dynastic family model with human capital externalities, fertility and endogenous growth.

By employing an endogenous growth model, this chapter investigates the public pension system for urban enterprise employees in China reformed in 2005. It examines the effects of the firm contribution rate and individual contribution rate on the per capita income growth rate, population growth rate, saving rate and education expense rate. Instead of pensions financed only by wage taxes in the above literature, it is assumed that in this model, the government levies pension taxes on each worker's wage and on each firm's payroll; and the pension taxes are proportional taxes. Part of individual's utility comes from her/his children's human capital, in other words, from the quality of children other than the number of children.

2. THE MODEL

Based on Zhang (1995, 2001), this model replaces the PAYG or fully funded public pension systems with China's partially funded one, and replaces the number of children in the utility function with children's human capital. There are numerous individuals and firms and a government in a closed economy. Each individual lives through three periods in life: childhood period, working period and retirement period. At the beginning of period t, L_t identical individuals of generation t enter the work force. Each individual of generation t have n_t children, hence, $L_{t+1} = n_t L_t$.

2.1. Individuals

Individuals develop their human capital in childhood period, and have no ability to make economic decision. Upon entering the work force, each individual represents one unit of labor. Rearing a child requires $v \in (0,1)$ units of labor. Hence, each individual supplies $(1 - vn_t) > 0$ units of labor to earn wage income. After making pension contributions, she/he consumes part of the income, pays education expenses for her/his children, and saves the remainder of income. In the retirement period, she/he consumes the savings with accrued interest, individual account benefits and social pool benefits.

Each individual derives utility from her/his working-period consumption $c_{2,t}$, retirement-period consumption $c_{3,t+1}$ and children's human capital. The utility is described by an additively separable logarithmic function. Thus, the utility maximization problem is:

$$\max_{\{s_t, n_t, e_t\}} U_t = \ln c_{2,t} + \beta \ln c_{3,t+1} + \gamma \ln(n_t h_{t+1}), \tag{1}$$

s.t.
$$c_{2,t} = (1-\tau-s_t)(1-vn_t)w_t - n_t e_t, \qquad (2)$$

$$c_{3,t+1} = (1+r_{t+1})s_t(1-vn_t)w_t + I_{t+1} + P_{t+1}, \qquad (3)$$

where $\beta \in (0,1)$ denotes the discount factor on the utility derived from retirement-period consumption, and $\gamma \in (0,1)$ that on the utility derived from children's human capital. Each individual's human capital of generation $t + 1$ is

$$h_{t+1} = Ae_t^\delta h_t^{1-\delta}, \qquad (4)$$

where $\delta \in (0,1)$ denotes the elasticity of human capital with respect to education expenses, $A > 0$ the productivity of human capital production. τ denotes the individual contribution rate, w_t the wage, s_t the saving rate, e_t the education expenses for each child, r_{t+1} the interest rate, I_{t+1} the individual account benefits, and P_{t+1} the social pool benefits.

The spokesman of National Population and Family Planning Commission of China (2007) said: China has not realized one child per family in practice, families having only one child was 35.9%, those having 1.5 children was 52.9%, and 11% of families were born with two or more children[4]. Hence, individual can choose the number of her/his children. Substituting equations (2) - (4) into equation (1), and letting the partial derivatives of equation (1) with respect to s_t, n_t and e_t be zero (only considering interior solutions) gives the first-order conditions for the utility maximization problem:

$$\beta \frac{1+r_{t+1}}{c_{3,t+1}} = \frac{1}{c_{2,t}}, \qquad (5)$$

$$\frac{e_t + (1-\tau-s_t)vw_t}{c_{2,t}} + \beta \frac{1+r_{t+1}}{c_{3,t+1}} s_t vw_t = \frac{\gamma}{n_t}, \qquad (6)$$

$$\gamma \frac{\delta}{e_t} = \frac{n_t}{c_{2,t}}. \qquad (7)$$

Equation (5) implies that the utility loss from reducing one unit of working-period consumption is equal to the utility gain from increasing $(1+r_{t+1})$ units of retirement-period consumption. Equation (6) implies that the utility loss from reducing working-period consumption and retirement-period consumption is equal to the utility gain from increasing children's human capital through increasing a child. Equation (7) implies that the utility loss

---

[4] Available at the Chinese government website: http://www.gov.cn/zxft/ft31/content_679733.htm.

from reducing working-period consumption is equal to the utility gain from raising child's human capital through increasing education expenses.

2.2. Firms

Firms produce a homogenous commodity in competitive markets. The production is described by Cobb-Douglas function $Y_t = DK_t^\theta (L_t l_t h_t)^{1-\theta}$, where Y_t is the output in period t, K_t the physical capital stock, l_t the amount of labor hired from each worker of generation t, $\theta \in (0,1)$ the physical capital share of income, $D > 0$ the productivity of physical capital production.

Firms make pension contributions at the rate of $\eta \in (0,1)$ on their payroll. According to the product distribution, one can get that $DK_t^\theta (L_t l_t h_t)^{1-\theta} = (1+r_t)K_t + (1+\eta)w_t L_t l_t$. Firms act competitively, renting physical capital to the point where the marginal product of physical capital is equal to its rental rate, and hiring labor to the point where the marginal product of labor is equal to $(1+\eta)w_t$:

$$1 + r_t = \theta D k_t^{\theta-1}, \tag{8}$$

$$w_t = \frac{1-\theta}{1+\eta} D k_t^\theta h_t, \tag{9}$$

where $k_t = K_t / (L_t l_t h_t)$ is the physical capital per unit of effective labor.

2.3. The Government

The individual contributions are saved in the individual accounts, respectively. The accumulation in an individual account is used to pay the individual when she/he retires in the next period as funded pension benefits.

$$I_{t+1} = (1+r_{t+1})\tau(1-vn_t)w_t. \tag{10}$$

The firm contributions are credited into the social pool account. The social pool fund is paid to the retirees in current period as PAYG pension benefits, $L_t P_{t+1} = \eta L_{t+1} l_{t+1} w_{t+1}$, or

$$P_{t+1} = \eta n_t l_{t+1} w_{t+1}. \tag{11}$$

2.4. Markets Clearing

Labor market clears when the demand for labor is equal to the supply:

$$l_t = 1 - vn_t. \quad (12)$$

The savings and individual contributions in period t generate the capital stock in period $t+1$:

$$K_{t+1} = L_t(\tau + s_t)(1 - vn_t)w_t. \quad (13)$$

3. EQUILIBRIUM ANALYSIS

A balanced growth equilibrium is a competitive equilibrium in which intensive variables such as the saving rate, population growth rate[5] and education expense rate for each child $\dfrac{e_t}{(1-vn_t)w_t}$ are constant, whereas extensive variables such as the wage, human capital, physical capital per worker, consumption and so on grow at the same endogenously determined and constant growth rate, g. The following analysis focuses on the balanced growth equilibrium.

3.1. Analytical Solutions

Combining equations (8), (9), (12) and (13) gives $\dfrac{w_{t+1}}{1+r_{t+1}} = \dfrac{1-\theta}{\theta(1+\eta)} \dfrac{(\tau + s_t)l_t w_t}{n_t l_{t+1}}$. In the balanced growth equilibrium,

$$\frac{w_{t+1}}{1+r} = \frac{1-\theta}{\theta(1+\eta)} \frac{(\tau + s)w_t}{n}. \quad (14)$$

Substituting equations (5) and (7) into equation (6), rearranging gives

$$e_t = v\delta \frac{1-\tau}{1-\delta} w_t. \quad (15)$$

Hence, in the balanced growth equilibrium, the education expense rate is

---

[5] That is $(L_{t+1}-L_t)/L_t = n_t-1$. Let $N_t = n_t - 1$, then the derivatives of N_t with respect to policy variables are equal to that of n_t.

$$r_e = \frac{v\delta}{1-\delta}\frac{1-\tau}{1-vn}. \tag{15'}$$

Substituting equations (2) and (15) into equation (7), rearranging gives

$$\frac{vn}{1-vn}\frac{1-\tau}{1-\delta} = \gamma\frac{1-\tau-s}{1+\gamma\delta}. \tag{7'}$$

Substituting equations (2), (3), (14) and (15) into equation (5), rearranging gives

$$(1-\tau-s) - \frac{\tau+s}{\beta\theta}\frac{\theta+\eta}{1+\eta} = \delta\frac{1-\tau}{1-\delta}\frac{vn}{1-vn}. \tag{5'}$$

Combining equations (7') and (5') gives

$$s = \frac{\mu}{\varphi} - \tau, \tag{16}$$

$$n = \frac{\gamma(1-\delta)}{v}\frac{\theta+\eta}{\gamma(1-\delta)(\theta+\eta)+(1-\tau)\varphi}, \tag{17}$$

where $\mu = \beta\theta(1+\eta)$, $\varphi = \mu + (1+\gamma\delta)(\theta+\eta)$.

Substituting equation (15) into equation (4), rearranging gives

$$\frac{h_{t+1}}{h_t} = A\left(v\delta\frac{1-\tau}{1-\delta}\frac{1-\theta}{1+\eta}D\right)^\delta k_t^{\delta\theta}. \tag{18}$$

Combining equations (9) and (13) gives

$$\frac{K_{t+1}/L_{t+1}}{K_t/L_t} = \frac{\tau+s}{n}\frac{1-\theta}{1+\eta}Dk_t^{\theta-1}. \tag{19}$$

Balanced growth equilibrium implies that $1+g = \frac{h_{t+1}}{h_t} = \frac{K_{t+1}/L_{t+1}}{K_t/L_t}$.

Combining equations (18) and (19) gives

$$g = \left[A^{1-\theta}\left(v\delta\frac{1-\tau}{1-\delta}\right)^{\delta(1-\theta)}\left(\frac{1-\theta}{1+\eta}D\right)^\delta\left(\frac{\tau+s}{n}\right)^{\delta\theta}\right]^{\frac{1}{1-\theta+\delta\theta}} - 1. \tag{20}$$

3.2. Effect of Firm Contribution Rate

Partially differentiating s, n, r_e and g with respect to η, respectively, gives

$$\frac{\partial s}{\partial \eta} = \frac{\beta\theta(1+\gamma\delta)(\theta-1)}{\varphi^2} < 0,$$

$$\frac{\partial n}{\partial \eta} = \frac{\gamma(1-\delta)}{v} \frac{\beta\theta(1-\tau)(1-\theta)}{[\gamma(1-\delta)(\theta+\eta)+(1-\tau)\varphi]^2} > 0,$$

$$\frac{\partial r_e}{\partial \eta} = \frac{v^2\delta}{(1-vn)^2} \frac{1-\tau}{1-\delta} \frac{\partial n}{\partial \eta} > 0,$$

$$\frac{\partial g}{\partial \eta} = \frac{(1+g)\delta}{1-\theta+\delta\theta} \left(-\frac{1}{1+\eta} - \frac{\theta}{n} \frac{\partial n}{\partial \eta} \right) < 0.$$

Raising the firm contribution rate decreases the saving rate and per capita income growth rate, whereas increases the population growth rate and education expense rate.

A rise in the firm contribution rate induces the fall in the wage, furthermore the decrease in the opportunity cost of rearing children, which leads to the increase in the population growth rate. The fall in the wage induces the decrease in the savings. Both the increase in the population growth rate and the decrease in the savings lead to the fall in the saving rate. The increase in the population growth rate decreases the denominator of equation (15'), hence, increases the education expense rate. The per capita income growth rate decreases because it is negatively related to the firm contribution rate and population growth rate by virtue of equation (20).

3.3. Effect of Individual Contribution Rate

Partially differentiating s, n, r_e and g with respect to τ, respectively, gives

$$\frac{\partial s}{\partial \tau} = -1,$$

$$\frac{\partial n}{\partial \tau} = \frac{\gamma(1-\delta)}{v} \frac{(\theta+\eta)\varphi}{[\gamma(1-\delta)(\theta+\eta)+(1-\tau)\varphi]^2} > 0,$$

$$\frac{\partial r_e}{\partial \tau} = \frac{v\delta}{(1-\delta)(1-vn)^2} \frac{(1-\tau)\varphi[\gamma(1-\delta)(\theta+\eta)-1]}{\gamma(1-\delta)(\theta+\eta)+(1-\tau)\varphi} < 0,$$

$$\frac{\partial g}{\partial \tau} = \frac{(1+g)\delta}{1-\theta+\delta\theta}\left(-\frac{1-\theta}{1-\tau} - \frac{\theta}{n}\frac{\partial n}{\partial \tau}\right) < 0.$$

Raising the individual contribution rate decreases the saving rate, education expense rate and per capita income growth rate, whereas increases the population growth rate.

The saving rate falls as much as the individual contribution rate rises because the mandatory savings (individual contributions) crowd out the voluntary savings by one-for-one. A rise in the individual contribution rate induces the decrease in the income, furthermore, the fall in the opportunity cost of rearing children, which leads to the increase in the population growth rate. Consequently, the per capita income growth rate decreases because it is negatively related to the population growth rate. The rise in the population growth rate decreases the denominator of equation (15'), and the numerator falls because of rise in the individual contribution rate. The effect of the individual contribution rate on the education expense rate depends on the magnitude of the relevant parameters. Since γ, δ, θ, $\eta \in (0, 1)$, thus $\gamma (1 - \delta) (\theta + \eta)$ is in the magnitude of 10^{-2}. Hence, $\partial r_e / \partial \tau < 0$. In the following section, we use different parameter values to check the effects by simulating.

4. NUMERICAL EXPERIMENT

4.1. Parameter Calibration

A period length is assumed to be 26 years in this OLG model. We assume that the discount factor per year on utility derived from retirement-period consumption is 0.980, hence, the discount factor per period is $\beta = 0.980^{26}$. Analogously, the discount factor per year on utility derived from children's human capital is 0.975, thus, the factor per period is $\gamma = 0.975^{26}$. The physical capital share of income is assumed to be 0.35.

Analogous to Yew and Zhang (2009), we assume that the elasticity of human capital with respect to education expenses $\delta = 0.3$, rearing a child requires $v = 0.17$ units of labor. As pointed out by Zhang (1995), for the purpose of this study, A and D can be assumed to be large enough that $g > 0$. What we hope to see here is how the per capita income growth rate changes with the policy variables. Hence, we can assume that $A = 8$ and $D = 7$.

According to the Chinese State Council documents, *State Council Decision on Establishing a Unified Basic Pension System for Enterprise Employees* (Chinese State Council Document 26 in 1997) and *State Council Decision on Improving the Basic Pension System for Enterprise Employees* (Chinese State Council Document 38 in 2005), the firm contribution rate $\eta = 20\%$, and the individual contribution rate $\tau = 8\%$. These values are baseline values of the parameters.

4.2. Effects of Policy Variables

Let the firm contribution rate be 20% at first. Substituting it and the baseline values of the other relevant parameters into equations (16), (17), (15') and (20), one can get s, n, r_e and g, respectively. Then let the firm contribution rate be 22%, repeating the above procedure gives the result shown in Table 1. n and g are values in period (26 years); s and r_e are ratios, their values in year are the same as that in period. Obviously, raising the firm contribution rate decreases the saving rate and per capita income growth rate, whereas increases the population growth rate and education expense rate.

Table 1. Effect of firm contribution rate

η	20%	22%
s	20.104%	19.718%
n	1.158	1.163
r_e	8.346%	8.355%
g	3.042	3.001

Analogously, let the individual contribution rate be 8% at first. Substituting it and the baseline values of the other relevant parameters into equations (16), (17), (15') and (20), one can get s, n, r_e and g, respectively. Then, let the individual contribution rate be 10%, repeating the above procedure gives the result shown in Table 2. Consequently, raising the individual contribution rate decreases the saving rate, education expense rate and per capita income growth rate, whereas increases the population growth rate. The numerical experiment completely verify the effects of the policy variables derived in Section 3.

Based on Tables 1 and 2, we can compute the elasticity of the four endogenous variables with respect to η and τ, respectively. The result is shown in Table 3. The absolute values of elasticity indicate that the effects of the firm contribution rate on the population growth rate, saving rate and education expense rate are smaller than that of the individual contribution rate; whereas the effect of the firm contribution rate on the per capita income growth rate is much greater than that of the individual contribution rate.

Changing the baseline values of θ, δ and v, one can repeat the above numerical experiment. It can be shown that the results about the effects of the policy variables on the endogenous variables and the sensitivities reflected by elasticity do not change.

Table 2. Effect of individual contribution rate

τ	8%	10%
s	20.104%	18.104%
n	1.158	1.179
r_e	8.346%	8.200%
g	3.042	3.006

Table 3. Elasticity of endogenous variables with respect to η and τ

	elasticity with respect to η	elasticity with respect to τ
s	-19.2%	-39.8%
n	4.3%	7.1%
r_e	1.1%	-7.0%
g	-13.5%	-4.8%

CONCLUSION

Employing the endogenous growth OLG model, this chapter investigates the public pension system for urban enterprise employees in China. We examine the effects of the firm contribution rate and individual contribution rate on the per capita income growth rate, population growth rate, saving rate and education expense rate. According to the situations in China, we calibrate the values of the relevant parameters to simulate the effects of the policy variables on the endogenous variables. We also examine the sensitivity of the endogenous variables with respect to the policy variables. Instead of a PAYG or fully funded public pension system in the literature, this chapter studies the partially funded one combining social pool account and individual accounts. Both firms and workers make pension contributions instead of only workers do in the literature.

The results are as follows. Raising the firm contribution rate decreases the per capita income growth rate and saving rate, whereas increases the population growth rate and education expense rate. Raising the individual contribution rate decreases the per capita income growth rate, saving rate and education expense rate, whereas increases the population growth rate. The numerical experiment not only verify the above effects, but also find that the effect of the firm contribution rate on the per capita income growth rate is much greater than that of the individual contribution rate, whereas the effects of the firm contribution rate on the population growth rate, saving rate and education expense rate are smaller than that of the individual contribution rate.

The above results have valuable implications. Based on the practical economy situations, keeping a stable, healthy and sustainable economic growth rate and rationally controlling the population growth rate are national essential policies of China in a quite long historical period. Reducing the saving rate and education expense rate are also the current economic aims. In order to promote economic growth and control population size, it is necessary to reduce the firm contribution rate and individual contribution rate. To decrease the saving rate, it is necessary to raise the firm contribution rate and individual contribution rate. To decrease the education expense rate, it is necessary to reduce the firm contribution rate and raise the individual contribution rate. Integrating the above economic and social goals, it has more advantages than disadvantages to reduce the firm contribution rate and raise the individual contribution rate.

The policy, reducing the firm contribution rate and raising the individual contribution rate can realize the several goals. It can further the economic growth because the growth rate is much more sensitive with respect to the firm contribution rate than to the individual contribution rate. The policy can also rationally control the population size. Because the positive effect of raising the individual contribution rate on the population can dominate the negative effect of reducing the firm contribution rate, rational rise in the population growth rate is consistent with the Chinese population policy announced in 2013, a couple with husband or wife is sole child in his or her own family before they get married is eligible to give birth to two children. The policy can reduce the saving rate because the effect of raising the individual contribution rate on the saving rate can cover the effect of reducing the firm contribution rate. Obviously, the policy can reduce the education expense rate because both reducing the firm contribution rate and raising the individual contribution rate can reduce the education expense rate.

Chapter 5

URBAN PUBLIC PENSION, EXOGENOUS FERTILITY AND ENDOGENOUS GROWTH

ABSTRACT

China has implemented a special population policy, so called family planning policy, for several decades. Hence, there is a point of view that says individuals cannot choose their number of children, i.e., the number of children is an exogenous variable that individuals cannot control. Assuming the viewpoint be correct, this chapter establishes a corresponding endogenous growth model to investigate China's public pension system for urban enterprise employees. We examine the effects of the firm contribution rate, individual contribution rate and population growth rate on the economic growth rate, saving rate and education expense ratio. Raising the firm contribution rate decreases the economic growth rate and saving rate, while increases the education expense ratio. Raising the individual contribution rate only decreases the saving rate. A rise in the population growth rate decreases the economic growth rate and education expense ratio. The effect of the firm contribution rate on the economic growth rate is much greater than that of the population growth rate, that on the saving rate is smaller than that of the individual contribution rate, and that on the education expense ratio is much smaller than that of the population growth rate. In order to promote the economic growth, decrease the saving rate and education expense ratio, it is necessary to reduce the firm contribution rate, raise the individual contribution rate and rationally control the population growth rate.

Keywords: urban public pension; exogenous fertility; endogenous growth

1. INTRODUCTION

In Chapter 4, we investigate the public pension system for urban enterprise employees by developing an endogenous growth OLG model, where both population growth rate and economic growth rate are endogenously determined. However, there is a point of view that says individual cannot choose her/his number of children. The reason is that China has implemented its special population policy, so called family planning policy for several decades. Each couple can only give birth to one child. Thus, individuals cannot choose their number of children. In other words, the number of children is an exogenous variable that individual cannot control. Provided that this viewpoint was correct, this chapter establishes a corresponding endogenous growth OLG model to investigate the public pension system for urban enterprise employees reformed in 2005. We examine the effects of the firm contribution rate, individual contribution rate and population growth rate on the economic growth rate, saving rate and education expense ratio.

Studying the relationship between the economic growth, population and public pension system should consider the following concrete situations: Firstly, as a developing country with low GDP per capita, China needs to keep a comparatively high economic growth rate. Secondly, since the beginning of 1980s, the residents' saving rate has been high, and the effective consumption demand was not enough. In the era of post-crisis of international finance, to promote the consumption, it is necessary to decrease the saving rate. Thirdly, Chinese generally pay much attention to their children's human capital, zealously invest in education to their children and satisfy for their children's high human capital. Finally, the ratio of education expenses to family income became higher and higher since the beginning of 1980s. The public hope to decrease the education expense ratio.

Many economists have studied the relation between economic growth and public pension with endogenous growth OLG model. Zhang and Zhang (1995, 1998), Wigger (1999a) transformed the capital per unit of effective labor into a constant and the production function into so-called "AK model" by adopting a special type of productivity. Instead of transforming the production function into "AK model", Zhang (1995, 2001), Yew and Zhang (2009) introduced human capital, which grows at the same rate with the physical capital per unit of labor in balanced growth equilibrium. However, to find the endogenous variables' solution, this chapter utilize the principle of physical capital should receive the same rate of return when allocated to both physical and human sectors of production.

2. THE MODEL

Based on Zhang (1995) and Yew and Zhang (2009), this model replaces PAYG or fully funded public pension systems with China's partially funded pension system, and takes the number of children as exogenous variable. There are numerous individuals and firms and a government in a closed economy. Each individual lives through three periods in life: childhood period, working period and retirement period. At the beginning of period t, L_t identical individuals of generation t enter the work force. Each individual has N children, hence, $L_{t+1} = NL_t$, and the population growth rate is $n = (L_{t+1} - L_t)/L_t = N - 1$.

2.1. Individuals

Individuals develop their human capital in childhood period, and have no ability to make economic decision. Upon entering the work force, each individual represents one unit of labor. Rearing a child requires $v \in (0,1)$ units of labor. Hence, each individual supplies $l = (1-vN) > 0$ units of labor to earn wage income. After making pension contributions, she/he consumes part of the income, pays education expenses for children, and saves the remainder of income. In the retirement period, she/he consumes the savings with accrued interest, individual account benefits and social pool benefits. Each individual derives utility from her/his working-period consumption $C_{2,t}$, retirement-period consumption $C_{3,t+1}$ and children's human capital. The utility is described by an additively separable logarithmic function. Thus, the utility maximization problem is:

$$\max_{\{s_t, E_t\}} U_t = \ln C_{2,t} + \beta \ln C_{3,t+1} + \gamma \ln(Nh_{t+1}), \qquad (1)$$

s.t.
$$C_{2,t} = (1 - \tau - s_t) w_t h_t - NE_t, \qquad (2)$$

$$C_{3,t+1} = R_{t+1} s_t w_t h_t + I_{t+1} + P_{t+1}, \qquad (3)$$

where $\beta \in (0,1)$ denotes the discount factor on the utility derived from retirement-period consumption, and $\gamma \in (0,1)$ that on the utility derived from children's human capital. Each individual's human capital of generation $t + 1$ is

$$h_{t+1} = A E_t^{\delta} h_t^{1-\delta}, \qquad (4)$$

where $\delta \in (0,1)$ is the elasticity of human capital with respect to education expenses, $A > 0$ is the productivity of human capital production. τ denotes the individual contribution rate, w_t the wage per unit of effective labor, s_t the saving rate, E_t the education expenses for each child, R_{t+1} the interest rate, I_{t+1} the individual account benefits, and P_{t+1} the social pool benefits.

Substituting equations (2) - (4) into equation (1), and letting the partial derivatives of equation (1) with respect to s_t and E_t be zero gives the first-order conditions for the utility maximization (only considering interior solutions):

$$\beta R_{t+1} C_{2,t} = C_{3,t+1}, \qquad (5)$$

$$\delta \gamma C_{2,t} = NE_t. \qquad (6)$$

Equation (5) implies that the utility loss from reducing one unit of working-period consumption is equal to the utility gain from increasing R_{t+1} units of retirement-period consumption. Equation (6) implies that the utility loss from reducing working-period consumption is equal to the utility gain from raising children's human capital through increasing education expenses.

2.2. Firms

Firms produce a homogenous commodity in competitive markets. The production is described by Cobb-Douglas function $Y_t = DK_t^{\theta} (L_t lh_t)^{1-\theta}$ or $y_t = Dk_t^{\theta} h_t^{1-\theta}$, where Y_t is the output in period t, K_t the physical capital stock at the beginning of period t, y_t the output per unit of labor, $k_t = K_t/(L_t l)$ the physical capital per unit of labor, $D > 0$ the productivity of physical capital production, $\theta \in (0,1)$ the physical capital share of income. As pointed out by Barro and Sala-I-Martin (2004), $\theta > \delta$, namely, the goods sector is relatively intensive in physical capital, and the education sector is relatively intensive in human capital.

Firms make pension contributions at the rate of $\eta \in (0,1)$ on their payroll. According to the product distribution, one can get that $DK_t^\theta (L_t lh_t)^{1-\theta} = R_t K_t + (1+\eta) w_t L_t lh_t$. Euler's theorem leads to the following results:

$$R_t = \theta D k_t^{\theta-1} h_t^{1-\theta}, \tag{7}$$

$$w_t = \frac{1-\theta}{1+\eta} D k_t^\theta h_t^{-\theta}. \tag{8}$$

2.3. The Government

The accumulation in an individual account is used to pay the individual when she/he retires in the next period as funded pension benefits.

$$I_{t+1} = R_{t+1} \tau w_t h_t. \tag{9}$$

The firm contributions are credited into the social pool account. The social pool fund is paid to the retirees in current period as PAYG pension benefits, $L_t P_{t+1} = \eta w_{t+1} L_{t+1} lh_{t+1}$, or

$$P_{t+1} = \eta N l w_{t+1} h_{t+1}. \tag{10}$$

2.4. Physical Capital Market

The savings and individual contributions in period t generate the physical capital stock in period $t + 1$:

$$N k_{t+1} = (\tau + s_t) w_t h_t. \tag{11}$$

3. DYNAMIC EQUILIBRIUM SYSTEM

A competitive equilibrium for this market economy is a sequence as $\{C_{2,t}, C_{3,t+1}, w_t, R_{t+1}, s_t, E_t, I_{t+1}, P_{t+1}, k_{t+1}, h_{t+1}\}_{t=0}^\infty$ that satisfies equations (1) - (11) for all t, given the initial conditions (k_0, h_0) and the parameter values of η and τ.

Substituting equations (2) - (3) and (6) - (11) into equation (5) and rearranging yields:

$$k_{t+1} = ak_t^\theta h_t^{1-\theta},\qquad(12)$$

where $a = \dfrac{1-\theta}{1+\eta}\dfrac{D}{N\varphi}$, $\varphi = 1+\mu$, $\mu = \dfrac{1+\delta\gamma}{\beta\theta}\left(\theta + \eta\dfrac{1-\theta}{1+\eta}\right)$.

Combining equations (2), (6) and (12) gives

$$E_t = \dfrac{l\delta\gamma}{1+\delta\gamma}\mu k_{t+1}.\qquad(6')$$

Substituting equation (6') into (4) yields

$$h_{t+1} = bk_{t+1}^\delta h_t^{1-\delta},\qquad(13)$$

where $b = A\left(\dfrac{l\delta\gamma\mu}{1+\delta\gamma}\right)^\delta$. Equations (12) and (13) constitute the dynamic equilibrium system to describe the economy.

Substituting equation (12) into equation (13) gives

$$h_{t+1} = ba^\delta k_t^{\theta\delta} h_t^{1-\theta\delta}.\qquad(14)$$

As pointed out by Barro and Sala-I-Martin (2004), physical capital must receive the same rate of return when allocated to either sector of production: $ba^\delta \theta\delta k_t^{\theta\delta-1} h_t^{1-\theta\delta} = \theta D k_t^{\theta-1} h_t^{1-\theta}$, or

$$h_t = \left(\dfrac{D}{\delta ba^\delta}\right)^{\frac{1}{\theta(1-\delta)}} k_t.\qquad(15)$$

Substituting equation (15) into equation (12) gives

$$k_{t+1} = Zk_t.\qquad(16)$$

where $Z = \left\{\dfrac{D^{1-\delta}}{(\delta A)^{1-\theta}}\left(\dfrac{1-\theta}{N}\right)^{\theta-\delta}\left(\dfrac{1+\delta\gamma}{l\delta\gamma}\right)^{\delta(1-\theta)}[(1+\eta)\varphi]^{\delta-\theta}\mu^{\delta(\theta-1)}\right\}^{\frac{1}{\theta(1-\delta)}}$. Therefore, the growth rate of k_t, h_t and y_t is

$$g = Z - 1 \qquad (17)$$

If $Z > 1$, the economy converges to a balanced growth equilibrium, in which intensive variables such as the saving rate, population growth rate and education expense ratio for each child $E_t/(lw_t h_t)$ are constant, whereas extensive variables such as the human capital, physical capital per unit of labor, consumption, etc., grow at the same endogenously determined and constant growth rate. The economy stagnates if $Z = 1$, and converges to $k = 0$ if $Z < 1$. The last two cases are meaningless because real economy grows in a period of 25 - 30 years even if it has transitory stagnation or degradation. The following analysis focuses on the balanced growth equilibrium.

Substituting equations (12) and (8) into equation (11) gives

$$s = \frac{1}{\varphi} - \tau. \qquad (18)$$

Combining equations (6'), (8) and (12) gives the education expense ratio

$$e = \frac{\delta \gamma}{1 + \delta \gamma} \frac{\mu}{\varphi N}. \qquad (19)$$

4. EFFECTS OF EXOGENOUS VARIABLES

4.1. Effect of Firm Contribution Rate

Partially differentiating g, s and e with respect to η, respectively, gives

$$\frac{\partial g}{\partial \eta} = -\frac{Z}{\theta(1-\delta)}\left(\frac{\theta-\delta}{1+\eta} + \left(\frac{\theta-\delta}{\varphi} + \delta\frac{1-\theta}{\mu}\right)\frac{1+\delta\gamma}{\beta\theta}\frac{1-\theta}{(1+\eta)^2}\right) < 0,$$

$$\frac{\partial s}{\partial \eta} = -\frac{(1+\delta\gamma)(1-\theta)}{\varphi^2 \beta\theta(1+\eta)^2} < 0,$$

$$\frac{\partial e}{\partial \eta} = \frac{\delta\gamma}{N}\frac{1-\theta}{\varphi^2 \beta\theta(1+\eta)^2} > 0.$$

Raising the firm contribution rate decreases the economic growth rate and saving rate, whereas increases the education expense ratio. A rise in the firm contribution rate induces the increase in the social pool benefits, furthermore the rise in the retirement-period consumption. To smooth the working-period consumption and retirement-period consumption, it is necessary to decrease the saving rate. The increment of the working-period consumption implies the rise in the education expense ratio by virtue of equation (6).

4.2. Effect of Individual Contribution Rate

Partially differentiating g, s and e with respect to τ, respectively, gives

$$\frac{\partial g}{\partial \tau} = 0,$$

$$\frac{\partial s}{\partial \tau} = -1,$$

$$\frac{\partial e}{\partial \tau} = 0.$$

Raising the individual contribution rate has no effect on the economic growth rate and education expense ratio but decreases the saving rate. The saving rate falls as much as the individual contribution rate rises because the mandatory savings (individual pension contributions) crowd out the voluntary savings by one-for-one. Equations (17) and (19) indicate that g and e are independent of τ. Hence, the individual contribution rate has no effect on the economic growth rate and education expense ratio.

4.3. Effect of population growth rate

Partially differentiating g, s and e with respect to n, respectively, gives

$$\frac{\partial g}{\partial n} = \frac{Z}{1-\delta} \frac{vN\theta(1-\delta)+\delta-\theta}{\theta Nl} < 0,$$

$$\frac{\partial s}{\partial n} = 0,$$

$$\frac{\partial e}{\partial n} = -\frac{\mu}{N^2\varphi} \frac{\delta\gamma}{1+\delta\gamma} < 0.$$

A rise in the population growth rate decreases the economic growth rate and education expense ratio, but has no effect on the saving rate. In the partial derivative, $vN\theta(1-\delta) + \delta - \theta < 0$ because $\theta > \delta$ and $v, N, \theta, \delta \in (0, 1)$. The economic growth rate falls because it is negatively related to the population growth rate by equation (17).

5. NUMERICAL EXPERIMENT

5.1. Parameter Calibration

A period length is assumed to be 26 years because it is usually in the interval of 25 - 30 years in the literature on OLG model. Analogous to Pecchenino and Pollard (2002), we assume that per year discount factor on the utility derived from retirement-period consumption is 0.980, hence, in a period, $\beta = 0.980^{26}$. Analogously, per year discount factor on the utility derived from children's human capital is 0.975, thus, $\gamma = 0.975^{26}$.

Analogous to Yew and Zhang (2009), we assume that the elasticity of human capital with respect to education expenses $\delta = 0.3$, rearing a child requires $v = 0.20$ units of labor. Assume a couple of urban adult residents have average 1.4 children, i.e., an individual has $N = 0.7$ children. The physical capital share of income is assumed to be 0.35 in China. What we hope to see here is how the economic growth rate changes with the exogenous variables. Hence, A and D can be normalized as 1.

According to the Chinese State Council documents, *State Council Decision on Establishing a Unified Basic Pension System for Enterprise Employees* (Chinese State Council Document 26 in 1997) and *State Council Decision on Improving the Basic Pension System for Enterprise Employees* (Chinese State Council Document 38 in 2005), the firm contribution rate $\eta = 20\%$, and the individual contribution rate $\tau = 8\%$. These are baseline values of the parameters.

5.2. Effects of Exogenous Variables and Sensitivities

Let the firm contribution rate be 18% at first. Substituting it and the baseline values of the other relevant parameters into equations (17), (18) and (19), one can get g, s and e, respectively. Then let the firm contribution rate be 20%, repeating the above procedure gives the result shown in Table 1. g is the value in period (26 years). s and e are ratios, their values in year are the same as in period. Obviously, raising the firm contribution rate decreases the economic growth rate and saving rate, whereas increases the education expense ratio.

Table 1. Effect of firm contribution rate

η	18%	20%	percentage increase
g	47.176	46.105	-2.27%
s	0.205	0.201	-2.00%
e	0.137	0.138	0.57%

Table 2. Effect of individual contribution rate

τ	8%	10%	percentage increase
g	46.105	46.105	0.00%
s	0.201	0.181	-9.95%
e	0.138	0.138	0.00%

Analogously, let the individual contribution rate be 8% at first. Substituting it and the baseline values of the other relevant parameters into equations (17), (18) and (19), we get g, s and e, respectively. Then, let the individual contribution rate be 10%, repeating the above procedure gives the result shown in Table 2. Raising the individual contribution rate has no effect on the economic growth rate and education expense ratio but decreases the saving rate. Doing numerical experiment with the baseline parameter values and the number of children 0.6 and 0.7, respectively, gives the effects of the population growth rate shown in Table 3. A rise in the population growth rate decreases the economic growth rate and education expense ratio, but has no effect on the saving rate. The experiments completely verify the effects of the exogenous variables derived in the above section.

Table 3. Effect of population growth rate

N	0.6	0.7	percentage increase
g	46.729	46.105	-1.34%
s	0.201	0.201	0.00%
e	0.161	0.138	-14.29%

Table 4. Elasticity of g, s and e with respect to η, τ and N

	η	τ	N
g	-20.44%	0.00%	-8.01%
s	-18.02%	-39.79%	0.00%
e	5.17%	0.00%	-85.71%

Based on Tables 1 - 3, we compute the elasticity of the endogenous variables with respect to η, τ and N, respectively. The result is shown in Table 4. The absolute values of the elasticity indicate that the effect of the firm contribution rate on the economic growth rate is much greater than that of the population growth rate, that on the saving rate is smaller than that of the individual contribution rate, and that on the education expense ratio is much smaller than that of the population growth rate.

CONCLUSION

Because there is a point of view that says individuals in China cannot choose their number of children, we suppose the viewpoint is correct temporarily. Taking population growth rate as exogenous variable, this chapter employs the endogenous growth OLG model to investigate the public pension system for urban enterprise employees in China. We examine the effects of the firm contribution rate, individual contribution rate and population growth rate on the economic growth rate, saving rate and education expense ratio. According to the circumstance in China, we estimate the values of relevant parameters to simulate the effects of the exogenous variables on the endogenous variables. We also examine the sensitivities of the endogenous variables with respect to the exogenous variables. Instead of a PAYG or fully funded public pension system in the literature, this chapter studies the partially funded one combining social pool and individual accounts. Both firms and employees make pension contributions instead of only employees do in the literature. To find the endogenous variables' solution, we utilize the principle of physical capital must receive the same rate of return when allocated to either sector of production, instead of the approach of human capital grows at the same rate with the physical capital per unit of labor in balanced growth equilibrium.

The results are as follows: Raising the firm contribution rate decreases the economic growth rate and saving rate, whereas increases the education expense ratio. Raising the individual contribution rate has no effect on the economic growth rate and education expense ratio but decreases the saving rate. A rise in the population growth rate decreases the economic growth rate and education expense ratio, but has no effect on the saving rate. The numericao experiments not only verify the above effects completely, but also find that the effect of the firm contribution rate on the economic growth rate is much greater than that of the population growth rate, that on the saving rate is smaller than that of the individual contribution rate, and that on the education expense ratio is much smaller than that of the population growth rate.

The above results imply some policy suggestion. Based on the practical economy situations in China, a developing country with low GDP per capita, high saving rate and high ratio of education expenses to family income should hold a comparatively high economic growth rate, reduce the saving rate and education expense ratio, especially in the era of post-crisis of international finance. In accordance with the effects of the firm contribution rate, individual contribution rate and population growth rate on the economic growth rate, saving rate and education expense ratio and their sensitivities, integrating the above economic goals gives the measures: to reduce the firm contribution rate, raise the individual contribution rate, and rationally control the population growth rate.

Chapter 6

URBAN PUBLIC PENSION, ENDOGENOUS FERTILITY AND ECONOMIC GROWTH

ABSTRACT

It is reasonable and correct to take fertility as an endogenous variable because each family can choose the number of children even if during the period while China carried out the strictest family planning policy. Employing an endogenous growth OLG model, we examine the effects of the contribution rates in the public pension system for urban enterprise employees on the per capita income growth rate, population growth rate, saving rate and education expense ratio in China. Raising the firm contribution rate decreases the per capita income growth rate and saving rate, whereas increases the population growth rate and education expense ratio. Raising the individual contribution rate under a threshold decreases the per capita income growth rate, but over the threshold increases the per capita income growth rate. Raising the individual contribution rate increases the population growth rate, whereas decreases the saving rate and education expense ratio. The effect of the individual contribution rate on the per capita income growth rate is very weak, whereas the effect of the firm contribution rate is very strong. The effects of the individual contribution rate on the population growth rate, saving rate and education expense ratio are near 3 times, 5 times and 11 times stronger than that of the firm contribution rate, respectively. It will do more good than harm to reduce the firm contribution rate and raise the individual contribution rate.

Keywords: urban public pension; endogenous fertility; endogenous growth

1. INTRODUCTION

The last chapter assumes that individuals cannot choose their number of children because China has implemented so called family planning policy for several decades, and takes population growth rate as exogenous variable. In fact, Chinese can choose their number of children. The spokesman of National Population and Family Planning Commission of China (2007) said: China has not realized one child per family in practice, families having only one child was 35.9%, those having 1.5 children was 52.9%, and 11% of families were born with two or more children[1]. Even if the government required each couple to give birth not more than one time, any couple can decide to give birth one time or no time. Therefore, it is reasonable and correct to take the number of children or population growth rate as endogenous variable.

China reformed its public pension system for urban enterprise employees in 1997 and 2005, respectively. According to the Chinese State Council Document 26 in 1997, *State Council Decision on Establishing a Unified Basic Pension System for Enterprise Employees* and the Chinese State Council Document 38 in 2005, *State Council Decision on Improving the Basic Pension System for Enterprise Employees*, the government establishes an individual account for each employee and a social pool for all employees and retirees. Each firm contributes 20% of its payroll to the social pool, while each employee contributes 8% of their wage to their individual account. The social pool fund is used to pay the current retirees as pay-as-you-go (PAYG) pension benefits, whereas the accumulation in an individual account is used to pay the individual when they retire as funded pension benefits. Each retiree receives funded pension benefits from their individual account and PAYG pension benefits from the social pool. This public pension system must affect the economic growth, population, residents' savings, etc.

For studying the relationship between the economic growth and public pension in China, it is necessary to echo the following practical situations: First, to recover from the international financial crisis, China needs to maintain a stable, healthy and sustainable economic growth. Second, household saving rate was very high and the effective consumption demand not enough in the last three decades. To promote the consumption, especially in the era of post-crisis of international finance, it is necessary to decrease the saving rate. Third, Chinese generally pay attention to not only their own welfare but also their children's human capital, enthusiastically invest in education to their children and satisfy for their children's high human capital. Fourth, the ratio of education expenses to family income has been becoming higher and higher. The public hope an obvious fall in the education expense ratio. Fifth, after the revised public pension system implementing some years, retirees will depend mainly on their own savings and the pension benefits, not on their children. Final, China has its special population policy.

There are a great deal of literature to study the relationship between economic growth, population and public pension with endogenous growth OLG model. For example, Zhang and Zhang (1995, 1998), Wigger (1999a), etc. A common feature of these studies is to transform the capital per unit of effective labor into a constant and the production function into so-called "AK model" by adopting a special type of productivity. Instead of that, Zhang (1995) introduced human capital, which grows at a same rate with the physical capital per unit of labor in balanced growth equilibrium. Zhang and Zhang (2003) examined the effects of unfunded social security with bequests, fertility and human capital by considering a mix of earnings-dependent and universal social security benefits. Yew and Zhang (2009) investigated the optimal scale of PAYG social security in a dynastic family model with human capital externalities, fertility and endogenous growth.

By employing an endogenous growth model, this chapter investigates the partially funded public pension system for urban enterprise employees in China. It examines the effects of the firm contribution rate and individual contribution rate on the per capita income growth rate,

---

[1] Available at the Chinese government website: http://www.gov.cn/zxft/ft31/content_ 679733.htm.

population growth rate, saving rate and education expense ratio. The approaches to find the analytical solution for endogenous variables are different from the above literature. This chapter utilizes the principle that physical capital must receive the same rate of return when allocated to either sector of production, instead of the assumption that human capital grows at the same rate with the physical capital per unit of labor in balanced growth equilibrium.

2. THE MODEL

A closed economy is composed of numerous individuals and firms and a government. Each individual lives through three periods in life: childhood period, working period and retirement period. At the beginning of period t, L_t identical individuals of generation t enter the work force. Each individual has N_t children, hence $L_{t+1} = N_t L_t$, and the population growth rate $n_t = (L_{t+1} - L_t) / L_t = N_t - 1$, which implies endogenous fertility.

2.1. Individuals

Individuals develop their human capital in childhood period, and have no ability to make economic decision. Upon entering the work force, each individual represents one unit of labor, uses $v \in (0,1)$ units of labor to rear each child and supplies $(1-vN_t) > 0$ units of labor to earn wage income. After making pension contributions, she/he consumes part of the income, pays education expenses for the children, and saves the remainder of income. In the retirement period, she/he consumes the savings with accrued interest, individual account benefits and social pool benefits.

Each individual derives utility from her/his working-period consumption $C_{2,t}$, retirement-period consumption $C_{3,t+1}$ and children's human capital. The utility is described by an additively separable logarithmic function. Thus, the utility maximization problem is:

$$\max_{\{s_t, N_t, E_t\}} U_t = \ln C_{2,t} + \beta \ln C_{3,t+1} + \gamma \ln(N_t h_{t+1}), \tag{1}$$

s.t.

$$C_{2,t} = (1 - \tau - s_t)(1 - vN_t)w_t h_t - N_t E_t, \tag{2}$$

$$C_{3,t+1} = R_{t+1} s_t (1 - vN_t) w_t h_t + I_{t+1} + P_{t+1}, \tag{3}$$

where $\beta \in (0,1)$ denotes the discount factor on the utility derived from retirement-period consumption, and $\gamma \in (0,1)$ that on the utility derived from children's human capital. They reflect individual preference. Each individual's human capital of generation $t + 1$ is

$$h_{t+1} = A E_t^{\delta} h_t^{1-\delta}, \tag{4}$$

where $\delta \in (0,1)$ is the elasticity of human capital with respect to education expenses, $A > 0$ the productivity of human capital production. τ denotes the individual contribution rate, w_t the wage per unit of effective labor, s_t the saving rate, E_t the education expenses for each child, R_{t+1} the rate of return to physical capital, I_{t+1} the individual account benefits, and P_{t+1} the social pool benefits.

Substituting equations (2) - (4) into equation (1) and letting the partial derivatives of equation (1) with respect to s_t, N_t and E_t be zero gives the first-order conditions for the utility maximization problem (only considering interior solutions):

$$\beta R_{t+1} C_{2,t} = C_{3,t+1}, \tag{5}$$

$$\frac{E_t + (1-\tau - s_t) v w_t h_t}{C_{2,t}} + \beta \frac{R_{t+1} s_t v w_t h_t}{C_{3,t+1}} = \frac{\gamma}{N_t}, \tag{6}$$

$$N_t E_t = \delta \gamma C_{2,t}. \tag{7}$$

Equation (5) implies that the utility loss from reducing one unit of working-period consumption is equal to the utility gain from increasing R_{t+1} units of retirement-period consumption. Equation (6) implies that the utility loss from reducing working-period consumption and retirement-period consumption is equal to the utility gain from increasing children's human capital through increasing a child. Equation (7) implies that the utility loss from reducing working-period consumption is equal to the utility gain from raising children's human capital through increasing one unit of education expenses.

2.2. Firms

Firms produce a homogenous commodity in competitive markets. The production is described by Cobb-Douglas function $Y_t = D K_t^\theta (L_t l_t h_t)^{1-\theta}$ or $y_t = D k_t^\theta h_t^{1-\theta}$, where Y_t is the output in period t, $D > 0$ the productivity of physical capital production, K_t the physical capital stock at the beginning of period t, l_t the amount of labor hired from each worker of generation t, $\theta \in (0,1)$ the physical capital share of income, $y_t = Y_t/(L_t l_t)$ the output per unit of labor, $k_t = K_t/(L_t l_t)$ the physical capital per unit of labor. $\theta > \delta$, namely, the goods sector is relatively intensive in physical capital, and the education sector is relatively intensive in human capital (Barro and Sala-I-Martin, 2004).

Firms make pension contributions at the rate of $\eta \in (0,1)$ on their payroll. The product is distributed into capital income, labor income with the firm contributions: $D K_t^\theta (L_t l_t h_t)^{1-\theta} = R_t K_t + (1+\eta) w_t L_t l_t h_t$. According to firms' profit maximization problem or by virtue of Euler's theorem, we have:

$$R_t = \theta D k_t^{\theta-1} h_t^{1-\theta}, \tag{8}$$

$$w_t = \frac{1-\theta}{1+\eta} Dk_t^\theta h_t^{-\theta}. \qquad (9)$$

2.3. The Government

The accumulation in an individual account is used to pay the individual when she/he retires in the next period as funded pension benefits.

$$I_{t+1} = R_{t+1}\tau(1-vN_t)w_t h_t. \qquad (10)$$

The social pool fund is paid to the retirees in current period as PAYG pension benefits, $L_t P_{t+1} = \eta w_{t+1} L_{t+1} l_{t+1} h_{t+1}$, or

$$P_{t+1} = \eta N_t l_{t+1} w_{t+1} h_{t+1}. \qquad (11)$$

2.4. Markets Clearing

Labor market clears when the demand for labor is equal to the supply:

$$l_t = 1 - vN_t. \qquad (12)$$

The savings and individual pension contributions in period t generate the physical capital stock at the beginning of period $t+1$:

$$(\tau + s_t)l_t w_t h_t = N_t l_{t+1} k_{t+1}. \qquad (13)$$

3. DYNAMIC EQUILIBRIUM SYSTEM

A competitive equilibrium for this market economy is a sequence as $\{C_{2,t}, C_{3,t+1}, w_t, R_{t+1}, s_t, E_t, I_{t+1}, P_{t+1}, k_{t+1}, h_{t+1}\}_{t=0}^\infty$ that satisfies equations (1) - (13) for all t, given the initial conditions (k_0, h_0) and the policy parameters, η and τ.

Substituting equations (5), (7) and (9) into equation (6) and rearranging gives

$$E_t = v\delta \frac{1-\tau}{1-\delta} \frac{1-\theta}{1+\eta} Dk_t^\theta h_t^{1-\theta}. \qquad (6')$$

Substituting equations (2) - (3) and (6) - (13) into equation (5) and rearranging yields

$$l_{t+1}k_{t+1} = a\frac{l_t}{N_t}k_t^\theta h_t^{1-\theta}, \tag{14}$$

where $a = \dfrac{1-\theta}{1+\eta}\dfrac{D}{\varphi}$, $\varphi = 1+\mu$, $\mu = \dfrac{1+\delta\gamma}{\beta\theta}\left(\theta + \eta\dfrac{1-\theta}{1+\eta}\right)$. Combining equations (7), (2) and (5) gives

$$E_t = \frac{\delta\gamma\mu}{1+\delta\gamma}l_{t+1}k_{t+1}. \tag{7'}$$

Substituting equation (7') into equation (4) yields

$$h_{t+1} = b(l_{t+1}k_{t+1})^\delta h_t^{1-\delta}, \tag{15}$$

where $b = A\left(\dfrac{\delta\gamma\mu}{1+\delta\gamma}\right)^\delta$. Combining equations (6') and (7') gives

$$\frac{\delta\gamma\mu}{1+\delta\gamma}l_{t+1}k_{t+1} = v\delta\frac{1-\tau}{1-\delta}\frac{1-\theta}{1+\eta}Dk_t^\theta h_t^{1-\theta}. \tag{16}$$

The system of three nonlinear first-order autonomous difference equations (14), (15) and (16) is the dynamic equilibrium system to describe the economy.

Substituting equation (14) into equation (16) gives

$$a\frac{l_t}{N_t} = i, \tag{16'}$$

where $i = vD\dfrac{1-\theta}{1+\eta}\dfrac{1-\tau}{1-\delta}\dfrac{1+\delta\gamma}{\gamma\mu}$. Substituting equation (12) into equation (16') gives

$$N = \frac{a}{i+va}, \text{ or } l = \frac{i}{i+va}. \tag{17}$$

That is, the number of children and supply of labor are dependent on the relevant parameters but independent of period.

Substituting equations (14) and (16') into equation (15) gives

$$h_{t+1} = bi^\delta k_t^{\theta\delta} h_t^{1-\theta\delta}. \tag{15'}$$

As pointed out by Barro and Sala-I-Martin (2004), physical capital must receive the same rate of return when allocated to either sector of production: $bi^\delta \theta \delta k_t^{\theta\delta-1} h_t^{1-\theta\delta} = \theta D k_t^{\theta-1} h_t^{1-\theta}$, or

$$h_t = \left(\frac{D}{\delta b}\right)^{\frac{1}{\theta(1-\delta)}} \cdot i^{-\frac{\delta}{\theta(1-\delta)}} \cdot k_t. \tag{18}$$

Substituting equations (17) and (18) into equation (14) and rearranging gives

$$k_{t+1} = Zk_t. \tag{19}$$

where $Z = \left(vD\dfrac{1-\theta}{1+\eta}\right)^{\frac{\theta-\delta}{\theta(1-\delta)}} \delta^{\frac{1-\theta}{\theta}} \left(\dfrac{D}{A}\right)^{\frac{1-\theta}{\theta(1-\delta)}} \left(\dfrac{1-\delta}{1-\tau}\right)^{\frac{\delta(1-\theta)}{\theta(1-\delta)}} \left(\dfrac{1+\delta\gamma}{\gamma}\dfrac{1-\tau}{1-\delta} + \dfrac{1}{1+\mu}\right).$

Therefore, the growth rate of k_t, h_t, y_t, etc., is

$$g = Z - 1. \tag{20}$$

If $Z > 1$, the economy converges to a balanced growth equilibrium, in which intensive variables such as the saving rate, population growth rate and education expense ratio for each child $E_t/(l_t w_t h_t)$ are constant, whereas extensive variables such as the physical capital per unit of labor, consumption, etc., grow at the same endogenously determined and constant growth rate. The economy stagnates if $Z = 1$, and converges to $k = 0$ if $Z < 1$. The last two cases are meaningless because real economy grows in a period of 25 - 30 years even if it has transitory stagnation or degradation. The following analysis focuses on the balanced growth equilibrium.

Substituting equations (9) and (14) into equation (13) gives

$$s = \frac{1}{\varphi} - \tau. \tag{21}$$

Combining equations (6') and (17) gives the education expense ratio

$$e = v\delta \frac{1-\tau}{1-\delta} \frac{i+va}{i}. \tag{22}$$

4. EFFECTS OF POLICY VARIABLES

4.1. Effect of Firm Contribution Rate

Partially differentiating g, N, s and e with respect to η, respectively, gives

$$\frac{\partial g}{\partial \eta} = -\frac{Z}{\theta(1+\eta)} \left(\frac{\theta-\delta}{1-\delta} + \left(\frac{1+\delta\gamma}{\gamma} \frac{1-\tau}{1-\delta} + \frac{1}{1+\mu} \right)^{-1} \frac{(1+\delta\gamma)(1-\theta)}{(1+\mu)^2 \beta(1+\eta)} \right) < 0,$$

$$\frac{\partial N}{\partial \eta} = \frac{ai(1+\delta\gamma)(1-\theta)}{(i+va)^2 \mu(1+\mu)\beta\theta(1+\eta)^2} > 0,$$

$$\frac{\partial s}{\partial \eta} = -\frac{(1+\delta\gamma)(1-\theta)}{\varphi^2 \beta\theta(1+\eta)^2} < 0,$$

$$\frac{\partial e}{\partial \eta} = \left(\frac{v}{i}\right)^2 \delta \frac{(1-\tau)ai(1+\delta\gamma)(1-\theta)}{(1-\delta)\mu(1+\mu)\beta\theta(1+\eta)^2} > 0.$$

Raising the firm contribution rate decreases the per capita income growth rate and saving rate, whereas increases the population growth rate and education expense ratio. A rise in the firm contribution rate induces the increase in the social pool benefits, which leads to a fall in the saving rate for smoothing the working-period consumption and retirement-period consumption. By virtue of Z in equation (20), the per capita income growth rate is inversely proportional to the firm contribution rate; hence, raising the firm contribution rate decreases the per capita income growth rate. A rise in the firm contribution rate decreases the labor income or the opportunity costs of labor, which induces a rise in the population growth rate. According to the definition of education expense ratio and equation (6'), the education expense ratio moves in the same direction with the population growth rate.

4.2. Effect of Individual Contribution Rate

Partially differentiating g, N, s and e with respect to τ, respectively, gives

$$\frac{\partial g}{\partial \tau} = \left(vD \frac{1-\theta}{1+\eta} \right)^{\frac{\theta-\delta}{\theta(1-\delta)}} \delta^{\frac{1-\theta}{\theta}} \left(\frac{D}{A} \right)^{\frac{1-\theta}{\theta(1-\delta)}} \left(\frac{1-\delta}{1-\tau} \right)^{\frac{\delta(1-\theta)}{\theta(1-\delta)}} \frac{1}{1-\delta} \left(\frac{\delta}{\theta} \frac{1-\theta}{1-\tau} - \frac{1+\delta\gamma}{\gamma} \right),$$

$$\frac{\partial N}{\partial \tau} = \frac{a(1+\delta\gamma)(1-\theta)vD}{(i+va)^2 \gamma(1-\delta)(1+\eta)\mu} > 0,$$

$$\frac{\partial s}{\partial \tau} = -1,$$

$$\frac{\partial e}{\partial \tau} = -\frac{\partial v}{1-\delta} < 0.$$

Raising the individual contribution rate increases the population growth rate, whereas decreases the saving rate and education expense ratio, the effect on the per capita income growth rate depends on the relevant parameters. A rise in the individual contribution rate decreases the disposal income or the opportunity costs of labor, which induces a rise in the population growth rate. The saving rate falls as much as the individual contribution rate rises because the mandatory savings (individual pension contributions) crowd out the voluntary savings by one-for-one. Raising the individual contribution rate on the one hand decreases the education expense ratio directly shown in equation (22), on the other hand increases the education expense ratio indirectly through increasing the population growth rate. The direct effect dominates the indirect effect induces the fall in the education expense ratio. Since the effect of the individual contribution rate on the per capita income growth rate depends on the relevant parameters, we examine it and check the above effects by simulations below.

5. NUMERICAL EXPERIMENT

5.1. Parameter Calibration

A period length is assumed to be 26 years in this OLG model. We assume that per year discount factor on the utility derived from retirement-period consumption is 0.980, hence, in a period, $\beta = 0.980^{26}$. Analogously, per year discount factor on the utility derived from children's human capital is 0.975, thus, in a period, $\gamma = 0.975^{26}$. According to the Chinese State Council Document 26 in 1997 and Chinese State Council Document 38 in 2005, the firm contribution rate $\eta = 20\%$ and the individual contribution rate $\tau = 8\%$.

We assume that the elasticity of human capital with respect to education expenses $\delta = 0.3$, rearing a child requires $v = 0.20$ units of labor. The physical capital share of income in China is assumed to be 0.35. What we hope to see here is how the endogenous variables change with the policy variables. Hence, A and D can be normalized as 1. These values are baseline values of the parameters.

5.2. Effects and their Intensities

Utilizing the baseline parameter values but η rising from 1% gradually to 20%, we simulate how g, N, s and e change along with η. Since the value of g is far more than that of N, s and e, they are displayed in different panels shown in Figure 1. Obviously, raising the firm contribution rate decreases the per capita income growth rate and saving rate, whereas increases the population growth rate and education expense ratio. g and N are values in period (26 years). s and e are ratios, their values in year are the same as in period.

Analogously, let τ rise from 1% gradually to 20%, simulating with them and the baseline values of the other relevant parameters gives the effect of the individual contribution rate shown in Figure 2. When the individual contribution rate is 12%, the per capita income growth rate is the minimum. Raising the individual contribution rate under 12% decreases the per capita income growth rate, but over 12% increases the per capita income growth rate. Raising the individual contribution rate increases the population growth rate, whereas decreases the saving rate and education expense ratio.

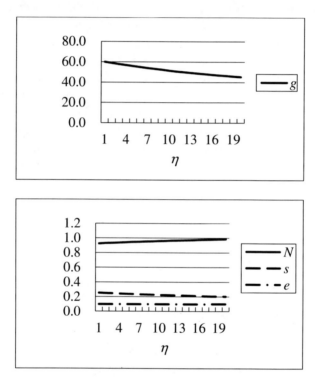

Figure 1. Effect of η on g, N, s and e.

The arc elasticity of each endogenous variable with respect to η and τ are shown in Table 1. The arc elasticity of g with respect to τ can be further investigated. It is -0.07% in [1%, 12%] and 0.15% in [12%, 20%], which means that the effect of the individual contribution rate on the per capita income growth rate is very weak. On the contrary, the effect of the firm contribution rate on the per capita income growth rate is very strong. The effect of the individual contribution rate on the population growth rate is near 3 times as large as that of the firm contribution rate. The effect of the individual contribution rate on the saving rate is near 5 times as large as that of the firm contribution rate. The effect of the individual contribution rate on the education expense ratio is about 11 times stronger than that of the firm contribution rate.

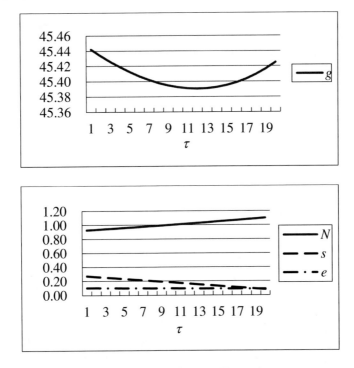

Figure 2. Effect of τ on g, N, s and e.

Table 1. Elasticity of endogenous variables with respect to η and τ

	elasticity with respect to η	elasticity with respect to τ
g	-15.22%	-0.02%
N	3.45%	9.37%
s	-12.97%	-59.65%
e	0.82%	-9.37%

CONCLUSION

Taking fertility as endogenous variable, this chapter employs the endogenous growth OLG model to investigate the public pension system for urban enterprise employees. We examine the effects of the firm contribution rate and individual contribution rate on the per capita income growth rate, population growth rate, saving rate and education expense ratio. According to the real situations of urban enterprises in China, we estimate the values of relevant parameters to simulate the effects of the policy variables on the endogenous variables. We also examine the sensitivities of the endogenous variables with respect to the policy variables. Instead of PAYG or fully funded public pension systems in the literature, this chapter studies the partially funded one combining social pool and individual accounts. Both firms and employees make pension contributions instead of only employees do in the literature. To find the endogenous variables' solution, we utilize the principle that physical capital must receive the same rate of return when allocated to either sector of production, instead of the approach of human capital grows at the same rate with the physical capital per unit of labor in balanced growth equilibrium.

The results are as the follows. Raising the firm contribution rate decreases the per capita income growth rate and saving rate, whereas increases the population growth rate and education expense ratio. Raising the individual contribution rate under a threshold decreases the per capita income growth rate, but over the threshold increases the per capita income growth rate. Raising the individual contribution rate increases the population growth rate, whereas decreases the saving rate and education expense ratio. The effect of the individual contribution rate on the per capita income growth rate is very weak, whereas the effect of the firm contribution rate is very strong. The effects of the individual contribution rate on the population growth rate, saving rate and education expense ratio are near 3 times, 5 times and 11 times stronger than that of the firm contribution rate, respectively.

Based on the practical situations of the economic and social development in China, a developing country with low GDP per capita and over-population needs to keep a stable, healthy and sustainable economic growth and rationally control the population size. In the era of post-crisis of international finance, China should promote consumption by decreasing the high saving rate and high ratio of education expenses to family income. Therefore, to increase the per capita income growth rate, it is necessary to reduce the firm contribution rate and individual contribution rate. To control rationally the population growth rate, it is necessary to reduce the firm contribution rate and individual contribution rate. To decrease the saving rate, it is necessary to raise the firm contribution rate and individual contribution rate. To decrease the education expense ratio, it is necessary to reduce the firm contribution rate and raise the individual contribution rate.

Integrating the effects of the policy variables on the endogenous variables and their intensities gives that it has more advantages than disadvantages to reduce the firm contribution rate and raise the individual contribution rate. The measure can upgrade the economic growth because the positive effect of reducing the firm contribution rate on the economic growth dominates the negative effect of raising the individual contribution rate since the elasticity of economic growth rate with respect to the firm contribution rate is much higher than the individual contribution rate. The measure of reducing the firm contribution rate and raising the individual contribution rate can rationally control the population size because the increase effect of raising the individual contribution rate dominates the decrease effect of reducing the firm contribution rate. And rational rise in the population growth rate is consistent with the population policy announced in 2013, which says that a couple with husband or wife is sole child in his or her own family before they get married is eligible to give birth to two children. The measure of reducing the firm contribution rate and raising the individual contribution rate can decrease the saving rate because the saving rate is much sensitive with respective to the individual contribution rate than to the firm contribution rate.

III. URBAN PENSION, EXOGENOUS MODEL, REPLACEMENT RATE

Chapter 7

OPTIMAL REPLACEMENT RATE OF URBAN PENSION UNDER POPULATION AGING[1]

ABSTRACT

Employing an OLG model with uncertain lifetime, this chapter investigates China's public pension system for urban enterprise employees. We examine the effects of the benefit replacement rates, life expectancy and population growth rate on the capital-labor ratio, social pool benefits, individual account benefits, consumption and utility. We also find the optimal social pool benefit replacement rate. Raising the individual account benefit replacement rate only increases the individual account benefits. Raising the social pool benefit replacement rate decreases the capital-labor ratio, individual account benefits, working-period consumption and utility, whereas increases the social pool benefits and retirement-period consumption. A rise in the life expectancy increases the capital-labor ratio, social pool benefits, individual account benefits and retirement-period consumption, whereas decreases the working-period consumption and utility. A fall in the population growth rate increases the capital-labor ratio, social pool benefits, individual account benefits, working-period consumption and utility, while decreases the retirement-period consumption. The optimal social pool benefit replacement rate rises in the joint case of risen life expectancy and fallen population growth rate. It will do more good than harm to raise the individual account benefit replacement rate, reduce the social pool benefit replacement rate, improve the living and medical conditions and control the population growth rate.

Keywords: urban public pension; replacement rate; life expectancy; population aging

1. INTRODUCTION

After publishing the *State Council Decision on Improving the Basic Pension System for Enterprise Employees* (Chinese State Council Document 38 in 2005), the Chinese government disclosed target replacement rate of pension benefits: "The target replacement

---

[1] By taking lifetime uncertainty into account, this chapter extends the paper, Urban Public Pension, Replacement Rates and Population Growth Rate in China, published in Insurance: Mathematics and Economics, 45 (2009) 230-235, which is available at www.elsevier.com/ locate/ime.

rate before the reform was 58.5%, where the social pool benefit replacement rate was 20% and the individual account benefit replacement rate 38.5%. The target replacement rate after the reform is 59.2%, where the social pool benefit replacement rate is 35% and the individual account benefit replacement rate 24.2%." The government has been increasing the pension benefits of enterprise retirees for recent ten years, and has pledged to continue increasing it. Hence, it is worth studying the effects of the public pension system on the economy and look for the optimal replacement rate.

To echo the reality of China, we study the replacement rates in the following situations: Firstly, impacted by the international financial crisis, the growth rate of China's GDP has fallen below 8% in 2012 and 2013. China has put economic growth at more important position. Secondly, the Chinese life expectancy has been rising because of improved living and medical conditions. Finally, the population growth rate has been falling mainly because China has carried out a special population policy for several decades. In general, the government required each couple to give birth not more than one time. In some special cases, a couple is eligible to give birth to two or more children. There are some ways for rural residents to become urban residents, e.g., graduated college students get jobs and military officers transfer to civilian works in urban areas; urbanization makes corresponding rural residents become urban residents, etc.

Pecchenino and Pollard (1997, 2002), Abel (1987), Sheshinski and Weiss (1981), Pecchenino and Utendorf (1999), and Zhang et al. (2001) used OLG models to investigate the relationship between uncertain lifetime, population growth rate and public pension system. Samuelson (1975) studied the optimum social security taxes in a life-cycle growth model by adjusting the capital-labor ratio to the modified golden rule level to maximize social welfare by controlling the social security taxes. The approach to find the optimal social security taxes is to equate the rate of interest to the growth rate of economy in a decentralized economy. Blanchard and Fischer (1989) elaborated the principle of social optimum, which is the Pareto Optimum. A social planner maximizes social welfare by rationally allocating social resources.

Introducing uncertain lifetime into the general equilibrium OLG model used by Yang (2009a), this chapter investigates the public pension system for urban enterprise employees in China. We examine the effects of the pension benefit replacement rates, life expectancy and population growth rate on the capital-labor ratio, pension benefits, consumption and utility. By comparing the equilibriums of the market economy and Pareto Optimum, we also seek the optimal policy variable that has effect on the capital-labor ratio. It is publicly recognized that the Chinese population aging peak will appear in 2030s. Hence, we look for the optimal policy variable value during the population aging peak. The results of this study suggest that the individual account benefit replacement rate should be raised, the social pool benefit replacement rate reduced, the living and medical conditions improved and the population growth rate controlled. The optimal social pool benefit replacement rate in 2030s while the population aging peak should be a little higher than the present target one.

2. THE MODEL

In this model, pay-as-you-go or fully funded pension systems in the literature are replaced by China's partially funded public pension system. A closed economy is composed of numerous individuals and firms and a government. The generation born at the beginning of period t is called generation t. The population grows at the rate of $n = N_t/N_{t-1} - 1$, where N_t is the population size of generation t.

2.1. Individuals

Each individual survives to the end of his/her working period certainly. His/her survival probability in retirement period is $p \in (0,1]$. In working period, each individual earns wage by supplying inelastically one unit of labor and makes pension contributions. It is possible for him/her to inherit some unintentional bequests from his/her parent. He/she consumes part of his/her income and saves the remainder. If he/she survives in the retirement period, then he/she consumes the savings with accrued interest, funded pension benefits and pay-as-you-go pension benefits. If he/she dies at the beginning of the retirement period, then his/her savings with accrued interest and funded pension benefits are inherited equally by his/her children as unintentional bequests.

Each individual derives utility from his/her working-period consumption c_{1t} and possible retirement-period consumption c_{2t+1}. The utility is described by an additively separable logarithmic function. Thus, the utility maximization problem is:

$$\max_{\{c_{1t}, c_{2t+1}, s_t\}} U_t = \ln c_{1t} + \theta p \ln c_{2t+1}, \tag{1}$$

s.t.
$$c_{1t} = (1-p)b_t + (1-\tau)w_t - s_t, \tag{2}$$

$$c_{2t+1} = (1 + r_{t+1})s_t + B_{t+1} + P_{t+1}, \tag{3}$$

$$(1+n)b_{t+1} = (1 + r_{t+1})s_t + B_{t+1}, \tag{4}$$

where $\theta \in (0,1)$ denotes the individual discount factor, w_t the wage, τ the individual contribution rate, s_t the savings, r_{t+1} the interest rate, B_{t+1} the individual account benefits, P_{t+1} the social pool benefits, and b_{t+1} the unintentional bequests inherited by each children.

Substituting equations (2) - (4) into equation (1), and letting the partial derivative of equation (1) with respect to s_t be zero gives the first-order condition for the utility maximization:

$$-c_{2t+1} + \theta p(1 + r_{t+1})c_{1t} = 0. \tag{5}$$

This familiar expression implies that the utility loss from reducing one unit of working-period consumption is equal to the utility gain from increasing $(1+r_{t+1})$ units of possible retirement-period consumption.

2.2. Firms

Firms produce a homogenous commodity in competitive markets. The production is described by Cobb-Douglas function $F(K_t, N_t) = AK_t^\alpha N_t^{1-\alpha}$ or $f(k_t) = Ak_t^\alpha$, where $F(K_t, N_t)$ is the output in period t, K_t the capital stock, $\alpha \in (0,1)$ the capital share of income, A the productivity, $k_t = K_t/N_t$ the capital-labor ratio, and $f(k_t)$ the output-labor ratio.

Firms make pension contributions at rate $\eta \in (0,1)$ on their payroll. According to the product distribution, one can get that $AK_t^\alpha N_t^{1-\alpha} = r_t K_t + (1+\eta)w_t N_t$. The first-order conditions for the profit maximization are

$$r_t = \alpha A k_t^{\alpha-1}, \tag{6}$$

$$w_t = (1-\alpha)A k_t^\alpha / (1+\eta). \tag{7}$$

2.3. The Government

The social pool fund is paid to the retirees in current period as pay-as-you-go pension benefits: $pN_{t-1}P_t = \eta w_t N_t$. Using the social pool benefit replacement rate ξ gives

$$P_t = \xi w_t = (1+n)\eta w_t / p, \tag{8}$$

thus

$$\eta = p\xi/(1+n). \tag{9}$$

The accumulation in individual account is used to pay the individual when he/she retires in the next period as funded pension benefits. Using the individual account benefit replacement rate μ gives

$$B_{t+1} = \mu w_{t+1} = (1+r_{t+1})\tau w_t, \tag{10}$$

thus

$$\tau = \frac{\mu}{1+r_{t+1}} \cdot \frac{w_{t+1}}{w_t}. \tag{11}$$

2.4. Dynamic Equilibrium System

The savings and individual pension contributions in period t generate the capital stock in period $t + 1$:

$$s_t + \tau w_t = (1+n)k_{t+1}. \tag{12}$$

A competitive equilibrium for the economy is a sequence as $\{c_{1t}, c_{2t+1}, w_t, r_{t+1}, s_t, B_{t+1}, P_t, b_t, k_{t+1}\}_{t=0}^{\infty}$ that satisfies equations (1) - (12) for all t, given the initial condition k_0 and the parameters, μ and ξ.

Substituting equations (2) - (4) and (6) - (12) into equation (5) gives a dynamic equilibrium system described by the following difference equation:

$$-\left(k_{t+1} + \alpha A k_{t+1}^{\alpha}\right) - \frac{\xi}{1+n+p\xi}(1-\alpha)Ak_{t+1}^{\alpha}$$
$$+ \theta p\left(1 + \alpha A k_{t+1}^{\alpha-1}\right)\left(\frac{1-p}{1+n}(k_t + \alpha A k_t^{\alpha}) + \frac{1}{1+n+p\xi}(1-\alpha)Ak_t^{\alpha} - k_{t+1}\right) = 0. \tag{13}$$

The stability condition for the dynamic system (referring to Appendix A) is

$$a + e < 0.$$

3. EFFECTS OF EXOGENOUS VARIABLES

In the steady state, the social pool benefits, individual account benefits, working-period consumption, retirement-period consumption and utility become

$$P = \xi \frac{1+n}{1+n+p\xi}(1-\alpha)Ak^{\alpha}, \tag{14}$$

$$B = \mu \frac{1+n}{1+n+p\xi}(1-\alpha)Ak^{\alpha}, \tag{15}$$

$$c_1 = (1-p)(k + \alpha A k^\alpha) + \frac{1+n}{1+n+p\xi}(1-\alpha)Ak^\alpha - (1+n)k, \quad (16)$$

$$c_2 = (1+n)\left[k + \alpha A k^\alpha + \frac{\xi}{1+n+p\xi}(1-\alpha)Ak^\alpha\right], \quad (17)$$

$$U = \ln c_1 + \theta p \ln c_2. \quad (18)$$

The individual account benefit replacement rate has no effect on the capital-labor ratio because the mandatory savings (the individual pension contributions) crowd out the voluntary savings by one-for-one. Obviously, raising the individual account benefit replacement rate only increases the individual account benefits, but has no effect on the social pool benefits, consumption and utility.

Totally differentiating the dynamic system around the steady state gives

$$(a+e)dk + id\xi + mdp + jdn = 0. \quad (19)$$

where

$$i = -\frac{1+n}{(1+n+p\xi)^2}(1-\alpha)Ak^\alpha - (1+\alpha Ak^{\alpha-1})\frac{\theta p^2}{(1+n+p\xi)^2}(1-\alpha)Ak^\alpha < 0,$$

$$m = \frac{\xi^2}{(1+n+p\xi)^2}(1-\alpha)Ak^\alpha + \theta(1+\alpha Ak^{\alpha-1})\left[\frac{1-p}{1+n}(k+\alpha Ak^\alpha) + \frac{1}{1+n+p\xi}(1-\alpha)Ak^\alpha - k\right]$$

$$-\theta p(1+\alpha Ak^{\alpha-1})\left[\frac{1}{1+n}(k+\alpha Ak^\alpha) + \frac{\xi}{(1+n+p\xi)^2}(1-\alpha)Ak^\alpha\right],$$

$$j = \frac{\xi}{(1+n+p\xi)^2}(1-\alpha)Ak^\alpha - \theta p(1+\alpha Ak^{\alpha-1})\left[\frac{1-p}{(1+n)^2}(k+\alpha Ak^\alpha) + \frac{1}{(1+n+p\xi)^2}(1-\alpha)Ak^\alpha\right].$$

Using equation (19) gives $\partial k/\partial \xi = -i/(a+e) < 0$. Raising the social pool benefit replacement rate decreases the capital-labor ratio. It can be shown that the effects of the social pool benefit replacement rate, life expectancy and population growth rate on the social pool benefits, individual account benefits, working-period consumption, retirement-period consumption and utility depend on the relevant parameters. Thus, we first calibrate the parameters, and then examine the effects by simulating.

3.1. Parameter Calibration

The capital share of income in China is assumed to be 0.35. Since what we want to see here is how the endogenous variables change relatively with the exogenous variables, the constant A can be normalized as 1. A period length in this model is assumed to be 30 years since the length is usually in the interval of 25 - 30 years in the literature on overlapping generations model. Assume that the individual discount factor per year is 0.98, which is similar to that used by Pecchenino and Pollard (2002). Hence, the individual discount factor per period is $\theta = 0.98^{30}$.

The public pension system for urban enterprise employees is different from that for rural residents, and only the former is studied in this chapter, so "Urban Population" is selected. Based on the "Population and Its Composition" in China Statistical Yearbook, which has in fact reflected immigration from rural areas, the population growth rate during the period from 1981 to 2011 is computed as $n \approx 2.425$.

The survival probability in retirement period is estimated by the life expectancy. According to the National Bureau of Statistics of China (2012), the life expectancy in 2010 is 74.83 years old. Since one period length is 30 years, the life-span from birth to the end of working-period is 60 years, and that from birth to the end of retirement period is 90 years. According to the concept of life expectancy, one can get $(1-p) \times 60 + p \times 90 = 74.83$, which gives $p \approx 49.43\%$. Although the choice of period length is arbitrary, it has to obey the following rule: Three periods should be longer than or equal to the life expectancy to ensure $p \leq 1$.

According to the official disclosure mentioned in the Introduction, the social pool benefit replacement rate, ξ, has been raised to 35%, and the individual account benefit replacement rate, μ, reduced to 24.2%. The above parameter values are baseline values.

3.2. Effect of Social Pool Benefit Replacement Rate

Utilizing the baseline parameter values but raising the social pool benefit replacement rate from 30% to 35% and 40%, respectively, we simulate how k, P, B, c_1, c_2, and U change along with ξ. The result is shown in Table 1. Raising the social pool benefit replacement rate decreases the capital-labor ratio, individual account benefits, working-period consumption and utility, whereas increases the social pool benefits and retirement-period consumption.

Table 1. Effect of social pool benefit replacement rate

ξ	30%	35%	40%
k	0.0088	0.0085	0.0082
P	0.0356	0.0408	0.0458
B	0.0287	0.0282	0.0277
c_1	0.1269	0.1252	0.1235
c_2	0.2942	0.2958	0.2973
U	-2.3943	-2.4066	-2.4188

3.3. Effect of Life Expectancy

Risen life expectancy means the survival probability in retirement period increased. According to the National Bureau of Statistics of China (2013), the life expectancies in 1990,

2000 and 2010 are 68.55, 71.40 and 74.83 years old, respectively. Use Excel to add a trend line on the curve of life expectancy, which is (*life expectancy*) = $65.54e^{0.043 \cdot (ordinal\ number)}$, R^2 of the trend line is 0.998. By the trend line, we forecast the life expectancies in 2020 and 2030, which are 77.84 and 81.26 years old, respectively. The corresponding survival probabilities in retirement period are 59.47% and 70.87%, respectively.

Simulating with the forecasted survival probabilities and the baseline parameter values gives the result shown in Table 2. A rise in the life expectancy induces the increase in the capital-labor ratio, social pool benefits, individual account benefits and retirement-period consumption, whereas the decrease in the working-period consumption and utility.

3.4. Effect of Population Growth Rate

According to the National Bureau of Statistics of China (2013), the sample of urban population from 2000 to 2011 gives a trend line, (*population*) = 2085·(*ordinal number*) + 43856, R^2 of the trend line is 0.999. By the trend line, we forecast the population in 2030 and 2035, and yield the population growth rates during 2000 - 2030 and 2005 - 2035, which are 1.363 and 1.115, respectively. Simulating with the forecasted population growth rates and the baseline parameter values gives the result shown in Table 3. A fall in the population growth rate increases the capital-labor ratio, social pool benefits, individual account benefits, working-period consumption and utility, while decreases the retirement-period consumption.

Table 2. Effect of life expectancy

p	49.43%	59.47%	70.87%
k	0.0085	0.0098	0.0109
P	0.0408	0.0425	0.0436
B	0.0282	0.0294	0.0302
c_1	0.1252	0.1200	0.1115
c_2	0.2958	0.3138	0.3275
U	-2.4066	-2.4964	-2.6256

Table 3. Effect of population growth rate

n	2.425	1.363	1.115
k	0.0085	0.0140	0.0163
P	0.0408	0.0476	0.0497
B	0.0282	0.0329	0.0344
c_1	0.1252	0.1498	0.1578
c_2	0.2958	0.2666	0.2592
U	-2.4066	-2.2552	-2.2105

3.5. Intensities of the Effects

It is easy to calculate the arc elasticity of the endogenous variables with respect to the exogenous variables. As shown in Table 4, the effect of population growth rate on the capital-labor ratio is stronger than that of the life expectancy, which in turn is stronger than that of the social pool benefit replacement rate. The effects on the social pool benefits rank in descending order as the social pool benefit replacement rate, population growth rate and life expectancy. Table 4 is compacter than the expressions in words.

4. SOCIAL OPTIMUM

Since the social pool benefit replacement rate has effect on the capital-labor ratio, it is possible to derive the optimal social pool benefit replacement rate. The method is to adjust the policy variable to make the capital-labor ratio achieve the modified golden rule level to maximize social welfare.

4.1. Social Welfare Maximization

The social welfare is defined as the sum of the lifetime utilities of all current and future generations (Groezen et al., 2003 also use an analogous social welfare function):

$$W = \theta p \ln c_{20} + \sum_{i=0}^{\infty} \rho^i (\ln c_{1i} + \theta p \ln c_{2i+1}). \tag{20}$$

Table 4. Elasticity of k, P, B, c_1, c_2, U with respect to ξ, p, n

	ξ	p	n
k	-23%	70%	-85%
P	87%	19%	-27%
B	-13%	19%	-27%
c_1	-10%	-33%	-31%
c_2	4%	29%	18%
U	-4%	-24%	-11%

where $\rho \in (0,1)$ denotes the social discount factor, which reflects the preference of social planner. The resource constraint is:

$$k_i + Ak_i^\alpha = (1+n)k_{i+1} + c_{1i} + pc_{2i}/(1+n). \tag{21}$$

The initial condition is that k_0 is given, and the terminal condition is $k_\infty = 0$.

The social planner maximizes the social welfare subject to the resource constraint, initial condition and terminal condition. The first-order conditions for the social welfare maximization problem are:

$$\theta(1+n)c_1^* = \rho c_2^*, \tag{22}$$

$$k^* = [(1+n-\rho)/\rho\alpha A]^{\frac{1}{\alpha-1}}, \qquad (23)$$

where the superscript * denotes the optimal steady state values of variables. The capital-labor ratio satisfying equation (23) is at the modified golden rule level, which means that the social welfare achieves the maximum.

In order to maximize the social welfare of the market economy in steady state, we control the policy variable to adjust the capital-labor ratio of the market economy in steady state to the modified golden rule level, namely, $k = k^*$. Substituting equation (23) into equation (13) and rearranging gives

$$\xi^* = \frac{\theta p(1-\alpha)(1+n-\rho) - \alpha(1+n)[\rho - \theta p(1-p-\rho)]}{p\alpha[\rho - \theta p(1-p-\rho)] + \rho(1-\alpha)(1+n-\rho)/(1+n)}. \qquad (24)$$

The optimal social pool benefit replacement rate depends on the individual discount factor, social discount factor, survival probability in retirement period, population growth rate, and capital share of income.

Table 5. ξ^* under different life expectancies

p	49.43%	59.47%	70.87%
ξ^*	35.00%	57.96%	74.79%

4.2. OPTIMAL SOCIAL POOL BENEFIT REPLACEMENT RATE

The effects of the life expectancy and population growth rate on the optimal social pool benefit replacement rate can be obtained by partially differentiating ξ^* with respective to p and n, respectively. It can be proven that these effects are dependent on the relevant parameter values. Hence, we estimate the parameter values and check the effects by simulating.

It is necessary to estimate first the social discount factor, which indicates how much the government weights different generations in its social welfare calculations. Hence, it should be estimated according to the government's regulations. Based on the disclosed target replacement rates, the optimal social pool benefit replacement rate adopted by the government is 35%. Substituting the relevant baseline parameter values into equation (24) and calculating repeatedly until the equation holds, we get $\rho \approx 0.3908$.

Case 1: Risen life expectancy. Simulating with the forecasted survival probabilities and the relevant baseline parameter values gives the result shown in Table 5. The optimal social pool benefit replacement rate rises with the life expectancy.

Case 2: Fallen population growth rate. Simulating with the forecasted population growth rates and the baseline parameter values gives the result shown in Table 6. The optimal social pool benefit replacement rate falls with the population growth rate.

Case 3: Risen life expectancy and fallen population growth rate. With the baseline parameter values, simulating four combinations of the forecasted life expectancies and population growth rates, respectively, gives the result shown in Table 7. The optimal social pool benefit replacement rate rises under the joint case of risen life expectancy and fallen population growth rate. The optimal rate in 2030s is around 37%.

Table 6. ξ^* under different population growth rates

n	2.425	1.363	1.115
ξ^*	35.00%	17.56%	13.34%

Table 7. ξ^* under different life expectancies and population growth rates

p	n	ξ^*	elasticity of ξ^* with respect to n	elasticity of ξ^* with respect to p
59.47%	1.363	33.05%	—	—
59.47%	1.115	27.08%	99%	—
70.87%	1.363	44.16%	—	165%
70.87%	1.115	36.87%	90%	175%

It is straightforward to compute the elasticity of ξ^* with respect to p and n. The elasticity of ξ^* with respect to p is much higher than that of ξ^* with respect to n. This implies that the optimal social pool benefit replacement rate is more sensitive to the life expectancy than to the population growth rate.

CONCLUSION

Employing the OLG model with uncertain lifetime, this chapter investigates the public pension system for urban enterprise employees in China. We examine the effects of the individual account benefit replacement rate, social pool benefit replacement rate, life expectancy and population growth rate on the capital-labor ratio, social pool benefits, individual account benefits, working-period consumption, retirement-period consumption and utility. By controlling the policy variable that has effect on capital-labor ratio to adjust the capital-labor ratio of the market economy to reach the modified golden rule level, we also find the optimal social pool benefit replacement rate.

The main results are as follows. Raising the individual account benefit replacement rate has no effect on the endogenous variables but increases the individual account benefits. Raising the social pool benefit replacement rate decreases the capital-labor ratio, individual account benefits, working-period consumption and utility, whereas increases the social pool benefits and retirement-period consumption. A rise in the life expectancy increases the capital-labor ratio, social pool benefits, individual account benefits and retirement-period consumption, whereas decreases the working-period consumption and utility. A fall in the population growth rate increases the capital-labor ratio, social pool benefits, individual account benefits, working-period consumption and utility, while decreases the retirement-period consumption. The intensities of the effects are shown in Table 4. The optimal social pool benefit replacement rate is dependent on the individual discount factor, social discount factor, survival probability in retirement period, population growth rate and capital share of income. It rises with the life expectancy, falls with the population growth rate, and rises under the joint case of risen life expectancy and fallen population growth rate because it is much more sensitive to the life expectancy than to the population growth rate.

The above results include some policy implications. (a) In the era of post-crisis of international finance, to increase investment to keep a stable, healthy and sustainable economic growth, it is necessary to reduce the social pool benefit replacement rate, improve the living and medical conditions and control the population growth rate. (b) To increase the social pool benefits, it is necessary to raise the social pool benefit replacement rate, improve the living and medical conditions and control the population growth rate. (c) To increase the individual account benefits, it is necessary to raise the individual account benefit replacement rate, reduce the social pool benefit replacement rate, improve the living and medical conditions and control the population growth rate. (d) To increase the working-period consumption, it is necessary to reduce the social pool benefit replacement rate and control the population growth rate. (e) To increase the retirement-period consumption, it is necessary to raise the social pool benefit replacement rate, improve the living and medical conditions and increase the population growth rate. (f) To raise the utility level, it is necessary to reduce the social pool benefit replacement rate and control the population growth rate.

Integrating the above goals and the intensities of the effects of the exogenous variables on the endogenous variables, it will do more good than harm to adopt the measures: raise the individual account benefit replacement rate, reduce the social pool benefit replacement rate, and improve the living and medical conditions and control the population growth rate. As shown in Table 4, the measures can promote the investment and furthermore recovery from international financial crisis.

The measures can also increase the individual account benefits, working-period consumption and retirement-period consumption. It is a pity for the measures to depress the social pool benefits because the negative effect of reducing the social pool benefit replacement rate dominates the positive effects of improving the living and medical conditions and controlling the population growth rate.

If the estimated social discount factor reflects the social planner's preference correctly, and the forecasted life expectancy in 2030s and population growth rate during 2005 - 2035 are accurate, then the optimal social pool benefit replacement rate in 2030s should be around 36%.

This social pool benefit replacement rate is a little higher than the present target one. The result is consistent with the fact for the government to increase continuously the pension benefits level of enterprise retirees in recent ten years.

APPENDIX A

Assume that there is unique, stable and nonoscillatory steady state equilibrium. In order to find the stability condition, we linearize the dynamic equilibrium system around the steady state (k). Some manipulation gives

$$a(k_{t+1}-k)+e(k_t-k)=0,$$

where

$$a = -(1+\alpha^2 Ak^{\alpha-1}) - \frac{\xi}{1+n+p\xi}(1-\alpha)\alpha Ak^{\alpha-1} - \theta p(1+\alpha Ak^{\alpha-1})$$

$$-\theta p(1-\alpha)\alpha Ak^{\alpha-2}\left[\frac{1-p}{1+n}(k+\alpha Ak^\alpha)+\frac{1}{1+n+p\xi}(1-\alpha)Ak^\alpha - k\right],$$

$$e = \theta p(1+\alpha Ak^{\alpha-1})\left[\frac{1-p}{1+n}(1+\alpha^2 Ak^{\alpha-1})+\frac{1}{1+n+p\xi}\alpha(1-\alpha)Ak^{\alpha-1}\right]>0.$$

The assumption that the equilibrium is unique, stable and nonoscillatory is equivalent to $0<\frac{k_{t+1}-k}{k_t-k}=-\frac{e}{a}<1$. Therefore, the stability condition is

$$a+e<0.$$

Chapter 8

ALTRUISTIC MOTIVES, LIFE EXPECTANCY AND URBAN PENSION REPLACEMENT RATES[1]

ABSTRACT

Altruistic motives within family are prevalent in China. Introducing altruistic motives into the last chapter's OLG model with uncertain lifetime, this chapter investigates the public pension system for urban enterprise employees. We examine the effects of the individual account benefit replacement rate, social pool benefit replacement rate, life expectancy and population growth rate on the capital-labor ratio, pension benefits, consumption and utility. We also find the optimal social pool benefit replacement rate. Raising the individual account benefit replacement rate only increases the individual account benefits. Raising the social pool benefit replacement rate increases the social pool benefits and retirement-period consumption, whereas decreases the capital-labor ratio, individual account benefits, working-period consumption and utility. A fall in the population growth rate increases the capital-labor ratio, social pool benefits, individual account benefits, working-period consumption and utility, whereas decreases the retirement-period consumption. A rise in the life expectancy decreases the six variables. The optimal social pool benefit replacement rate falls in case of either risen life expectancy or fallen population growth rate. It further falls under the joint case of risen life expectancy and fallen population growth rate. It will do more good than harm to raise the individual account benefit replacement rate, reduce the social pool benefit replacement rate and control the population growth rate.

Keywords: altruistic motive; uncertain lifetime; urban public pension; replacement rate

1. INTRODUCTION

It is familiar to see that in ordinary Chinese families, the old usually present gifts to their children when they get married or buy houses, and leave bequests to their children when the

---

[1] This chapter is revised from the paper, Altruistic Motives, Uncertain Lifetime and Urban Public Pension Replacement Rates, published in Optimization: A Journal of Mathematical Programming and Operations Research, 61: 2, 209 - 221, which is available at www.tandfonline.com.

old pass away. The last chapter has introduced the target replacement rates of the public pension system for urban enterprise employees reformed in 2005: "The target replacement rate before the reform was 58.5%, in which the social pool benefit replacement rate was 20% and the individual account benefit replacement rate 38.5%. The target replacement rate after the reform is 59.2%, in which the social pool benefit replacement rate is 35% and the individual account benefit replacement rate 24.2%." The government has been increasing the pension benefits in recent ten years, and has expressed to continue increasing it. If the altruistic motives are taken into account, what effect will change, and how about the policy suggestion, especially the optimal social pool benefit replacement rate?

It is worth studying the replacement rate based on the following actual situations in China: Firstly, Chinese generally have altruistic motives. For example, the young, when get married, usually get gifts from their parents; the old, when pass away, usually leave bequests to their children. Secondly, the Chinese life expectancy has been rising because of improved living and medical conditions. Thirdly, the growth rate of China's economy has fallen evidently in the last several years. As a developing country with lower per capita GDP, China needs to keep an appropriately high economic growth rate. Finally, the population growth rate has fallen because mainly of the Chinese special population policy implemented before 2013: A couple generally is required to have not more than one child. In some special cases, a couple is eligible to give birth to two or more children.

Some literature used OLG model with altruistic motive and uncertain lifetime to study social security pensions. Sheshinski and Weiss (1981) examined the annuity aspect of social security within the framework of an OLG model. Abel (1987a) solved the consumption and portfolio decision problem of a consumer who lives for either one period or two periods. Blanchard and Fischer (1989) examined the effect of an unfunded social security if current generations care about the welfare of future generations to the extent that they make positive bequests. Abel (1989) demonstrated the effect of a lump-sum tax on debt neutrality in an OLG model. There was not any production sector in these models. Altig and Davis (1993) developed implications of two-sided altruism in a three-period OLG framework, and showed how unfunded social security interventions can significantly depress aggregate capital accumulation. Fuster (2000) studied how the lack of an annuities market affects saving behavior and intergenerational transfers in a dynastic OLG economy. It was found that the answer to this question depends crucially on altruism. Samuelson (1975) studied the optimum social security in a life-cycle growth model by adjusting the capital-labor ratio to the modified golden rule level to maximize social welfare. Blanchard and Fischer (1989) elaborated the principle of social optimum. A social planner maximizes social welfare by rationally allocating social resources.

Introducing altruistic motives and uncertain lifetime into the OLG model used by Yang (2009a), this chapter investigates the public pension system for urban enterprise employees in China. We examine the effects of the benefit replacement rates, life expectancy and population growth rate on the capital-labor ratio, pension benefits, consumption and utility. By controlling the policy variable, one can adjust the capital-labor ratio in market economy to the modified golden rule level to maximize social welfare. Furthermore, it enables us to find the optimum social allocation. Comparing the market economy equilibrium with the optimum social allocation, we look for the optimal social pool benefit replacement rate. In the model of this chapter, as real life, the government levies pension taxes on each worker's wage and on each firm's payroll with a proportional schedule.

2. THE MODEL

This chapter introduces production sector into Abel's (1987) model. A closed economy is composed of numerous individuals and firms and a government. The generation born at the beginning of period t is called generation t. The population grows at the rate of $n = (N_t / N_{t-1}) - 1$, where N_t is the population size of generation t.

2.1. Individuals

Each individual survives to the end of his/her working period certainly, but survives in retirement period with probability $p \in (0,1]$. In the working period, each individual earns wage by supplying inelastically one unit of labor and makes pension contributions. He/she gets bequests or gifts from his/her parent, consumes part of the income and saves the remainder. If he/she survives in his/her retirement period, he/she distributes the savings with accrued interest, individual account benefits and social pool benefits between his/her consumption and the gifts to his/her children. If he/she dies at the beginning of the retirement period, then his/her savings with accrued interest and individual account benefits are inherited equally by his/her children as bequests.

Each individual derives utility from his/her working-period consumption c_{1t}, possible retirement-period consumption c_{2t+1}, and bequests b_{t+1}^D or gifts b_{t+1}^S. The utility is described by an additively separable logarithmic function. Thus, the utility maximization problem is:

$$\text{Max} \quad U_t = \ln c_{1t} + \theta p \ln c_{2t+1} + \delta(1-p)\ln b_{t+1}^D + \delta p \ln b_{t+1}^S, \tag{1}$$

s.t.
$$c_{1t} = \frac{(1-p)b_t^D + pb_t^S}{1+n} + (1-\tau)w_t - s_t, \tag{2}$$

$$c_{2t+1} + b_{t+1}^S = (1+r_{t+1})s_t + B_{t+1} + P_{t+1}, \tag{3}$$

$$b_{t+1}^D = (1+r_{t+1})s_t + B_{t+1}, \tag{4}$$

where $\theta \in (0,1)$ denotes the individual discount factor, $\delta \in (0,1)$ the altruism intensity, w_t the wage, τ the individual contribution rate, s_t the savings, r_{t+1} the interest rate, B_{t+1} the individual account benefits, and P_{t+1} the social pool benefits. Without losing generality, assume that $\theta > \delta$ since there is a limit to each individual's altruism.

Substituting equations (2) - (4) into equation (1), and letting the partial derivatives of equation (1) with respect to s_t and c_{2t+1} be zero gives the first-order conditions for the utility maximization:

$$\delta(1+r_{t+1})\left(\frac{1-p}{b_{t+1}^D} + \frac{p}{b_{t+1}^S}\right) = \frac{1}{c_{1t}}, \qquad (5)$$

$$\theta b_{t+1}^S = \delta c_{2t+1}. \qquad (6)$$

Equation (5) implies that the utility loss from reducing one unit of working-period consumption is equal to the utility gain from increasing $(1+r_{t+1})$ units of bequests or gifts. Equation (6) implies that the utility loss from reducing one unit of gifts is equal to the utility gain from increasing one unit of retirement-period consumption.

2.2. Firms

Firms produce a homogenous commodity in competitive markets. The production is described by Cobb-Douglas function $Y_t = AK_t^\alpha N_t^{1-\alpha}$ or $y_t = Ak_t^\alpha$, where Y_t is the output in period t, K_t the capital stock, $\alpha \in (0,1)$ the capital share of income, A the productivity, y_t the output-labor ratio, and $k_t = K_t / N_t$ the capital-labor ratio.

Firms make pension contributions at a rate of $\eta \in (0,1)$ on their payroll. According to the product distribution, one can get that $AK_t^\alpha N_t^{1-\alpha} = r_t K_t + (1+\eta)w_t N_t$. By virtue of Euler Theorem, we get:

$$r_t = \alpha A k_t^{\alpha-1}, \qquad (7)$$

$$w_t = \frac{(1-\alpha)Ak_t^\alpha}{1+\eta}. \qquad (8)$$

2.3. The Government

The social pool fund is paid to the retirees in current period as pay-as-you-go pension benefits: $pN_{t-1}P_t = \eta w_t N_t$. Using the concept of social pool benefit replacement rate ξ gives

$$P_t = \xi w_t = \frac{1+n}{p}\eta w_t, \qquad (9)$$

or

$$\eta = \frac{p\xi}{1+n}. \qquad (10)$$

The accumulation in an individual account is used to pay the individual when he/she retires in the next period as funded pension benefits. Using the concept of individual account benefit replacement rate μ gives

$$B_{t+1} = \mu w_{t+1} = (1+r_{t+1})\tau w_t, \tag{11}$$

or

$$\tau = \frac{\mu}{1+r_{t+1}} \cdot \frac{w_{t+1}}{w_t}. \tag{12}$$

2.4. Dynamic Equilibrium System

The savings and individual pension contributions in period t generate the capital stock in period $t + 1$:

$$s_t + \tau w_t = (1+n)k_{t+1}. \tag{13}$$

Substituting equations (2) - (4) and (7) - (13) into equations (5) - (6) and rearranging gives a dynamic equilibrium system described by the following difference equation:

$$\left[k_t + Ak_t^\alpha - (1+n)k_{t+1} - \frac{p\theta}{\theta+\delta}\left(k_t + \alpha Ak_t^\alpha + \xi \frac{1-\alpha}{1+n+p\xi} Ak_t^\alpha \right) \right] \cdot$$

$$\left[(1-p)\frac{\delta}{\theta+\delta}\left(k_{t+1} + \alpha Ak_{t+1}^\alpha + \xi \frac{1-\alpha}{1+n+p\xi} Ak_{t+1}^\alpha \right) + p\left(k_{t+1} + \alpha Ak_{t+1}^\alpha \right) \right]$$

$$= \frac{1+n}{\theta+\delta}k_{t+1}\left(k_{t+1} + \alpha Ak_{t+1}^\alpha + \xi \frac{1-\alpha}{1+n+p\xi} Ak_{t+1}^\alpha \right) \tag{14}$$

Assume that there is unique, stable and nonoscillatory steady state equilibrium (e.g., Blanchard and Fischer, 1989, p. 96). The stability condition refers to Appendix A.

3. COMPARATIVE STATICS

The individual account benefit replacement rate has no effect on the capital-labor ratio because the mandatory savings (individual pension contributions) crowd out the voluntary savings by one-for-one[2]. However, the social pool benefit replacement rate has effect on the

---

[2] Some literature (e.g., Blanchard and Fischer,1989; Abel, 1987; etc.) has pointed out: the neutrality of infra-marginal changes in the compulsory saving in individual accounts (the compulsory saving is still below the desired private saving rate).

capital-labor ratio because it appears in the dynamic equilibrium system. When the system converges to its steady state, the pension benefits, consumption and utility become:

$$P = \xi \frac{1+n}{1+n+p\xi}(1-\alpha)Ak^\alpha, \qquad (9')$$

$$B = \mu \frac{1+n}{1+n+p\xi}(1-\alpha)Ak^\alpha, \qquad (11')$$

$$c_1 = Ak^\alpha - nk - \frac{p\theta}{\theta+\delta}\left(k + \alpha Ak^\alpha + \xi \frac{1-\alpha}{1+n+p\xi}Ak^\alpha\right), \qquad (2')$$

$$c_2 = \frac{\theta}{\theta+\delta}(1+n)\left(k + \alpha Ak^\alpha + \xi \frac{1-\alpha}{1+n+p\xi}Ak^\alpha\right), \qquad (3')$$

$$U = \ln c_1 + \theta p \ln c_2 + \delta(1-p)\ln[(1+n)(k + \alpha Ak^\alpha)] + \delta p \ln(\delta c_2/\theta). \qquad (1')$$

Obviously, raising the individual account benefit replacement rate has no effect on the endogenous variables but increases the individual account benefits. The effects of the social pool benefit replacement rate, life expectancy and population growth rate on the endogenous variables can be obtained by partially differentiating k, P, B, c_1, c_2 and U with respect to ξ, p and n, respectively. It can be shown that the effects depend on values of the parameters. Hence, we estimate the parameter values at first, and then examine the effects by simulating.

3.1. Parameter Calibration

Because a period length is usually in the interval of 25 - 30 years in the literature on OLG model, this model sets a period length of 26 years. Analogous to Pecchenino and Pollard (2002), we assume that the individual discount factor per year is 0.985, and the altruism intensity per year 0.965. Hence, the individual discount factor per period is $\theta = 0.985^{26}$, and the altruism intensity per period $\delta = 0.965^{26}$. The capital share of income in China is assumed to be 0.35. Since what we want to see here is how the endogenous variables change with the exogenous variables, the constant A can be normalized as 1. The survival probability in retirement period is estimated by the life expectancy. According to UN Secretariat (2007), the life expectancy of Chinese people in 2000 - 2005 is 72.0 years old. Since one period length is 26 years, the life-span from birth to the end of working-period is 52 years. The life-span from birth to the end of retirement period is 78 years. According to the concept of life expectancy, one can get $(1-p) \times 52 + p \times 78 = 72.0$, which gives $p \approx 76.92\%$. Although the choice of period length is arbitrary, it has to obey the following rule: Three times of the period length should be longer than or equal to the life expectancy to ensure $p \leq 1$.

Based on the caliber of "Urban Population", the population growth rate during 1980 - 2006 is computed as $n \approx 2.045$ according to the "Population and Its Composition" in China Statistical Yearbook, which has in fact reflected immigration from rural areas. According to the reform of the public pension system in 2005, the social pool benefit replacement rate ξ has been raised from 20% to 35%, and the individual account benefit replacement rate μ reduced from 38.5% to 24.2%. The above estimated values are benchmark values of the parameters.

3.2. Effect of Social Pool Benefit Replacement Rate

Let the social pool benefit replacement rate be 20%. Substituting the benchmark parameter values into equation (14) in steady state and calculating repeatedly until the equation holds, we get the capital-labor ratio, $k \approx 0.0455$. Substituting it and the benchmark parameter values into equations (9'), (11'), (2'), (3'), (1') gives the values of the five endogenous variables. Then, let the social pool benefit replacement rate be 28% and 35%, respectively. Repeating the above procedure yields the result shown in Table 1. Raising the social pool benefit replacement rate decreases the capital-labor ratio[3], individual account benefits, working-period consumption and utility, whereas increases the social pool benefits and retirement-period consumption. A rise in the social pool benefit replacement rate induces the increase in the social pool benefits, which in turn leads to the increase in the retirement-period consumption but the decrease in the savings and furthermore the decrease in the capital-labor ratio. This will decrease the wage, furthermore decrease the individual account benefits and working-period consumption.

Table 1. Effect of social pool benefit replacement rate

ξ	20%	28%	35%
k	0.0448	0.0431	0.0418
P	0.0417	0.0565	0.0688
B	0.0505	0.0489	0.0476
c_1	0.1601	0.1582	0.1566
c_2	0.3386	0.3418	0.3445
U	-2.9510	-2.9567	-2.9619

Table 2. Effect of life expectancy

p	76.92%	80.77%	84.62%
k	0.0418	0.0417	0.0415
P	0.0688	0.0684	0.0681
B	0.0476	0.0473	0.0471
c_1	0.1566	0.1524	0.1481
c_2	0.3445	0.3439	0.3432
U	-2.9619	-3.0318	-3.1028

---

[3] Pecchenino and Pollard (2002) also established a negative effect of increasing the replacement rate for pay-as-you-go component of a pension system.

3.3. Effect of Life Expectancy

Risen life expectancy implies that the survival probability in retirement period increases. According to UN Secretariat (2007), the life expectancy of Chinese people in 2005 - 2010 is 73.0 years old, and that in 2010 - 2015 is 74.0 years old. Hence, the survival probabilities in retirement period are computed to be 80.77% and 84.62%, respectively. Simulating with the estimated survival probabilities and the benchmark parameter values gives the result shown in Table 2. A rise in the life expectancy induces the decrease in the capital-labor ratio[4], social pool benefits, individual account benefits, working-period consumption, retirement-period consumption and utility.

A rise in the life expectancy decreases the social pool benefits because of the social pool fund budget. This in turn decreases the retirement-period consumption and gifts. The fall in the expected bequests (stemmed from risen life expectancy) and the fall in the gifts induce the decrease in the working-period consumption and savings, which in turn leads to the decrement in the capital-labor ratio, furthermore the decrease in the wage and then the individual account benefits.

3.4. Effect of Population Growth Rate

Using the same method to estimate the population growth rate during 1980 - 2006, we estimate the population growth rate during 1984 - 2010 and that during 1989 - 2015. They are 1.789 and 1.617, respectively. In the estimation, the urban population in 2015 is predicted with the urban population in each year from 2000 to 2013 and the TREND function in Microsoft Excel. Simulating with the estimated population growth rates and the benchmark parameter values gives the result shown in Table 3. A fall in the population growth rate leads to the increase in the capital-labor ratio, social pool benefits, individual account benefits, working-period consumption and utility, whereas the decrease in the retirement-period consumption. A fall in the population growth rate induces the increase in the capital-labor ratio because of concentrating effect. The rise in the capital-labor ratio increases the wage, furthermore the social pool benefits and individual account benefits. For utility maximization, the rise in the pension benefits decreases the savings. The retirement-period consumption decreases when the negative effect of decreased savings dominates the positive effect of increased pension benefits. The rise in the wage and the fall in the savings both lead to the increase in the working-period consumption.

4. PARETO OPTIMUM

4.1. Social Welfare Maximization

The fact that the social pool benefit replacement rate has effect on the capital-labor ratio implies that controlling the replacement rate can adjust the capital-labor ratio in market

---

[4] Pecchenino and Pollard (2002) also established the possibility for economies with higher longevity to have lower physical capital stocks.

economy to the modified golden rule level. Social welfare is the sum of lifetime utilities of all current and future generations (Blanchard and Fischer, 1989; and Groezen et al., 2003; also use an analogous social welfare function):

Table 3. Effect of Population Growth Rate

n	2.045	1.789	1.617
k	0.0418	0.0478	0.0528
P	0.0688	0.0716	0.0737
B	0.0476	0.0495	0.0509
c_1	0.1566	0.1653	0.1720
c_2	0.3445	0.3414	0.3396
U	-2.9619	-2.9169	-2.8827

$$W = \theta p \ln c_{20} + \delta(1-p)\ln b_0^D + \delta p \ln b_0^S \\ + \sum_{i=0}^{\infty} \rho^i \left[\ln c_{1i} + \theta p \ln c_{2i+1} + \delta(1-p)\ln b_{i+1}^D + \delta p \ln b_{i+1}^S \right], \quad (15)$$

where $\rho \in (0,1)$ is the social discount factor, which reflects the preference of social planner. The resource constraint is

$$k_i + Ak_i^\alpha = (1+n)k_{i+1} + c_{1i} + p\frac{c_{2i}}{1+n}, \quad (16)$$

The initial condition is that k_0 is given, and the terminal condition is $k_\infty = 0$.

The social planner maximizes the social welfare subject to the resource constraint, the initial and terminal conditions. The first-order conditions for the social welfare maximization problem are:

$$\theta(1+n)c_1^* = \rho c_2^*, \quad (17)$$

$$1 + \alpha A(k^*)^{\alpha-1} = \frac{1+n}{\rho} \quad \text{or} \quad k^* = \left(\frac{1+n-\rho}{\rho \alpha A}\right)^{\frac{1}{\alpha-1}}, \quad (18)$$

where the superscript * denotes the optimal steady state values of variables. The capital-labor ratio satisfying equation (18) is at the modified golden rule level, which means that the social welfare reaches the maximum.

In order to maximize the social welfare of the market economy in steady state, we control the policy variable to adjust the capital-labor ratio of the market economy in steady state to the modified golden rule level, namely, $k = k^*$. Substituting equation (18) into equation (14) and rearranging gives

$$p\theta\delta(1-p)\varphi^2 + \left[p^2\theta\frac{1+n}{\rho}+(1+n)+\delta(1-p)\left(n-\frac{1+n-\rho}{\rho\alpha}\right)\right]\varphi + p\frac{1+n}{\rho}\left(n-\frac{1+n-\rho}{\rho\alpha}\right) = 0 \quad (19)$$

where $\varphi = \dfrac{1}{\theta+\delta}\left(\dfrac{1+n}{\rho}+\xi^*\dfrac{1-\alpha}{1+n+p\xi^*}\cdot\dfrac{1+n-\rho}{\rho\alpha}\right)$.

The optimal social pool benefit replacement rate depends on the individual discount factor θ, altruism intensity δ, survival probability in retirement period p, capital share of income α, population growth rate n, and social discount factor ρ.

4.2. Optimal Social Pool Benefit Replacement Rate

The effects of the life expectancy and population growth rate on the optimal social pool benefit replacement rate can be obtained by partially differentiating ξ^* with respective to p and n, respectively. It can be shown that these effects are dependent on the relevant parameter values. We will check the effects by simulation.

It is necessary to estimate the social discount factor at first, which indicates how much the government weights different generations in its social welfare calculations. Hence, it should be estimated according to the government's regulations. The target replacement rate of social pool benefits is 35%, which is the optimal social pool benefit replacement rate adopted by the government. Substituting the above relevant parameter values into equation (19) and calculating repeatedly until the equation holds, we get $\rho \approx 0.8102$.

Case 1: Risen life expectancy. When the survival probability is 80.77%, substituting it and the benchmark values of the other parameters into equation (19) gives $\xi^* \approx 33.35\%$. Analogous simulation gives that ξ^* is 32.71% when the survival probability is 84.62%. As shown in Table 4, the optimal social pool benefit replacement rate falls when the life expectancy has risen.

Case 2: Fallen population growth rate. As mentioned above, the estimated population growth rate during 1984 - 2010 and that during 1989 - 2015 are 1.789 and 1.617, respectively. Simulating with the estimated population growth rates and the benchmark values of the other parameters gives the result shown in Table 5. The optimal social pool benefit replacement rate falls with the population growth rate.

Case 3: Risen life expectancy and fallen population growth rate. With the benchmark values of θ, δ, α and ρ, simulating the four combinations of the above survival probabilities and population growth rates gives the result shown in Table 6. The optimal social pool benefit replacement rate further falls under the joint condition of risen life expectancy and fallen population growth rate

Table 4. ξ^* under risen life expectancies

p	76.92%	80.77%	84.62%
ξ^*	35.00%	33.35%	32.71%

Table 5. ξ^* under fallen population growth rates

n	2.045	1.789	1.617
ξ^*	35.00%	24.40%	17.15%

Table 6. ξ^* under different life expectancies and population growth rates

p	n	ξ^*
80.77%	1.789	24.10%
80.77%	1.617	16.95%
84.62%	1.789	23.58%
84.62%	1.617	16.54%

CONCLUSION

Taking altruistic motives into account, this chapter employs an OLG model with uncertain lifetime to investigate the public pension system for urban enterprise employees in China. We examine the effects of the individual account benefit replacement rate, social pool benefit replacement rate, life expectancy and population growth rate on the capital-labor ratio, social pool benefits, individual account benefits, working-period consumption, retirement-period consumption and utility. By controlling the policy variable that has effect on the capital-labor ratio to adjust the capital-labor ratio in market economy to the modified golden rule level, we also find the optimal social pool benefit replacement rate. At last, we check the effects of the life expectancy and population growth rate on the optimal social pool benefit replacement rate.

The results are as follows: Raising the individual account benefit replacement rate can only increase the individual account benefits. Raising the social pool benefit replacement rate decreases the capital-labor ratio, individual account benefits, working-period consumption and utility, whereas increases the social pool benefits and retirement-period consumption. A rise in the life expectancy induces the decrease in the capital-labor ratio, social pool benefits, individual account benefits, working-period consumption, retirement-period consumption and utility. A fall in the population growth rate leads to the increase in the capital-labor ratio, social pool benefits, individual account benefits, working-period consumption and utility, whereas the decrease in the retirement-period consumption. The optimal social pool benefit replacement rate depends on the individual discount factor, altruism intensity, survival probability in retirement period, capital share of income, population growth rate and social discount factor. The simulations show that the optimal social pool benefit replacement rate falls in the case of risen life expectancy or fallen population growth rate. It further falls under the joint condition of risen life expectancy and fallen population growth rate. This is different from the result derived from the model without considering altruistic motives.

These results have some policy implications: (a) In order to keep an appropriately high economic growth rate, it is necessary to reduce the social pool benefit replacement rate and control the population growth rate. (b) To increase the social pool benefits, it is necessary to raise the social pool benefit replacement rate and control the population growth rate. (c) To increase the individual account benefits, it is necessary to raise the individual account benefit replacement rate, reduce the social pool benefit replacement rate and control the population growth rate. (d) To increase the consumption of workers, it is necessary to reduce the social pool benefit replacement rate and control the population growth rate. (e) To increase the consumption of retirees, it is necessary to raise the social pool benefit replacement rate and increase the population growth rate. (f) To increase the utility level, it is necessary to reduce the social pool benefit replacement rate and control the population growth rate.

Integrating the above economic goals, it will do more good than harm to raise the individual account benefit replacement rate, reduce the social pool benefit replacement rate and control the population growth rate. The optimal social pool benefit replacement rate should fall under the joint condition of risen life expectancy and fallen population growth rate. Taking altruistic motives into account affects the conclusion about the optimal social pool benefit replacement rate derived in the last chapter. It implies that the optimal social pool benefit replacement rate should be lower than the target rate mentioned at the beginning of this chapter during the period of population aging peak.

APPENDIX A

In order to find the stability condition, we linearize the dynamic system around the steady state (k). Some manipulation gives $adk_{t+1} + edk_t = 0$, where

$$a = \frac{1+n}{\theta+\delta}\left(k + \alpha Ak^\alpha + \frac{\xi(1-\alpha)}{1+n+p\xi}Ak^\alpha\right) \cdot [1+(1-p)\delta]$$

$$+ \frac{1+n}{\theta+\delta}\left(k + \alpha^2 Ak^\alpha + \frac{\xi(1-\alpha)}{1+n+p\xi}\alpha Ak^\alpha\right) + (1+n)p(k + \alpha Ak^\alpha)$$

$$+ \left[nk - Ak^\alpha + \frac{p\theta}{\theta+\delta}\left(k + \alpha Ak^\alpha + \frac{\xi(1-\alpha)}{1+n+p\xi}Ak^\alpha\right)\right].$$

$$e = -\left[(1+\alpha Ak^{\alpha-1}) - \frac{p\theta}{\theta+\delta}\left(1 + \alpha^2 Ak^{\alpha-1} + \frac{\xi(1-\alpha)}{1+n+p\xi}\alpha Ak^{\alpha-1}\right)\right] \cdot$$

$$\left[\frac{(1-p)\delta}{\theta+\delta}\left(k + \alpha Ak^\alpha + \frac{\xi(1-\alpha)}{1+n+p\xi}Ak^\alpha\right) + p(k + \alpha Ak^\alpha)\right]$$

$$< 0$$

The assumption that the equilibrium is unique, stable and nonoscillatory is equivalent to $0 < \dfrac{dk_{t+1}}{dk_t} = -\dfrac{e}{a} < 1$. Therefore, the stability condition is

$$a+e>0.$$

IV. Rural Pension, Exogenous Model

Chapter 9

BASIC OLG MODEL FOR RURAL PUBLIC PENSION

ABSTRACT

Employing an exogenous OLG model, this chapter investigates the public pension system for rural residents in China. We examine the effects of the individual contribution rate, village subsidy rate, local government allowance rate, basic benefit rate and population growth rate on the capital-labor ratio, per capita consumption and pension benefits. Raising the individual contribution rate only increases the per capita pension benefits. Both raising the village subsidy rate and raising the local government allowance rate increase the capital-labor ratio, per capita consumption and pension benefits. Raising the basic benefit rate decreases the capital-labor ratio and per capita consumption, while increases the pension benefits. A rise in the population growth rate decreases the capital-labor ratio, per capita consumption and pension benefits. It has more advantages than disadvantages to raise the individual contribution rate and village subsidy rate, maintain the present basic benefit rate and accordingly raise the local government allowance rate by adjusting fiscal expenditure structure, and control the population growth rate.

Keywords: rural public pension; per capita consumption; pension benefits

1. INTRODUCTION

The Chinese central government issued the *State Council Opinions on Establishing Unified Basic Pension System for Urban and Rural Residents* (Chinese State Council Document 8 in 2014) in February 2014 to merge the new-type rural public pension system and the public pension system for non-employed urban residents, and establish a unified public pension system for rural residents and non-employed urban residents. The participants in the non-employed citizen pension system was more than 23 million and that in the new-type rural public pension system amounted to 460 million by the end of 2012. Obviously, the coverage and influence of the new-type rural public pension system is far greater than that of the non-employed citizen pension system. Furthermore, to solve the existing problems in the new-type rural public pension system is of great importance for rural residents and non-employed urban residents. Therefore, this book still focuses on the public pension system for rural residents.

The Chinese State Council Document 8 in 2014 stipulates: Participants make pension contributions by choosing one of the twelve levels as they like, 100, 200, 300, 400, 500, 600, 700, 800, 900, 1,000, 1,500, and 2,000 Yuan per participant per year. Villages subsidize the individual contributions according to the decision of villagers' meeting. Local governments allowance the individual contributions with a standard not less than 30 Yuan per participant per year for participants who choose the lowest contribution level, and 60 Yuan for participants who choose the level of 500 Yuan or more. The individual contributions, village subsidies and local government allowances are accumulated in the participants' individual accounts. Each retiree (participant above the age of 60) can draw individual account benefits from her or his individual account, and get basic pension benefits from the central government and local government. The central government pays full basic benefits decided by the central government to retirees in western and central China, and a half of that to those in eastern China[1]. The provincial governments in eastern areas pay another half of the full basic benefits decided by the central government. Local governments can pay additional basic benefits to the retirees according to the local situations. The rural public pension system is expected to reduce the rural poverty, narrow the income gap between urban and rural areas, and promote the domestic consumption.

The public pension system for rural residents has the following problems in present period: The pension benefits are very low; most of participants choose the lowest pension contribution level; the village subsidies and local government allowances are also very low; and the incentive mechanism is inefficient. Although there are additional subsidy policies on the basic pension benefits, the strength of the policies is not strong. The public pension system has not enough attraction for potential participants to join in. Thereby, it is urgent to strengthen the incentive mechanism of the rural public pension system, and promote its financing ability and the pension benefit level.

Doing research on the rural public pension should be based on the following concrete situations in China. Firstly, the pension benefit level should be raised. The basic pension benefits are 55 Yuan per retiree per month, which is much lower than the per capita net annual income of rural residents. Secondly, world economy has been recovering slowly after the international financial crisis. China's economy was also affected. The growth rate has come down significantly in recent three years, and the downside pressure remains. Although the quality and efficiency of economic development have got unparalleled attention now, the economic growth rate should not be ignored, because it affects employment, income and social stability. It relies on expanding domestic demand to maintain a stable, healthy and sustainable growth after the financial crisis. Finally, although China is implementing a new population policy, a couple can give birth to two children if husband or wife is only one child in his or her own family before they get married. The new population policy is unlikely to induce dramatic increase in the rural population growth rate.

Regarding public pension and consumption and capital accumulation, Barro (1974) applied an OLG model to argue that if individuals in successive generations were linked by bequests, changes in the stock of government debt or in social security programs would have

---

[1] The reason is not explained in public. Perhaps it is because the eastern rural areas are richer than the central and western rural areas.

no effect on the steady state capital stock. Feldstein (1974) used an extended life-cycle model to analyze the impact of social security on the individual's simultaneous decision about retirement and saving, and concluded that social security would reduce the capital-labor ratio in models that do not admit a bequest motive. Blanchard and Fischer (1989) used an OLG model to study pay-as-you-go (PAYG) social security system, and showed that a PAYG social security system prevents the rate of capital accumulation and reduces the steady state capital stock. Blanchard and Fischer (1989) also showed that a fully funded social security system has no effect on total savings and capital accumulation. The reason is that the increase in social security savings is exactly offset by a decrease in private savings in such a way that the sum of the two is equal to the previous level of private savings. Zhang and Zhang (1998) analyzed the effects of social security on savings, fertility, and per capita income growth with three specifications of utility functions: Individuals' utility is solely a function of their own consumption of goods; individuals derive direct utility from the number of children they have but not the utility of their descendants; individuals also derive direct utility from the utility of their offspring. With the specification that individuals only care about their own consumptions, it is shown that in the presence of intergenerational transfers, higher (lower) social security taxes lead to lower (higher) fertility, lower (higher) gift ratio and higher (lower) growth. However, the above literature study PAYG or fully funded public pensions based on developed countries.

There is also some literature in China to study public pension system with OLG model. Wang et al. (2001) used computable general equilibrium model to examine the impacts of various design options for pension system reform on the sustainability of the system and on overall economy growth. Within a framework of an endogenous growth OLG model, Yang (2009b) examined the effects of China's partially funded public pension system on the fertility, economic growth and family old-age security, and finds the optimal firm contribution rate interval to rationally control population size, promote economic growth and encourage some material support from the young to the old within family. Yang (2011a) investigated China's public pension system for urban enterprise employees and examines the effects of the benefit replacement rate, life expectancy and population growth rate on the capital-labor ratio, pension benefits, consumption and utility. Kang (2012) compared the effects of improving pension contribution rate and postponing retirement age on capital stock per worker, personal and social pooling account pension level and other economic variables within a framework of general equilibrium OLG model. However, what the literature studied is the basic public pension system for enterprise employees in China. It is hard to find the studies regarding China's public pension system for rural residents.

Consulting the above literature and according to reality of the public pension system for rural residents, this chapter investigates the rural basic pension system by employing an OLG model. It examines the effects of the individual contribution rate, village subsidy rate, local government allowance rate, basic benefit rate and population growth rate on the capital-labor ratio, per capita consumption and pension benefits. Only individuals make pension contributions in the models of the literature. However in our exogenous overlapping generations model, according to China's real rural situations, peasants make contributions, villages subsidize and local governments allowance the contributions. Utilizing the data such as China Statistical Yearbook, the Chinese State Council Documents on rural public pension system, etc., we estimate the relevant parameter values, simulate the effects, and analyze the strengths of the effects.

2. THE MODEL

This chapter adopts Diamond's (1965) two-period OLG model. A closed economy is composed of numerous individuals and firms, and a government. Each individual lives for two periods: working period and retirement period. The generation born at the beginning of period t is called generation t. The work force grows at the rate of $n = (N_t / N_{t-1}) - 1$, where N_t is the work force size of generation t.

2.1. Individuals

Each individual earns labor income by supplying inelastically one unit of labor, makes pension contributions, consumes part of her income, and saves the remainder of the income during her working period. In the retirement period, she consumes her savings with accrued interest, individual account benefits and basic benefits.

Each individual derives utility from the working-period consumption $c_{1,t}$ and retirement-period consumption $c_{2,t+1}$. By choosing the consumption and savings, each individual maximizes own utility:

$$\max\nolimits_{\{c_{1t}, c_{2t+1}, s_t\}} U_t = u(c_{1t}) + \theta u(c_{2t+1}), \tag{1}$$

s.t.
$$c_{1t} = (1-\tau)w_t - s_t, \tag{2}$$

$$c_{2t+1} = (1+r_{t+1})s_t + I_{t+1} + J_{t+1}, \tag{3}$$

where $\theta \in (0,1)$ is the individual discount factor, $\tau \in (0,1)$ the individual contribution rate, w_t the labor income, s_t the savings, r_{t+1} the interest rate, I_{t+1} individual account benefits, and J_{t+1} the basic benefits. $u(\cdot)$ is an increasing and strictly concave function: $u'(\cdot) > 0$, $u''(\cdot) < 0$.

The first-order condition for the utility maximization problem is:

$$-u'(c_{1t}) + \theta(1+r_{t+1})u'(c_{2t+1}) = 0. \tag{4}$$

This familiar expression implies that the utility loss from reducing one unit of working-period consumption is equal to the utility gain from increasing $(1+r_{t+1})$ units of retirement-period consumption.

2.2. Villages

Villages produce a homogenous commodity in competitive markets. The production function $F(K_t, N_t) = N_t f(k_t)$ is homogeneous of degree one, where K_t is the capital stock, $k_t = K_t/N_t$ the capital-labor ratio and $f(k_t)$ the output-labor ratio. $f(k_t)$ exhibits positive and diminishing marginal product: $f'(k_t) > 0$, $f''(k_t) < 0$. The marginal product of capital approaches infinity as capital goes to 0 and approaches 0 as capital goes to infinity: $\lim_{k_t \to 0} f'(k_t) = \infty$ and $\lim_{k_t \to \infty} f'(k_t) = 0$.

Based on villages' total labor income, villages provide subsidies to the individual contributions at rate $\eta \in (0,1)$, and local governments provide allowances at rate $\zeta \in (0,1)$. The central government and local governments together pay retirees for the basic benefits at the basic benefit rate of $j \in (0,1)$.

The village subsidies, local government allowances and basic benefits root in peasants' labor fruit in long term.

Hence, the product is distributed into capital income, labor income with the subsidies, allowances and basic benefits: $F(K_t, N_t) = r_t K_t + (1 + \eta + \zeta + j) N_t w_t$. By virtue of Euler's theorem, we have:

$$r_t = f'(k_t), \tag{5}$$

$$w_t = \frac{f(k_t) - k_t f'(k_t)}{1 + \eta + \zeta + j}. \tag{6}$$

2.3. The Government

The accumulation in an individual account, come from the individual contributions, village subsidies, local government allowances and their accrued interests, is used to pay the individual when she or he retires in the next period as funded pension benefits:

$$I_{t+1} = (1 + r_{t+1})(\tau + \eta + \zeta) w_t. \tag{7}$$

The central government and local governments pay retirees for the basic benefits: $N_{t-1} J_t = j N_t w_t$, or

$$J_t = (1 + n) j w_t. \tag{8}$$

2.4. The Capital Market

The savings and individual pension contributions, village subsidies and local government allowances in period t generate the capital stock in period $t + 1$: $K_{t+1} = N_t[s_t + (\tau + \eta + \zeta)w_t]$, or

$$(1+n)k_{t+1} = s_t + (\tau + \eta + \zeta)w_t. \tag{9}$$

2.5. Dynamic equilibrium

Given the initial condition k_0 and the values of policy parameters τ and η, a competitive equilibrium for the economy is a sequence as $\{c_{1t}, c_{2t+1}, s_t, w_t, r_t, I_{t+1}, J_t, k_{t+1}\}_{t=0}^{\infty}$ that satisfies equations (1) - (9) for all t.

Substituting equations (2), (3) and (5) - (9) into equation (4) gives a dynamic equilibrium system described by the following difference equation:

$$-u'\left((1+\eta+\zeta)\frac{f(k_t)-k_t f'(k_t)}{1+\eta+\zeta+j} - (1+n)k_{t+1}\right)$$
$$+\theta[1+f'(k_{t+1})] \cdot u'\left((1+n)k_{t+1}[1+f'(k_{t+1})] + (1+n)j\frac{f(k_{t+1})-k_{t+1}f'(k_{t+1})}{1+\eta+\zeta+j}\right) = 0 \tag{10}$$

Assume that there is unique, stable and nonoscillatory steady state equilibrium. In order to find the stability condition, we linearize the dynamic system around the steady state (k). Some manipulation gives

$$a(k_{t+1}-k) + b(k_t - k) = 0$$

where

$$a = (1+n)u_1'' + \theta f'u_2' + \theta(1+f')(1+n)\left[(1+f'+kf'') - \frac{jkf''}{1+\eta+\zeta+j}\right]u_2'',$$

$$b = \frac{1+\eta+\zeta}{1+\eta+\zeta+j}kf''u_1'' > 0.$$

The assumption that the equilibrium is unique, stable and nonoscillatory is equivalent to $0 < \frac{k_{t+1}-k}{k_t - k} = -\frac{b}{a} < 1$. Therefore, the stability condition is:

$$a + b < 0. \tag{11}$$

3. COMPARATIVE STATICS

Totally differentiating the dynamic system around the steady state gives:

$$(a+b)dk + gd\eta + id\zeta + edj + hdn = 0, \tag{12}$$

where, let $\sigma = \eta + \zeta$ for simplicity,

$$g = -j\frac{f-kf'}{(1+\sigma+j)^2}[u_1'' + \theta(1+f')(1+n)u_2''] > 0,$$

$$i = -j\frac{f-kf'}{(1+\sigma+j)^2}[u_1'' + \theta(1+f')(1+n)u_2''] > 0,$$

$$e = (1+\sigma)\frac{f-kf'}{(1+\sigma+j)^2}[u_1'' + \theta(1+f')(1+n)u_2''] < 0,$$

$$h = ku_1'' + \theta(1+f')\left[k(1+f') + j\frac{f-kf'}{1+\sigma+j}\right]u_2'' < 0.$$

Define $c_t = \frac{N_t c_{1t} + N_{t-1} c_{2t}}{N_t} = c_{1t} + \frac{c_{2t}}{1+n}$ as per capita consumption of the work force, and $B_t = I_t + P_t$ as pension benefits of each retiree in period t. After the economy converging to the steady state equilibrium, the per capita consumption and pension benefits become:

$$c = f - nk, \tag{13}$$

$$B = [(1+f')(\tau+\sigma) + (1+n)j]\frac{f-kf'}{1+\sigma+j}. \tag{14}$$

3.1. Effect of Individual Contribution Rate

Because the voluntary savings are crowded out by one-for-one when the individual contributions (or mandatory savings) increase, the individual contribution rate does not appear in the dynamic system and has no effect on the capital-labor ratio. Thereby, $\partial k/\partial \tau = 0$. Partially differentiating c and B with respect to τ, respectively, and using the stability condition gives

$$\frac{\partial c}{\partial \tau} = 0,$$

$$\frac{\partial B}{\partial \tau} = (1+f')\frac{f-kf'}{1+\sigma+j} > 0.$$

The per capita consumption is a function of the capital-labor ratio, and the individual contribution rate has no effect on the capital-labor ratio. Hence, it has no effect on the per capita consumption. The pension benefits are composed of the individual account benefits and basic benefits. Raising the individual contribution rate increases the individual account benefits and has no effect on the basic benefits, hence as a whole increases the pension benefits.

3.2. Effects of Village Subsidy Rate and Local Government Allowance Rate

Partially differentiating k, c and B with respect to η, respectively, and using the stability condition gives:

$$\frac{\partial k}{\partial \eta} = -\frac{g}{a+b} > 0,$$

$$\frac{\partial c}{\partial \eta} = (f'-n)\frac{\partial k}{\partial \eta},$$

$$\frac{\partial B}{\partial \eta} = \frac{f-kf'}{(a+b)(1+\sigma+j)^2} \{\Phi_1\},$$

where

$$\{\Phi_1\} = [(1+f')(1-\tau)+(f'-n)j] \cdot [(1+n)u_1'' + \theta u_2' f'']$$
$$+ [(1+f')(1-\tau)(1+\sigma)k + (f'-n)j(1+\sigma)k + (\tau+\sigma)(f-k)j - (1+n)j^2 k] \frac{f''u_1''}{1+\sigma+j}$$
$$+ [(1+f')(1-\tau)+(f'-n)j]\varphi(1+f')(1+n)(1+f'+kf'')u_2''$$
$$+ [(\tau+\sigma)(f-k)+(1+f')(1-\tau)k + (f'-1-2n)jk]\varphi(1+f')(1+n)\frac{jf''u_2''}{1+\sigma+j}$$

Raising the village subsidy rate increases the capital-labor ratio, also increases the per capita consumption if the interest rate is higher than the population growth rate, but the effect on the pension benefits is dependent on the parameter values. A rise in the village subsidy rate increases directly the capital-labor ratio, and decreases indirectly the labor income.

Because the direct effect dominates the indirect effect, raising the village subsidy rate increases the capital-labor ratio. Under the condition of $f' > n$, namely, the interest rate is higher than the population growth rate, from equation (13), one can see that raising the village subsidy rate increases the per capita consumption. Equation (14) shows that raising the village subsidy rate decreases directly the labor income and increases the individual account benefits, while increases the capital-labor ratio and decreases the interest rate. The four effects mix to make the total effect on the pension benefits be ambiguous.

Observing equations (10) and (12) and the expressions of g and i yields that η and ζ play a same role, that is, the functions of the two policy variables in the model are identical. It implies that the partial derivatives of k, c and B with respect to ζ are the same as that with respect to η. In other words, the effect of ζ on the capital-labor ratio, per capita consumption and pension benefits are the same as that of η. Thereby, raising the local government allowance rate increases the capital-labor ratio, also increases the per capita consumption if the interest rate is higher than the population growth rate, but the effect on the pension benefits is dependent on the parameter values.

3.3. Effect of Basic Benefit Rate

Partially differentiating k, c and B with respect to j, respectively, and using the stability condition gives:

$$\frac{\partial k}{\partial j} = -\frac{e}{a+b} < 0,$$

$$\frac{\partial c}{\partial j} = (f' - n)\frac{\partial k}{\partial j},$$

$$\frac{\partial B}{\partial j} = \frac{f - kf'}{(a+b)(1+\sigma+j)^2}\{\Phi_2\},$$

where

$$\{\Phi_2\} = [(1+n)(1+\sigma) - (1+f')(\tau+\sigma)] \cdot [(1+n)u_1'' + \theta u_2' f'']$$

$$+ \left\{ \begin{array}{l} [(1+n)(1+\sigma) - (1+f')(\tau+\sigma)] \cdot \dfrac{1+\sigma}{1+\sigma+j} k \\ -(1+\sigma)\left[\dfrac{f-kf'}{1+\sigma+j}(\tau+\sigma) - \dfrac{[(1+f')(\tau+\sigma) + (1+n)j]k}{1+\sigma+j} \right] \end{array} \right\} f''u_1''$$

$$+ [(1+n)(1+\sigma) - (1+f')(\tau+\sigma)] \cdot \theta(1+f')^2(1+n)u_2''$$

$$+ [(1+n)(1+\sigma+j)k - (f-kf')(\tau+\sigma)]\frac{\theta(1+f')(1+n)(1+\sigma)}{1+\sigma+j} f''u_2''.$$

Raising the basic benefit rate decreases the capital-labor ratio, also decreases the per capita consumption if the interest rate is higher than the population growth rate, but the effect on the pension benefits is dependent on the parameter values. A rise in the basic benefit rate decreases the labor income furthermore the savings, both of them make the capital-labor ratio fall. Under the condition of $f' > n$, namely, the interest rate is higher than the population growth rate, from equation (13), one can get that raising the basic benefit rate decreases the per capita consumption. Equation (14) shows that raising the basic benefit rate has directly positive effect on the basic pension benefits, decreases directly the labor income, indirectly decreases the capital-labor ratio and increases the interest rate. The four effects mix to make the total effect on the pension benefits be ambiguous.

3.4. Effect of Population Growth Rate

Partially differentiating k, c and B with respect to n, respectively, and using the stability condition gives:

$$\frac{\partial k}{\partial n} = -\frac{h}{a+b} < 0,$$

$$\frac{\partial c}{\partial n} = (f' - n)\frac{\partial k}{\partial n} - k,$$

$$\frac{\partial B}{\partial n} = \frac{1}{(a+b)(1+\sigma+j)}\{\Phi_3\},$$

where

$$\{\Phi_3\} = kf''u_1''\left\{j(f - kf')\frac{1+\sigma}{1+\sigma+j} + k[(1+f')(\tau+\sigma)+(1+n)j]\right\}$$
$$+ j(f - kf')[(1+n)u_1'' + \theta u_2' f'' + \theta(1+f')^2(1+n)u_2'']$$
$$+ \theta(1+f')kf''u_2''\left\{j(f - kf')(1+n)\frac{1+\sigma}{1+\sigma+j} + [(1+f')(\tau+\sigma)+(1+n)j]\left[k(1+f') + j\frac{f-kf'}{1+\sigma+j}\right]\right\}$$

A rise in the population growth rate decreases the capital-labor ratio, also decreases the per capita consumption if the interest rate is higher than the population growth rate, but the effect on the pension benefits is dependent on the parameter values. The capital-labor ratio falls in the case of rise in the population growth rate because of the dilution effect from population growth. Under the condition of the interest rate is higher than the population growth rate, from equation (13), one can see that a rise in the population growth rate decreases the per capita consumption. Equation (14) shows that a rise in the population growth rate indirectly decreases the capital-labor ratio and labor income, but increases the interest rate. Taking the positive effect of a rise in the population growth rate on the basic benefits into account, the four effects mix to make the total effect on the pension benefits be ambiguous. Some effects of the exogenous variables on the endogenous variables are dependent on the parameter values; hence we estimate first the parameters and then check the effects by simulations below.

4. NUMERICAL EXPERIMENT

Suppose that the utility is described by a logarithmic function, $u(c) = \ln c$, and the production by Cobb-Douglas function, $f(k) = Ak^\alpha$, where A denotes the productivity, and α the capital share of income. Thus, the dynamic equilibrium system becomes

$$\frac{(1+\sigma+j)(1+\theta)}{(1-\alpha)A}k_{t+1} + \frac{jk_{t+1}^\alpha}{1+\alpha Ak_{t+1}^{\alpha-1}} = \theta\frac{1+\sigma}{1+n}k_t^\alpha. \tag{15}$$

4.1. Parameter Setting

A period length in this model is assumed to be 28 years because the length is usually in the interval of 25 - 30 years in the literature on OLG model, and the data resulted from the Third National Population Census in 1982 and the Sixth National Population Census in 2010 are adopted in this model. Analogous to Pecchenino and Pollard (2002), we assume that per year discount factor on the utility derived from retirement-period consumption is 0.985, hence, the factor per period is $\theta = 0.985^{28}$.

The capital share of income is usually to be estimated as 0.3 in developed countries. The labor in China is comparatively cheaper, thus the labor share of income is lower, while the capital share of income is higher than that in developed countries. Hence, it is proper to assume that α in China is 0.35. Since the technological progress is not reflected in this model, and what we want to see here is how the endogenous variables change relatively with the five exogenous variables, the constant A can be normalized as 1.

"Rural Employed Population" in China Statistical Yearbook is selected. The rural work force growth rate in the period from 1982 to 2010^2 is computed to be $n = 41418/33867 - 1$ according to the Third National Population Census in 1982 and the Sixth National Population Census in 2010 in China Statistical Yearbook.

At present, the annual contributions per participant are 183 Yuan and the monthly pension benefits per retiree 82 Yuan (Gao, 2013). The net annual income per rural resident is 6977.29 Yuan, hence the individual contribution rate is $\tau = 183/6977.29$. According to equation (8) and the basic benefits per year $J = 12 \times 82$ Yuan, one can compute the basic benefit rate, $j = J/[(1+n)w] \approx 11.532\%$. The Chinese State Council Document 8 in 2014 stipulates: Local governments allowance the individual contributions with a standard not less than 30 Yuan per participant per year for participants who choose the lowest contribution

---

[2] Although the Chinese rural public pension came out in 2009, peasants above the age of 60 have gotten the pension benefits because they had contributed to the pension system when they were young via say price scissors of industrial and agricultural products, agriculture taxation, etc.

level, and 60 Yuan for participants who choose the contribution level of 500 Yuan or more. Villages subsidize the individual contributions according to the decision of villagers' meeting. Because the allowances in different regions are different from each other and there are no authorized data, we assume the local government allowance to each participant per year is 45 Yuan. Thus, the local government allowance rate is $\zeta = 45/6977.29$. The village subsidies are lower than the local government allowances. The subsidies are assumed to be 30 Yuan per participant per year; hence the village subsidy rate is $\eta = 30/6977.29$. The above estimated values are benchmark values of the parameters.

4.2. Simulations

Simulating with the benchmark parameter values but raising the individual contribution rate from 2.62% gradually to 4.62% gives the result shown in Table 1. Raising the individual contribution rate increases the pension benefits, and has no effect on the capital-labor ratio and per capita consumption.

Table 1. Effect of individual contribution rate

τ	2.62%	3.12%	3.62%	4.12%	4.62%
k	0.06869	0.06869	0.06869	0.06869	0.06869
c	0.37634	0.37634	0.37634	0.37634	0.37634
B	0.05693	0.06029	0.06368	0.06707	0.07045

Table 2. Effect of village subsidy rate

η	0.43%	0.63%	0.83%	1.03%	1.23%
k	0.06869	0.06872	0.06876	0.06879	0.06883
c	0.37634	0.37641	0.37647	0.37653	0.37659
B	0.05693	0.05818	0.05943	0.06068	0.06192

Simulating with the benchmark parameter values but raising the village subsidy rate from 0.43% gradually to 1.23% gives the result shown in Table 2. It is shown that raising the village subsidy rate increases the capital-labor ratio, per capita consumption and pension benefits.

Simulating with the benchmark parameter values but raising the local government allowance rate from 0.64% gradually to 1.84% gives the result shown in Table 3. Raising the local government allowance rate increases the capital-labor ratio, per capita consumption and pension benefits.

Simulating with the benchmark parameter values but raising the basic benefit rate from 11.53% gradually to 15.53% gives the result shown in Table 4. Raising the basic benefit rate increases the pension benefits, and decreases the capital-labor ratio and per capita consumption.

Simulating with the benchmark parameter values but raising the population growth rate from 22.3% gradually to 26.30% gives the result shown in Table 5. A rise in the population growth rate decreases the capital-labor ratio, per capita consumption and pension benefits.

Table 3. Effect of local government allowance rate

ς	0.64%	0.94%	1.24%	1.54%	1.84%
k	0.06869	0.06874	0.06879	0.06885	0.06890
c	0.37634	0.37644	0.37653	0.37662	0.37672
B	0.05693	0.05878	0.06065	0.06251	0.06436

Table 4. Effect of basic benefit rate

j	11.53%	12.53%	13.53%	14.53%	15.53%
k	0.06869	0.06716	0.06567	0.06424	0.06285
c	0.37634	0.37360	0.37091	0.36826	0.36565
B	0.05693	0.05894	0.06088	0.06276	0.06457

Table 5. Effect of population growth rate

n	22.30%	23.30%	24.30%	25.30%	26.30%
k	0.06869	0.06795	0.06724	0.06653	0.06584
c	0.37634	0.37436	0.37240	0.37047	0.36857
B	0.05693	0.05688	0.05683	0.05678	0.05673

Table 6. Elasticity of k, c and B with respect to the exogenous variables

	τ	η	ς	j	n
k	0	0.2%	0.3%	-30.1%	-25.7%
c	0	0.1%	0.1%	-9.8%	-12.7%
B	38.5%	8.7%	12.7%	42.6%	-2.1%

Based on the above simulations, it is straightforward to examine the intensities of the effects of the exogenous variables on k, c and B. The arc elasticity of k, c and B with respect to τ, η, ς, j and n are shown in Table 6. The absolute values reflect the effect intensities, and the signs the effect directions. The effect of the basic benefit rate on the capital-labor ratio is the largest, the others ranking in descending order are the population growth rate, local government allowance rate and village subsidy rate. The effect of the population growth rate on the per capita consumption is the largest, the others ranking in descending order are the basic benefit rate, local government allowance rate and village subsidy rate. The effect of the basic benefit rate on the pension benefits is the largest, the others ranking in descending order are the individual contribution rate, local government allowance rate, village subsidy rate and population growth rate.

CONCLUSION

This chapter investigates the public pension system for rural residents in China by employing the general equilibrium OLG model. It examines the effects of the individual contribution rate, village subsidy rate, local government allowance rate, basic pension benefit rate and population growth rate on the capital-labor ratio, per capita consumption and pension benefits. According to the circumstances in rural areas of China, we estimate the values of relevant parameters, and simulate the above effects and the sensitivities of the endogenous variables with respect to the exogenous variables. Besides that participants make pension contributions, villages subsidize and local governments allowance the individual contributions.

The main results are as follows. Raising the individual contribution rate increases the pension benefits, and has no effect on the capital-labor ratio and per capita consumption. Raising both the village subsidy rate and local government allowance rate increases the capital-labor ratio, per capita consumption and pension benefits. Raising the basic benefit rate increases the pension benefits, while decreases the capital-labor ratio and per capita consumption. A rise in the population growth rate decreases the capital-labor ratio, per capita consumption and pension benefits. The effect of the basic benefit rate on the capital-labor ratio is the largest, the others ranking in descending order are the population growth rate, local government allowance rate and village subsidy rate. The effect of the population growth rate on the per capita consumption is the largest, the others ranking in descending order are the basic benefit rate, local government allowance rate and village subsidy rate. The effect of the basic benefit rate on the pension benefits is the largest, the others ranking in descending order are the individual contribution rate, local government allowance rate, village subsidy rate and population growth rate.

Dragged down by the international financial crisis, world economy recovered very slowly, and China's economic growth rate fell evidently and the downside risk still exists. In order to maintain a stable, healthy and sustainable development of the economy, China needs to expand domestic demand, which includes consumption and investment. To enhance attraction of the public pension system for rural residents, China must strengthen its incentive mechanism. Hence, it is necessary to take measures from entrance and exit of the public pension system. That is to say, to enhance the subsidies and allowances at the entrance and raise the pension benefits at the exit. According to the above results, we can obtain the following judgments: In order to increase the capital accumulation and residents' consumption, it is necessary to reduce the basic benefit rate and population growth rate, and raise the local government allowance rate and village subsidy rate. To increase the pension benefits, it is necessary to raise the individual contribution rate, village subsidy rate, local government allowance rate and basic benefit rate, while reduce the population growth rate.

Integrating the effects of the exogenous variables and their intensities, it has more advantages than disadvantages to adopt the following measures: raising the individual contribution rate, village subsidy rate and local government allowance rate, maintaining the present basic benefit rate, and reducing appropriately the population growth rate. The measures of reducing the population growth rate, raising the village subsidy rate and local government allowance rate can increase the consumption and capital accumulation. Raising the individual contribution rate, village subsidy rate and local government allowance rate, and reducing the population growth rate can increase the pension benefit level in a large scale.

In order to raise the local government allowance rate and maintain the present basic benefit rate, it is necessary to adjust the present fiscal expenditure structure. The local governments can lower the growth speed of the additional basic pension benefits paid by the governments, or temporarily stop raising the additional basic pension benefits. The saved fiscal resources can accordingly be used to increase the allowances to the individual contributions. In other words, transfer a part of subsidies to the exit of the public pension system for rural residents to the entrance of the system. Such a measure can raise the local government allowance rate. Once rural residents see the governments have increased allowances to participants' contributions, the more the individual contributions are the more the government allowances, the participants can recognize the rise in their own interests or benefits. They will increase confidence to future pension benefits, hence raise their contribution level and furthermore realize the goal of rise in the individual contribution rate. The rise in the village subsidy rate relies on growth and grandness of village collective economy. Controlling the population growth rate depends on the Chinese special population policy. The results from this model indicate it is not suitable to relax the population policy greatly. Lower population growth rate is not only helpful to control the size of rural population, but also has positive effect on the capital accumulation and residents' consumption.

Chapter 10

GIFT MOTIVE AND RURAL PUBLIC PENSION

ABSTRACT

Taking gift motive into account, this chapter investigates the public pension system for rural residents in China by employing an exogenous OLG model. We examine the effects of the individual contribution rate, village subsidy rate, local government allowance rate, basic benefit rate and population growth rate on the capital-labor ratio and gifts. The individual contribution rate, village subsidy rate, local government allowance rate and basic benefit rate have no effect on the capital-labor ratio. If the interest rate is higher than the population growth rate, both raising the village subsidy rate and raising the local government allowance rate decrease the gifts, raising the basic benefit rate increases the gifts, and a rise in the population growth rate decreases the capital-labor ratio. The material support from children to their parents should gradually decrease, while the pension benefits come from the rural public pension system should gradually increase in the future. It will do more good than harm to raise the village subsidy rate, maintain the present basic benefit rate and accordingly raise the local government allowance rate by adjusting fiscal expenditure structure. In order to maintain a stable, healthy and sustainable economic growth, China needs to enlarge domestic demand. Hence, it is necessary to raise moderately the population growth rate. This is consistent with the population policy announced in 2013, a couple with husband or wife is sole child in his or her own family before they get married is eligible to give birth to two children.

Keywords: rural public pension; gift motive

1. INTRODUCTION

In this chapter, we take a new element, gift motive, into account. In the last chapter, we did not consider altruistic motive. Chinese rural residents are imbued with a sense of filial duty in which children are reared to care for their parents in old-age. Children appreciate their parents for bringing them up. This is a tacit agreement in rural families. However, net transfers of wealth within family in general run from the young to the old because the Chinese rural economy has been growing so rapid that the income of the working generation is much more than that of the retired generation. Thereby, we introduce gifts or material support from children to their parents into the last chapter's model.

The last chapter has introduced the public pension system for rural residents regulated by the *State Council Opinions on Establishing Unified Basic Pension System for Urban and Rural Residents* (Chinese State Council Document 8 in 2014). Participants make pension contributions, villages subsidize and local governments allowance the individual contributions, all of which are accumulated in the participants' individual accounts. Each retiree (participant above the age of 60) can draw individual account benefits from her or his individual account and get basic benefits from the central government and local governments. The public pension system for rural residents is expected to reduce the rural poverty, narrow the income gap between urban and rural areas, and promote the domestic consumption.

We investigate the effect of the public pension system for rural residents under the following real circumstances: First, Chinese rural residents are altruistic through gifts that run from the yong to the old in families. When the rural public pension system covers the rural areas all over the country, the idea to rear children for old-age material support should gradually be changed. Rural retirees should gradually reduce material support from their children, but depend on the rural public pension benefits. Second, impacted by the international financial crisis, the growth rate of China's gross domestic product (GDP) has fallen below 8% in 2012 and 2013. As a developing country with low per capita GDP, China needs to keep a comparatively rapid economic growth.

Some literature used OLG model with altruistic motive to study social security. Sheshinski and Weiss (1981) examined the annuity aspect of social security within the framework of an OLG model. Abel (1987a) solved the consumption and portfolio decision problem of a consumer who can hold his wealth in the form of riskless bonds and actuarially fair annuities. Abel (1989) demonstrated the effect of a lump-sum tax on debt neutrality. There was no production sector in these models. Fuster (2000) studied how the lack of an annuities market affects savings behavior and intergenerational transfers in a dynastic OLG economy. Zhang et al. (2001) examined how mortality decline affects long-run steady state growth by assuming actuarially fair annuity markets in an OLG model with uncertain lifetime and social security.

Introducing gift motive into the model of the last chapter and consulting the above literature, this chapter investigates the public pension system for rural residents by employing an OLG model. It examines the effects of the individual contribution rate, village subsidy rate, local government allowance rate, basic benefit rate and population growth rate on the capital-labor ratio and gifts. Instead of only individuals make pension contributions in the models of the literature, we catch up with China's real rural situations in our exogenous OLG model by assuming that participants make contributions and villages subsidize and local governments allowance the individual contributions.

2. THE MODEL

A closed economy is composed of numerous individuals and firms, and a government. Each individual lives for two periods: working period and retirement period. The generation born at the beginning of period t is called generation t. The work force grows at the rate of $n = (N_t / N_{t-1}) - 1$, where N_t is the work force size of generation t.

2.1. Individuals

Each individual earns labor income by supplying inelastically one unit of labor, makes pension contributions, consumes part of his or her income, presents his or her parent some gifts that are in fact material support to the retiree in family, and saves the remainder of the income during his or her working period. In the retirement period, he or she consumes his or her savings with accrued interest, individual account benefits, basic benefits and gifts from her children.

Each individual derives utility from his or her working-period consumption $c_{1,t}$, retirement-period consumption $c_{2,t+1}$ and his or her parent's retirement-period consumption. An adult can only care his or her parent's retirement-period consumption and is not able to concern the bypast working-period consumption. Each individual maximizes his or her utility by choosing savings, gifts and consumption:

$$\max_{\{s_t, Q_t, C_{1,t}, C_{2,t+1}\}} U_t = u(c_{1,t}) + \beta u(c_{2,t+1}) + \gamma u(c_{2,t}), \tag{1}$$

s.t.
$$c_{1,t} = (1-\tau)w_t - s_t - Q_t, \tag{2}$$

$$c_{2,t+1} = (1+r_{t+1})s_t + I_{t+1} + J_{t+1} + (1+n)Q_{t+1}, \tag{3}$$

where $\beta \in (0,1)$ denotes the discount factor on the utility derived from his or her retirement-period consumption, $\gamma \in (0,1)$ the discount factor on the utility derived from his or her parent's retirement-period consumption, $\tau \in (0,1)$ the individual contribution rate, w_t the labor income, Q_t the gifts to her parent, s_t the savings, r_{t+1} the interest rate, I_{t+1} individual account benefits, J_{t+1} the basic benefits, and Q_{t+1} the gifts from children.

Substituting equations (2) and (3) into equation (1), and letting the partial derivatives of equation (1) with respect to s_t and Q_t be zero gives the first-order conditions for the utility maximization problem:

$$-u'(c_{1,t}) + \beta(1+r_{t+1})u'(c_{2,t+1}) = 0, \tag{4}$$

$$-u'(c_{1,t}) + \gamma(1+n)u'(c_{2,t}) = 0. \tag{5}$$

Equation (4) implies that the utility loss from reducing one unit of working-period consumption is equal to the utility gain from increasing $(1+r_{t+1})$ units of retirement-period consumption. Equation (5) implies that the utility loss from reducing one unit of working-period consumption is equal to the utility gain from increasing $(1+n)$ units of parent's retirement-period consumption.

2.2. Villages

Villages produce a homogenous commodity in competitive markets. The production function $Y_t = F(K_t, N_t)$ or $y_t = f(k_t)$ is homogeneous of degree one, where Y_t is the output in period t, K_t the physical capital stock, $k_t = K_t/N_t$ the capital-labor ratio, and y_t the output-labor ratio. The production function $f(k_t)$ exhibits not only constant returns to scale, but also positive and diminishing marginal product, i.e., $f'(k_t) > 0$, $f''(k_t) < 0$. The marginal product of capital approaches infinity as capital goes to 0 and approaches 0 as capital goes to infinity: $\lim_{k_t \to 0} f'(k_t) = \infty$ and $\lim_{k_t \to \infty} f'(k_t) = 0$.

Based on villages' total labor income, villages provide pension contribution subsidies at a rate of $\eta \in (0,1)$, and local governments provide allowances at a rate of $\zeta \in (0,1)$. The central government and local governments together pay rural retirees the basic benefits at a basic benefit rate of $j \in (0,1)$. The village subsidies, local government allowances and basic benefits root in peasants' labor fruit in long term. Hence, the product is distributed into capital income, labor income with the subsidies, allowances and basic benefits: $F(K_t, N_t) = r_t K_t + (1 + \eta + \zeta + j) N_t w_t$. By virtue of Euler's theorem, we have:

$$r_t = f'(k_t), \qquad (6)$$

$$w_t = \frac{f(k_t) - k_t f'(k_t)}{1 + \eta + \zeta + j}. \qquad (7)$$

2.3. The Government

The accumulation in an individual account, coming from the individual contributions, village subsidies and local government allowances, is used to pay the individual when the individual retires in the next period as funded pension benefits:

$$I_{t+1} = (1 + r_{t+1})(\tau + \eta + \zeta) w_t. \qquad (8)$$

The central government and local governments pay rural retirees the basic benefits: $N_{t-1} J_t = j N_t w_t$, or

$$J_t = j(1 + n) w_t. \qquad (9)$$

2.4. Dynamic Equilibrium

According to Blanchard and Fischer (1989) or Barro and Sala-I-Martin (2004), the savings and individual contributions, village subsidies and local government allowances in period t generate the capital stock in period $t + 1$: $K_{t+1} = N_t[s_t + (\tau + \eta + \zeta)w_t]$, or

$$(1+n)k_{t+1} = s_t + (\tau + \eta + \zeta)w_t. \tag{10}$$

Given the initial condition k_0 and values of the policy parameters τ, η, ζ and j, a competitive equilibrium for the economy is a sequence as $\{c_{1t}, c_{2t+1}, s_t, w_t, r_t, I_{t+1}, J_t, k_{t+1}\}_{t=0}^{\infty}$ that satisfies equations (1) - (10) for all t.

Substituting equations (2), (3) and (6) - (10) into equations (4) and (5) gives a dynamic equilibrium system described by the following system of difference equations:

$$-u'\left((1+\eta+\zeta)\frac{f(k_t)-k_t f'(k_t)}{1+\eta+\zeta+j} - (1+n)k_{t+1} - Q_t\right)$$
$$+ \beta[1+f'(k_{t+1})]u'\left((1+n)\left\{k_{t+1}[1+f'(k_{t+1})] + j\frac{f(k_{t+1})-k_{t+1}f'(k_{t+1})}{1+\eta+\zeta+j} + Q_{t+1}\right\}\right) = 0 \tag{11}$$

$$-u'\left((1+\eta+\zeta)\frac{f(k_t)-k_t f'(k_t)}{1+\eta+\zeta+j} - (1+n)k_{t+1} - Q_t\right)$$
$$+ \gamma(1+n)u'\left((1+n)\left\{k_t[1+f'(k_t)] + j\frac{f(k_t)-k_t f'(k_t)}{1+\eta+\zeta+j} + Q_t\right\}\right) = 0 \tag{12}$$

Assume that there is steady state equilibrium. In order to find the stability condition, we linearize the dynamic system around the steady state (k). Some manipulation gives

$$a\hat{k}_{t+1} + e\hat{k}_t + g\hat{Q}_{t+1} + h\hat{Q}_t = 0, \tag{13}$$

$$i\hat{k}_{t+1} + l\hat{k}_t + q\hat{Q}_t = 0, \tag{14}$$

where, $\hat{k}_t = (k_t - k)$, $\hat{Q}_t = (Q_t - Q)$, etc. for notation simplicity, and let $u'_1 = u'(c_1)$, $u''_1 = u''(c_1)$, etc.,

$$a = (1+n)u''_1 + \beta u'_2 f'' + \beta(1+f')(1+n)\left(1+f'+\frac{1+\eta+\zeta}{1+\eta+\zeta+j}kf''\right)u''_2,$$

$$e = \frac{1+\eta+\zeta}{1+\eta+\zeta+j} kf''u_1'' > 0,$$

$$g = \beta(1+f')(1+n)u_2'',$$

$$h = u_1'',$$

$$i = (1+n)u_1'',$$

$$l = \frac{1+\eta+\zeta}{1+\eta+\zeta+j} kf''u_1'' + \gamma(1+n)^2\left(1+f'+\frac{1+\eta+\zeta}{1+\eta+\zeta+j}kf''\right)u_2'',$$

$$q = u_1'' + \gamma(1+n)^2 u_2''.$$

Rearranging equations (13) and (14) gives

$$\hat{k}_{t+2} + a_1\hat{k}_{t+1} + a_2\hat{k}_t = 0,$$

where $a_1 = \dfrac{gl+hi-qa}{gi}$, $a_2 = \dfrac{hl-qe}{gi}$.

The assumption that the system converges to a steady state is equivalent to (see Samuelson, 1955, p.436)

$$1+a_1+a_2 > 0,$$

$$1-a_1+a_2 > 0,$$

$$a_2 < 1.$$

This is the stability condition.

Rearranging $1+a_1+a_2 > 0$ gives

$$\frac{q(a+e)-(g+h)(i+l)}{-gi} = \frac{\Delta}{-gi} > 0.$$

Because

$$-gi < 0,$$

Therefore

$$\Delta < 0.$$

3. COMPARATIVE STATICS

Totally differentiating equations (11) and (12) around the steady state gives:

$$(a+e)dk + (g+h)dQ + md\eta + pd\zeta + vdj + zdn = 0, \quad (15)$$

$$(i+l)dk + qdQ + xd\eta + \alpha d\zeta + \theta dj + \varphi dn = 0, \quad (16)$$

where

$$m = \frac{-j(f-kf')}{(1+\eta+\zeta+j)^2}\left[u_1'' + \beta(1+f')(1+n)u_2''\right] > 0, \qquad p = m,$$

$$v = \frac{(1+\eta+\zeta)(f-kf')}{(1+\eta+\zeta+j)^2}\left[u_1'' + \beta(1+f')(1+n)u_2''\right] < 0,$$

$$z = ku_1'' + \beta(1+f')\left[k(1+f') + j\frac{f-kf'}{1+\eta+\zeta+j} + Q\right]u_2'' < 0,$$

$$x = \frac{-j(f-kf')}{(1+\eta+\zeta+j)^2}\left[u_1'' + \gamma(1+n)^2 u_2''\right] > 0, \qquad \alpha = x,$$

$$\theta = \frac{(1+\eta+\zeta)(f-kf')}{(1+\eta+\zeta+j)^2}\left[u_1'' + \gamma(1+n)^2 u_2''\right] < 0$$

$$\varphi = ku_1'' + \gamma u_2' + \gamma(1+n)\left[k(1+f') + j\frac{f-kf'}{1+\eta+\zeta+j} + Q\right]u_2''.$$

Rewriting equations (15) and (16) as

$$\begin{pmatrix} a+e & g+h \\ i+l & q \end{pmatrix}\begin{pmatrix} dk \\ dQ \end{pmatrix} + \begin{pmatrix} m \\ x \end{pmatrix}d\eta + \begin{pmatrix} p \\ \alpha \end{pmatrix}d\zeta + \begin{pmatrix} v \\ \theta \end{pmatrix}dj + \begin{pmatrix} z \\ \varphi \end{pmatrix}dn = 0. \quad (17)$$

Therefore (referring to Appendix A),

$$\Delta = \begin{vmatrix} a+e & g+h \\ i+l & q \end{vmatrix} < 0;$$

$$\Delta_1 = \begin{vmatrix} m & g+h \\ x & q \end{vmatrix} = qm - (g+h)x = 0;$$

$$\Delta_2 = \frac{-j(f-kf')}{(1+\eta+\zeta+j)^2}\left\{\beta u_2' f''\left[u_1'' + \gamma(1+n)^2 u_2''\right] + (1+n)[\beta(1+f') - \gamma(1+n)](f'-n)u_1'' u_2''\right\} < 0,$$
if $f' > n$;

$$\Delta_3 = \begin{vmatrix} v & g+h \\ \theta & q \end{vmatrix} = vq - \theta(g+h) = 0;$$

$$\Delta_4 = \frac{(1+\eta+\zeta)(f-kf')}{(1+\eta+\zeta+j)^2}\left\{(f'-n)(1+n)[\beta(1+f') - \gamma(1+n)]u_1'' u_2'' + \beta u_2' f''\left[u_1'' + \gamma(1+n)^2 u_2''\right]\right\} > 0, \text{ if } f' > n;$$

$$\Delta_5 = [\beta(1+f') - \gamma(1+n)]u_1'' u_2''\left[k(f'-n) + j\frac{f-kf'}{1+\eta+\zeta+j} + Q\right] - \gamma u_2'[u_1'' + \beta(1+f')(1+n)u_2''] > 0,$$
if $f' > n$;

$$\Delta_6 = [\gamma(1+n) - \beta(1+f')]\left\{(1+n)\left[j\frac{f-kf'}{1+\eta+\zeta+j} + Q - \frac{1+\eta+\zeta}{1+\eta+\zeta+j}k^2 f''\right] + \frac{1+\eta+\zeta}{1+\eta+\zeta+j}kf''\left[k(1+f') + j\frac{f-kf'}{1+\eta+\zeta+j} + Q\right]\right\}u_1'' u_2''$$
$$+ \beta u_2' f''\left\{ku_1'' + \gamma u_2' + \gamma(1+n)\left[k(1+f') + j\frac{f-kf'}{1+\eta+\zeta+j} + Q\right]u_2''\right\}$$
$$+ \gamma u_2' \beta(1+f')(1+n)\left(1 + f' + \frac{1+\eta+\zeta}{1+\eta+\zeta+j}kf''\right)u_2'' + \left[(1+n) + \frac{1+\eta+\zeta}{1+\eta+\zeta+j}kf''\right]\gamma u_2' u_1''$$

Using Cramer's rule yields:

$$\frac{\partial k}{\partial \eta} = -\frac{\Delta_1}{\Delta} = 0,$$

$$\frac{\partial Q}{\partial \eta} = -\frac{\Delta_2}{\Delta} < 0, \text{ if } f' > n,$$

$$\frac{\partial k}{\partial j} = -\frac{\Delta_3}{\Delta} = 0,$$

$$\frac{\partial Q}{\partial j} = -\frac{\Delta_4}{\Delta} > 0, \text{ if } f' > n,$$

$$\frac{\partial k}{\partial n} = -\frac{\Delta_5}{\Delta} > 0, \text{ if } f' > n,$$

$$\frac{\partial Q}{\partial n} = -\frac{\Delta_6}{\Delta}.$$

The individual contribution rate does not appear in the dynamic system because the mandatory savings (individual contributions) crowd out the voluntary savings by one-for-one. Hence, it has no effect on the capital-labor ratio and gifts, that is, $\frac{\partial k}{\partial \tau} = \frac{\partial Q}{\partial \tau} = 0$.

The village subsidy rate has no effect on the capital-labor ratio. Raising the village subsidy rate decreases the gifts if the interest rate is higher than the population growth rate. The neutrality reflected by the effect on the capital-labor ratio is caused by the gift motive, which has been proved by Barro (1974). Raising the village subsidy rate increases the accumulation in individual account. It enables retirees to reduce gifts from their children.

Because $p = m$ and $\alpha = x$, the effect of local government allowance rate on the capital-labor ratio and gifts is the same as that of the village subsidy rate. Observing equations (11) and (12) yields that η and ζ play the same role. Their functions in the model are identical. Hence, the partial derivatives of k and Q with respect to ζ equal that with respect to η. Hence, the effects of ζ on the endogenous variables are the same as that of η. Thereby, raising the local government allowance rate decreases the gifts if the interest rate is higher than the population growth rate, but has no effect on the capital-labor ratio.

The basic benefit rate has no effect on the capital-labor ratio. Raising the basic benefit rate increases the gifts if the interest rate is higher than the population growth rate. Raising the basic benefit rate increases the income in retirement period, which enables workers to present more gifts to their parents.

A rise in the population growth rate increases the capital-labor ratio if the interest rate is higher than the population growth rate, but the effect on the gifts is dependent on the parameter values.

CONCLUSION

Taking gift motive into account, this chapter investigates the public pension system for rural residents in China by employing the general equilibrium OLG model. It examines the effects of the individual contribution rate, village subsidy rate, local government allowance rate, basic pension benefit rate and population growth rate on the capital-labor ratio and gifts. The differences from the previous studies are as follows: First, this chapter uses an exogenous OLG model and introduces gift motive into the model of the last chapter. Second, apart from individuals make pension contributions, villages subsidize and local governments allowance the individual contributions.

The main results are as follows. The policy variables, the individual contribution rate, village subsidy rate, local government allowance rate and basic pension benefit rate have no effect on the capital-labor ratio. If the interest rate is higher than the population growth rate, both raising the village subsidy rate and raising the local government allowance rate decrease the gifts, raising the basic benefit rate increases the gifts, and a rise in the population growth rate decreases the capital-labor ratio. The effect of the population growth rate on the gifts is dependent on the parameter values.

Chinese rural residents have the philosophy of rearing children for old-age. For Chinese rural families, material support from children to parents is a common phenomenon. The rural public pension system can help the rural residents to transfer their old philosophy. The material support from children should gradually decrease and the pension benefits from the public pension system should gradually increase in the future. According to the above results, it is reasonable to raise the village subsidy rate and local government allowance rate, and reduce the basic benefit rate. In present situation, the basic benefit rate is still low. It is better to raise the village subsidy rate, and maintain the present basic benefit rate and accordingly raise the local government allowance rate by adjusting the fiscal expenditure structure.

Impacted by the international financial crisis, world economy recovered very slowly, China's economic growth fell evidently and its downside risk still exists. In order to maintain a stable, healthy and sustainable development of the economy, China needs to expand domestic demand, which includes consumption and investment. According to the above results, we can obtain the following judgments: To increase the capital accumulation, it is necessary to raise moderately the population growth rate. This result of the present model is consistent with the Chinese new population policy announced in 2013, a couple with husband or wife is only one child in his or her own family before they get married is eligible to give birth to two children. The new population policy has positive effect on the capital accumulation.

APPENDIX A

$$a+e = (1+n)u_1'' + \beta u_2' f'' + \beta(1+f')^2(1+n)u_2'' + \frac{1+\eta+\zeta}{1+\eta+\zeta+j} kf''[u_1'' + \beta(1+f')(1+n)u_2'']$$

$$i+l = (1+n)u_1'' + \gamma(1+n)^2(1+f')u_2'' + \frac{1+\eta+\zeta}{1+\eta+\zeta+j} kf''[u_1'' + \gamma(1+n)^2 u_2'']$$

$$\Delta_2 = \begin{vmatrix} a+e & m \\ i+l & x \end{vmatrix}$$

$$= \frac{-j(f-kf')}{(1+\eta+\zeta+j)^2} \{\beta u_2' f''[u_1'' + \gamma(1+n)^2 u_2''] + (1+n)[\beta(1+f') - \gamma(1+n)](f'-n)u_1'' u_2''\} < 0$$

,

if $f' > n$,

$$\Delta_4 = \begin{vmatrix} a+e & v \\ i+l & \theta \end{vmatrix}$$

$$= \frac{(1+\eta+\zeta)(f-kf')}{(1+\eta+\zeta+j)^2}\{(f'-n)(1+n)[\beta(1+f')-\gamma(1+n)]u_1''u_2'' + \beta u_2'f''[u_1'' + \gamma(1+n)^2 u_2'']\}$$

$$\Delta_5 = \begin{vmatrix} z & g+h \\ \varphi & q \end{vmatrix}$$

$$= [\beta(1+f')-\gamma(1+n)]u_1''u''\left[k(f'-n)+j\frac{f-kf'}{1+\eta+\zeta+j}+Q\right] - \gamma u_2'[u_1'' + \beta(1+f')(1+n)u_2''] > 0$$

if $f' > n$.

$$\Delta_6 = \begin{vmatrix} a+e & z \\ i+l & \varphi \end{vmatrix}$$

$$= [\gamma(1+n)-\beta(1+f')]u_1''u_2''\left\{(1+n)\left[j\frac{f-kf'}{1+\eta+\zeta+j}+Q-\frac{1+\eta+\zeta}{1+\eta+\zeta+j}k^2 f''\right] + \frac{1+\eta+\zeta}{1+\eta+\zeta+j}kf''\left[k(1+f')+j\frac{f-kf'}{1+\eta+\zeta+j}+Q\right]\right\}$$

$$+ \beta u_2'f''\left\{ku_1'' + \gamma u_2' + \gamma(1+n)\left[k(1+f')+j\frac{f-kf'}{1+\eta+\zeta+j}+Q\right]u_2''\right\}$$

$$+ \gamma u_2'\beta(1+f')(1+n)\left(1+f'+\frac{1+\eta+\zeta}{1+\eta+\zeta+j}kf''\right)u_2'' + \left[(1+n)+\frac{1+\eta+\zeta}{1+\eta+\zeta+j}kf''\right]\{\gamma u_2' u_1''\}$$

.

V. Rural Pension, Endogenous Growth Model

Chapter 11

RURAL PUBLIC PENSION, HUMAN CAPITAL AND ENDOGENOUS GROWTH

ABSTRACT

Employing an endogenous growth model, this chapter investigates China's public pension system for rural residents. We examine the effects of the individual contribution rate, village subsidy rate, local government allowance rate and basic benefit rate on the labor income growth rate, population growth rate, saving rate, consumption ratio, and education expense ratio. The negative effect of the individual contribution rate on the labor income growth and population growth is not strong. The negative effects of the village subsidy rate and local government allowance rate on the saving rate are strong, and that on the labor income growth are weak; their positive effects on the consumption ratio and population growth are not strong. The negative effect of the basic benefit rate on the saving rate is very strong, and that on the population growth and labor income growth is not strong; its positive effect on the consumption ratio is comparatively strong. It is necessary to raise the village subsidy rate and local government allowance rate by a comparatively big margin, increase the basic benefit rate by a small margin, and reasonably decrease the individual contribution rate.

Keywords: rural public pension; human capital; endogenous growth

1. INTRODUCTION

The last two chapters used exogenous OLG model to study the public pension system for rural residents. This chapter will investigate the pension system with endogenous growth model. We will study the effects of the rural public pension system on economic growth, rural consumption, etc. by taking the following real circumstances: First, Chinese rural residents are imbued with a sense of filial duty in which children are reared to care for their parents in old-age. Children appreciate their parents for bringing them up. Second, intergenerational net wealth tends to transfer from the young to the old because the working generation's incomes are more than that of the retired generation. Third, rural residents attach importance not only to their own consumption, but also to education for their children and satisfy for their children's high human capital. Final, a couple of rural residents that produce only one child who is a girl is eligible to give birth to one additional child. A couple with husband or wife is sole one child in his or her own family before they get married is eligible to give birth to two children. Rural residents generally have more children than urban residents.

A lot of literature studied the relationship between economic growth, population and public pension using OLG model with endogenous growth. Zhang and Zhang (1995) used an endogenous growth model to examine the effects on fertility and output growth rates of three kinds of PAYG social security systems. Zhang and Zhang (1998) applied an endogenous growth model with three specifications of utility functions to analyze the effects of social security on savings, fertility and per capita income growth. Wigger (1999a) showed that small sized public pensions stimulate per capita income growth, but further increases in public pensions reduce it. A common feature of these studies is to transform the capital per unit of effective labor into a constant and the production function into "AK model" by adopting a special type of productivity. Zhang (1995) examined the effects of social security on the growth of per capita income and fertility. Instead of transforming the production function into "AK model", Zhang introduced human capital, which grows at the same rate with the physical capital per unit of labor in balanced growth equilibrium. Zhang (2001) used the same approach to compare long-run implications for growth and fertility of four types of taxation for social security with positive bequests. Zhang et al. (2001) examined the impacts of mortality decline on long-run growth in an endogenous growth model with social security.

By employing an endogenous growth model, this chapter investigates the public pension system for rural residents in China. It examines the effects of the individual contribution rate, village subsidy rate, local government allowance rate and basic benefit rate on the labor income growth, population growth, saving rate, consumption ratio, and education expense ratio. According to the real rural situations, we estimate the values of relevant parameters and check the effects by simulations. There are three differences between this chapter and the above literature: Firstly, the literature studied PAYG or fully funded public pension systems, whereas this chapter investigates a partially funded one. Secondly, only employees make pension contributions in the models of the literature, whereas participants, villages and local governments do in this model. Finally, part of individual's utility comes from her or his children's human capital, instead of the number of children.

2. THE MODEL

There are numerous individuals and villages and a government in a closed economy. Each individual lives through three periods in life: childhood period, working period and retirement period. At the beginning of period t, L_t identical individuals of generation t enter the work force. Each individual of generation t have N_t children, hence, $L_{t+1} = N_t L_t$.

2.1. Individuals

Individuals develop their human capital in childhood period, and have no ability to make economic decision. Upon entering the work force, each individual represents one unit of labor. Rearing a child requires $v \in (0,1)$ units of labor. Hence, each individual supplies the rest of labor $(1-vN_t) > 0$ to earn labor income. After making pension contributions, she/he consumes part of the income, pays education expenses for her/his children, and saves the remainder of income. In the retirement period, she/he consumes the savings with accrued interest, individual account benefits, and basic benefits.

Each individual derives utility from her/his working-period consumption $C_{2,t}$, retirement-period consumption $C_{3,t+1}$, and children's human capital. Each individual maximizes her/his utility by choosing the saving rate, number of children and education expenses. Thus, the utility maximization problem is:

$$\max_{\{s_t, N_t, E_t\}} U_t = \ln C_{2,t} + \beta \ln C_{3,t+1} + \gamma \ln(N_t h_{t+1}), \tag{1}$$

s.t.
$$C_{2,t} = (1-\tau-s_t)(1-vN_t)W_t - N_t E_t, \tag{2}$$

$$C_{3,t+1} = R_{t+1} s_t (1-vN_t)W_t + I_{t+1} + J_{t+1}, \tag{3}$$

where β and γ denote the discount factors on the utilities derived from her/his retirement-period consumption, and children's human capital, respectively. Since there is a limit to each individual's altruism, it is proper to assume that $1 > \beta > \gamma > 0$ without losing generality. Each individual's human capital of generation $t+1$ is

$$h_{t+1} = A E_t^\delta h_t^{1-\delta}, \tag{4}$$

where $\delta \in (0,1)$ is the elasticity of human capital with respect to education expenses, $A > 0$ is the productivity of human capital production. $\tau \in (0,1)$ denotes the individual contribution rate, W_t the labor income per unit of labor, s_t the saving rate, E_t the education expenses for each child, R_{t+1} the rental rate for physical capital, I_{t+1} the individual account benefits, and J_{t+1} the basic benefits.

Substituting equations (2) - (4) into equation (1), and letting the partial derivatives of equation (1) with respect to s_t, N_t, E_t and Q_t be zero (only considering interior solutions) gives the first-order conditions for the utility maximization problem:

$$\beta \frac{R_{t+1}}{C_{3,t+1}} = \frac{1}{C_{2,t}}, \tag{5}$$

$$\frac{E_t + (1-\tau-s_t)vW_t}{C_{2,t}} + \beta \frac{R_{t+1} s_t v W_t}{C_{3,t+1}} = \frac{\gamma}{N_t}, \tag{6}$$

$$\frac{\delta \gamma}{E_t} = \frac{N_t}{C_{2,t}}. \tag{7}$$

Equation (5) implies that the utility loss from reducing one unit of working-period consumption is equal to the utility gain from increasing R_{t+1} units of retirement-period consumption. Equation (6) implies that the utility loss from reducing working-period consumption and retirement-period consumption is equal to the utility gain from increasing children's human capital through increasing a child. Equation (7) implies that the utility loss from reducing working-period consumption is equal to the utility gain from raising child's human capital through increasing a unit of education expenses.

2.2. Villages

Villages produce a homogenous commodity in competitive markets. The production is described by Cobb-Douglas function $Y_t = DK_t^\theta (L_t l_t h_t)^{1-\theta}$, where Y_t is the output in period t, K_t the physical capital stock, l_t the amount of labor hired from each peasant of generation t, $\theta \in (0,1)$ the physical capital share of income, $D > 0$ the productivity of physical capital production.

Based on villages' total labor income, villages provide subsidies to the individual contributions at a rate of $\eta \in (0,1)$ and local governments provide allowances at a rate of $\zeta \in (0,1)$. The central government and local governments together pay rural retirees the basic benefits at a basic benefit rate of $j \in (0,1)$. According to the product distribution, one can get that $DK_t^\theta (L_t l_t h_t)^{1-\theta} = R_t K_t + (1+\eta+\zeta+j) L_t l_t W_t$. By virtue of Euler's theorem, we have:

$$R_t = \theta D k_t^{\theta-1}, \tag{8}$$

$$W_t = (1-\theta) D k_t^\theta h_t / (1+\eta+\zeta+j), \tag{9}$$

where $k_t = K_t / (L_t l_t h_t)$ is the physical capital per unit of effective labor.

2.3. The Government

The accumulation in an individual account is used to pay the individual when she/he retires in the next period as funded pension benefits:

$$I_{t+1} = R_{t+1} (\tau + \eta + \zeta)(1 - v N_t) W_t. \tag{10}$$

The central government and local governments together pay retirees the basic benefits: $L_{t-1}J_t = jL_t l_t W_t$, or

$$J_t = jN_{t-1} l_t W_t. \tag{11}$$

2.4. Markets Clearing

Labor market clears when the demand for labor is equal to the supply:

$$l_t = 1 - vN_t. \tag{12}$$

The savings and individual pension contributions, village subsidies and local government allowances in period t generate the capital stock in period $t + 1$:

$$K_{t+1} = L_t(s_t + \tau + \eta + \zeta) l_t W_t. \tag{13}$$

3. EQUILIBRIUM ANALYSIS

The following analysis focuses on balanced growth equilibrium. For convenience, we define the following ratios: $c_2 = \dfrac{C_{2,t}}{l_t W_t}$ is working-period consumption ratio, $c_3 = \dfrac{C_{3,t+1}}{l_t W_t}$ retirement-period consumption ratio, and $e = \dfrac{E_t}{l_t W_t}$ education expense ratio. A balanced growth equilibrium is a competitive equilibrium in which intensive variables such as the saving rate, consumption ratio and population growth rate[1] are constant, whereas extensive variables such as the labor income, human capital, physical capital per unit of labor, consumption grow at the same endogenously determined and constant growth rate, g.

Combining equations (8) and (9) gives:

$$\frac{W_{t+1}}{R_{t+1}} = \frac{1-\theta}{1+\eta+\zeta+j} \cdot \frac{s_t + \tau + \eta + \zeta}{\theta N_t l_{t+1}} l_t W_t. \tag{14}$$

Substituting equation (7) into equation (2), rearranging gives

$$(1+\delta\gamma)C_{2,t} = (1-\tau-s_t) l_t W_t. \tag{2'}$$

---

[1] That is $(L_{t+1}-L_t)/L_t = N_t-1$. Let $n_t = N_t-1$, then the derivatives of N_t with respect to the policy variables are equal to that of n_t.

Substituting equations (2'), (3), (10), (11) and (14) into equation (5), rearranging gives

$$s = \frac{\theta\beta(1+\eta+\zeta+j)-(1+\delta\gamma)(\eta+\zeta)[j+\theta(1+\eta+\zeta)]}{\theta\beta(1+\eta+\zeta+j)+(1+\delta\gamma)[j+\theta(1+\eta+\zeta)]} - \tau. \qquad (15)$$

Rearranging equation (2') gives:

$$c_2 = \frac{1-(s+\tau)}{1+\delta\gamma} \qquad (16)$$

Substituting equations (5) and (7) into equation (6), rearranging gives:

$$\frac{1-\delta}{\delta}E_t = (1-\tau)vW_t. \qquad (6')$$

Using the defined ratios and substitute them into equation (12), rearranging gives:

$$N = \frac{(1-\delta)\gamma c_2}{v[(1-\tau)+(1-\delta)\gamma c_2]}. \qquad (17)$$

Using the defined ratios, equations (7) and (17), rearranging gives:

$$e = \delta v \frac{(1-\tau)+(1-\delta)\gamma c_2}{1-\delta}. \qquad (18)$$

Substituting equation (9) into equation (4), rearranging gives

$$\frac{h_{t+1}}{h_t} = A\left(el\frac{1-\theta}{1+\eta+\zeta+j}D\right)^\delta k_t^{\vartheta}. \qquad (4')$$

Combining equations (9) and (13), rearranging gives:

$$\frac{K_{t+1}/L_{t+1}}{K_t/L_t} = \frac{s+\tau+\eta+\zeta}{1+\eta+\zeta+j}\frac{1-\theta}{\alpha N}Dk_t^{\theta-1}. \qquad (13')$$

Balanced growth equilibrium implies $1+g = \frac{h_{t+1}}{h_t} = \frac{K_{t+1}/L_{t+1}}{K_t/L_t}$. Substituting equation (4') into equation (13'), rearranging gives:

$$g = \left[A^{\frac{1-\theta}{\delta}} D \frac{1-\theta}{1+\eta+\zeta+j} \left(v\delta \frac{1-\tau}{1-\delta} \right)^{1-\theta} \left(\frac{s+\tau+\eta+\zeta}{N} \right)^{\theta} \right]^{\frac{\delta}{1-\theta+\delta\theta}} - 1. \quad (19)$$

4. EFFECTS OF POLICY VARIABLES

4.1. Effect of Individual Contribution Rate

Partially differentiating s, c_2, N, e and g with respect to τ, gives:

$$\frac{\partial s}{\partial \tau} = -1,$$

$$\frac{\partial c_2}{\partial \tau} = 0,$$

$$\frac{\partial N}{\partial \tau} = \frac{(1-\delta)\gamma c_2}{v[(1-\tau)+(1-\delta)\gamma c_2]^2} > 0,$$

$$\frac{\partial e}{\partial \tau} = -\frac{\delta v}{1-\delta} < 0,$$

$$\text{sign}\left(\frac{\partial g}{\partial \tau}\right) = \text{sign}\left(\frac{\partial}{\partial \tau}\left[\frac{(1-\tau)^{1-\theta}}{N^{\theta}}\right]\right), \frac{\partial g}{\partial \tau} < 0.$$

Raising the individual contribution rate decreases the saving rate, education expense ratio and labor income growth rate, whereas increases the population growth rate, but has no effect on the consumption ratio. The individual contributions, which are mandatory savings, crowd out the voluntary savings by one-for-one. Hence, raising the individual contribution rate decreases the saving rate, and the partial derivative of saving rate with respect to the individual contribution rate is minus one. Since the total savings composed of the mandatory savings and voluntary savings do not change, the individual contribution rate has no effect on the consumption ratio. Raising the individual contribution rate decreases the opportunity cost to rear children, and increases the number of children and population growth rate. The labor income growth rate is negatively related to the number of children, hence falls when the individual contribution rate rises. The dilution effect of risen number of children decreases the education expense ratio.

4.2. Effect of Village Subsidy Rate

Partially differentiating s, c_2, N, e and g with respect to η, gives:

$$\frac{\partial s}{\partial \eta} = (1+\delta\gamma)\frac{\theta[\beta+(1+\delta\gamma)][-\theta(1+\eta+\zeta+j)^2 - (1+j)j(1-\theta)] + j(1-\theta)\{\theta[\beta-(1+\delta\gamma)(1+2\eta+2\zeta+j)] - (1+\delta\gamma)j(1-\theta)\}}{\{\theta\beta(1+\eta+\zeta+j)+(1+\delta\gamma)[j+\theta(1+\eta+\zeta)]\}^2} < 0,$$

$$\frac{\partial c_2}{\partial \eta} = -\frac{1}{1+\delta\gamma}\frac{\partial s}{\partial \eta} > 0,$$

$$\frac{\partial N}{\partial \eta} = \frac{(1-\tau)(1-\delta)\gamma}{v[(1-\tau)+(1-\delta)\gamma c_2]^2}\frac{\partial c_2}{\partial \eta} > 0,$$

$$\frac{\partial e}{\partial \eta} = \delta v \gamma \frac{\partial c_2}{\partial \eta} > 0,$$

$$\text{sign}\left(\frac{\partial g}{\partial \eta}\right) = \text{sign}\left(\frac{\partial}{\partial \eta}\left[\frac{(s+\tau+\eta+\zeta)^\theta}{(1+\eta+\zeta+j)N^\theta}\right]\right), \quad \frac{\partial g}{\partial \eta} < 0.$$

Raising the village subsidy rate decreases the saving rate and labor income growth rate, whereas increases the consumption ratio, population growth rate and education expense ratio. A rise in the village subsidy rate decreases the labor income, and furthermore the saving rate. The fall in the saving rate leads to the rise in the consumption ratio reflected by equation (16), which in turn induces a rise in the population growth rate and education expense ratio. The labor income growth rate falls because it is negatively related to the population growth rate.

4.3. Effect of Local Government Allowance Rate

Partially differentiating s, c_2, N, e and g with respect to ζ, gives:

$$\frac{\partial s}{\partial \zeta} = \frac{\partial s}{\partial \eta},$$

$$\frac{\partial c_2}{\partial \zeta} = \frac{\partial c_2}{\partial \eta},$$

$$\frac{\partial N}{\partial \zeta} = \frac{\partial N}{\partial \eta},$$

$$\frac{\partial e}{\partial \zeta} = \frac{\partial e}{\partial \eta},$$

$$\frac{\partial g}{\partial \zeta} = \frac{\partial g}{\partial \eta}.$$

Raising the local government allowance rate decreases the saving rate and labor income growth rate, whereas increases the consumption ratio, population growth rate and education expense ratio. The interpretation is analogous to that for the effect of the village subsidy rate.

4.4. Effect of Basic Benefit Rate

Partially differentiating s, c_2, N, e and g with respect to j, gives:

$$\frac{\partial s}{\partial j} = \frac{(\theta-1)\theta\beta(1+\delta\gamma)(1+\eta+\zeta)^2}{\{\theta\beta(1+\eta+\zeta+j)+(1+\delta\gamma)[j+\theta(1+\eta+\zeta)]\}^2} < 0,$$

$$\frac{\partial c_2}{\partial j} = -\frac{1}{1+\delta\gamma}\frac{\partial s}{\partial j} > 0,$$

$$\frac{\partial N}{\partial j} = \frac{(1-\tau)(1-\delta)\gamma}{v[(1-\tau)+(1-\delta)\gamma c_2]^2}\frac{\partial c_2}{\partial j} > 0,$$

$$\frac{\partial e}{\partial j} = \delta v \gamma \frac{\partial c_2}{\partial j} > 0,$$

$$\text{sign}\left(\frac{\partial g}{\partial j}\right) = \text{sign}\left(\frac{\partial}{\partial j}\left[\frac{(s+\tau+\eta+\zeta)^\theta}{(1+\eta+\zeta+j)N^\theta}\right]\right), \quad \frac{\partial g}{\partial j} < 0.$$

Raising the basic benefit rate decreases the saving rate and labor income growth rate, whereas increases the consumption ratio, population growth rate and education expense ratio. A rise in the basic benefit rate decreases the labor income, hence decreases the saving rate. A fall in the saving rate induces the rise in the consumption ratio, which in turn leads to a rise in the population growth rate and education expense ratio. The rise in the population growth rate makes the labor income growth rate fall because they are negatively related to each other.

5. EFFECT STRENGTH

5.1. Parameter Calibration

Analogous to Yew and Zhang (2009), we assume that the elasticity of human capital with respect to education expenses $\delta = 0.25$, rearing a child requires $v = 0.24$ units of labor. As pointed out by Zhang (1995), for the purpose of this study, A and D can be assumed to be large enough that $g > 0$. What we hope to see here is how the endogenous variables change with the policy variables. Hence, we can assume that $A = 8$ and $D = 9$. Analogous to Zhang et al. (2001), Pecchenino and Pollard (2002), Barro and Sala-I-Martin (2004), etc., the physical capital share of income in rural areas of China is low, we assume that $\theta = 0.16$.

According to the Chinese State Council Document 32 in 2009 and China Statistical Yearbook, the individual contribution rate is estimated to be $\tau \approx 7\%$, the village subsidy rate $\eta \approx 4\%$, and the local government allowance rate $\zeta \approx 3\%$. A couple of peasants have average 2.3 children, namely, a peasant has 1.15 children. Based on the basic pension benefits, the number of children and the net labor income per rural resident, and by virtue of equation (11), the basic benefit rate is estimated to be $j \approx 14\%$.[2]

A period length in this model is assumed to be 25 years because the length is usually in the interval of 25 - 30 years in the literature on OLG model. Analogous to Pecchenino and Pollard (2002), we assume that per year discount factor on the utility derived from retirement-period consumption is 0.980, hence the discount factor per period is $\beta = 0.980^{25}$. Analogously, per year discount factor on the utility derived from children's human capital is 0.975, thus the discount factor per period is $\gamma = 0.975^{25}$. These are benchmark values of the parameters.

5.2. Simulations

The policy parameters, τ, η, ζ and j are generally not higher than 50% in practice. The following simulations are limited in the interval. Simulating with the benchmark parameter values but raising the individual contribution rate from 0% gradually to 50% gives the result shown in Figure 1. They are displayed in two panels because the values of s, c_2 and e are much lower than that of g and N. Obviously, raising the individual contribution rate decreases the labor income growth rate, saving rate and education expense ratio, whereas increases the population growth rate, but has no effect on the consumption ratio.

---

[2] Lack of authorized relevant data leads to some arbitrariness for the parameter values.

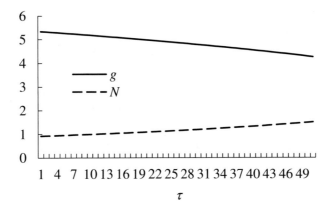

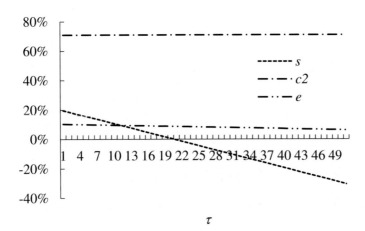

Figure 1. Effect of τ on g, N, s, c_2 and e.

Analogously, simulating with the benchmark parameter values but raising the village subsidy rate from 0% gradually to 50% gives the result shown in Figure 2. Raising the village subsidy rate decreases the labor income growth rate and saving rate, whereas increases the population growth rate, consumption ratio and education expense ratio.

In the same way, simulating with the benchmark parameter values but raising the local government allowance rate from 0% gradually to 50%. It is shown that the figure is almost the same as Figure 2. Hence, the effect of the local government allowance rate is almost the same as that of the village subsidy rate.

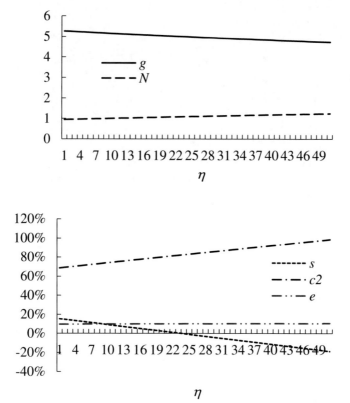

Figure 2. Effect of η on g, N, s, c_2 and e.

Finally, simulating with the benchmark parameter values but raising the basic benefit rate from 0% gradually to 50% gives the result shown in Figure 3. Raising the basic benefit rate decreases the labor income growth rate and saving rate, whereas increases the population growth rate, consumption ratio and education expense ratio.

The arc elasticity of the endogenous variables with respect to the exogenous variables is shown in Table 1. The effect of the individual contribution rate on the labor income growth rate is the strongest, which exceeds the sum of the effects of the village subsidy rate and local government allowance rate, and that of the basic benefit rate is weaker than the sum of the two. The effect of the individual contribution rate on the population growth rate is approximately equal to the sum of the effects of the village subsidy rate and local government allowance rate, and about 3 times of that of the basic benefit rate. The effect of the village subsidy rate on the saving rate is the strongest, the others ranking in descending order as the local government allowance rate, individual contribution rate and basic benefit rate. The effects of the village subsidy rate, local government allowance rate and basic benefit rate on the consumption ratio are almost equal to each other. The effect of the individual contribution rate on the education expense ratio is the strongest, which is about 2 times of the sum of that of the village subsidy rate, local government allowance rate and basic benefit rate.

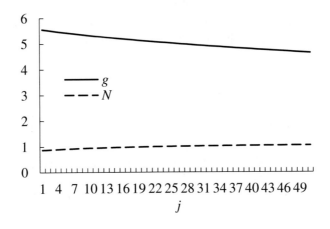

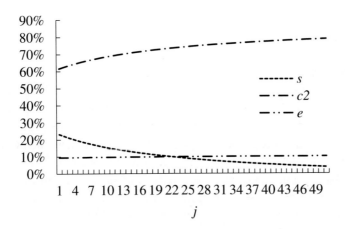

Figure 3. Effect of j on g, N, s, c_2 and e.

Table 1. Elasticity of endogenous variables with respect to policy variables

	τ	η	ς	j
s	-4.66	-10.35	-7.31	-0.72
c_2	0.00	0.18	0.18	0.12
N	0.24	0.13	0.13	0.09
e	-0.24	0.05	0.05	0.03
g	-0.11	-0.05	-0.05	-0.09

CONCLUSION

Employing the endogenous growth OLG model, this chapter investigates the public pension system for rural residents of China. It examines the effects of the individual contribution rate, village subsidy rate, local government allowance rate and basic benefit rate on the labor income growth rate, population growth rate, saving rate, consumption ratio, and education expense ratio. According to the situations in rural areas of China, we estimate the values of relevant parameters and simulate the sensitivities of the endogenous variables with respect to the policy variables.

The results are as follows: Raising the individual contribution rate decreases the labor income growth rate, saving rate and education expense ratio, whereas increases the population growth rate, but has no effect on the consumption ratio. Raising the village subsidy rate, local government allowance rate and basic benefit rate all decreases the labor income growth rate and saving rate, whereas increases the population growth rate, consumption ratio and education expense ratio. The effect of the individual contribution rate on the labor income growth rate is the strongest, which exceeds the sum of the effects of the village subsidy rate and local government allowance rate, and that of the basic benefit rate is weaker than the sum of the two. The effect of the individual contribution rate on the population growth rate is approximately equal to the sum of the effects of the village subsidy rate and local government allowance rate, and about 3 times of that of the basic benefit rate. The effect of the village subsidy rate on the saving rate is the strongest, the others ranking in descending order as the local government allowance rate, individual contribution rate and basic benefit rate. The effects of the village subsidy rate, local government allowance rate and basic benefit rate on the consumption ratio are almost equal to each other. The effect of the individual contribution rate on the education expense ratio is the strongest, which is about 2 times of the sum of that of the village subsidy rate, local government allowance rate and basic benefit rate.

The above results have important implications. According to the actuality in rural areas of China, it is urgent to promote the rural economic growth, rationally control the population size, increase the consumption ratio, decrease the saving rate, and depress the education expense ratio. Hence, it is necessary to adopt the following measures: raise the village subsidy rate and local government allowance rate by a comparatively big margin, increase the basic benefit rate by a small margin, and reasonably decrease the individual contribution rate.

Chapter 12

RURAL PUBLIC PENSION, UNCERTAIN LIFETIME AND ENDOGENOUS GROWTH

ABSTRACT

Taking uncertain lifetime into account, this chapter employs an endogenous growth OLG model with gift motive to investigate the rural public pension system in China. We examine the effects of the life expectancy, individual contribution rate, village subsidy rate, local government allowance rate and basic benefit rate on the labor income growth rate, population growth rate, saving rate, consumption ratio, education expense ratio, gift ratio and bequest ratio. Integrating the effects and their intensities, and considering the economic and social development goals in rural China, it will do more good than harm to raise the basic benefit rate, local government allowance rate and village subsidy rate, reduce the individual contribution rate, and improve the living and medical conditions.

Keywords: rural public pension; uncertain lifetime; family transfers

1. INTRODUCTION

Persons are always confronted with death probability. Especially, retirees are in face of higher mortality. Therefore, we introduce lifetime uncertainty into the endogenous growth model with gift motive of the last chapter. In addition, Chinese rural residents' life expectancy has been rising because their living and medical conditions have been improved. The *State Council Guidelines on New-Type Rural Public Pension Trials* (Chinese State Council Document 32 in 2009) is expected to reduce the rural poverty, narrow the income gap between the urban and rural areas, and promote the economic growth. Under the condition of taking lifetime uncertainty into account, what are the effects of the rural pension system and how about the effect intensities?

It was in OLG model with endogenous growth for much literature to study the relationship between economic growth, population and public pension. A common feature of the studies such as Zhang and Zhang (1995, 1998), Wigger (1999a), etc. is to transform the capital per unit of effective labor into a constant and production function into the so-called "*AK* model" by adopting a special type of productivity. Zhang (1995) introduced human capital, which grows at the same rate with the physical capital per unit of labor in balanced growth equilibrium. Zhang (2001) used the same approach to compare long-run implications for growth and fertility. Yew and Zhang (2009) investigated the optimal scale of PAYG social security in a dynastic family model with human capital externalities, fertility and endogenous growth. Pecchenino and Pollard (2002), Zhang et al. (2003), etc. introduced lifetime uncertainty into OLG models to investigate rising longevity, economic growth and public pension.

By employing an endogenous growth model, this chapter investigates the rural public pension system in China. It examines the effects of the life expectancy, individual contribution rate, village subsidy rate, local government allowance rate and basic benefit rate on the labor income growth rate, population growth rate, saving rate, consumption ratio, education expense ratio, gift ratio and bequest ratio. According to the real rural situations, we estimate the values of relevant parameters and check the effects by simulations. In addition to participants making pension contributions, villages subsidize and local governments allowance to the individual contributions in this model.

2. THE MODEL

There are numerous individuals and villages and a government in a closed economy. Each individual survives to the end of her working period certainly, but survives in retirement period with a probability of $p \in (0,1]$. At the beginning of period t, L_t identical individuals of generation t enter the work force. Each individual of generation t have N_t children, hence, $L_{t+1} = N_t L_t$.

2.1. Individuals

Individuals develop their human capital in childhood period, and have no ability to make economic decision. Upon entering the work force, each individual represents one unit of labor. Rearing a child requires $v \in (0,1)$ units of labor. Hence, each individual supplies $(1-vN_t) > 0$ units of labor to earn labor income. After making pension contributions, she/he consumes part of the income, pays education expenses for her/his children, gives her/his parent possible gifts, and saves the remainder of income. If she/he survives in her/his retirement period, she/he consumes the savings with accrued interest, individual account benefits, basic benefits and gifts from her/his children. If she/he dies at the beginning of her/his retirement period, her/his savings with accrued interest and individual account benefits are inherited equally by her/his children as unintentional bequests.

Each individual derives utility from her/his working-period consumption $C_{2,t}$, retirement-period consumption $C_{3,t+1}$, children's human capital and her/his parent's retirement-period consumption. An adult can only care her/his parent's retirement-period consumption and not be able to concern bypass working-period consumption. Each individual maximizes her/his utility by choosing saving rate, number of children, education expenses and gifts to her/his parent. The utility maximization problem is:

$$\max_{\{s_t, N_t, E_t, Q_t\}} U_t = \ln C_{2,t} + p\beta \ln C_{3,t+1} + \gamma \ln(N_t h_{t+1}) + p\alpha \ln C_{3,t}, \quad (1)$$

s.t.
$$C_{2,t} = (1 - \tau - s_t)(1 - vN_t)W_t - N_t E_t - pQ_t + (1-p)B_t, \quad (2)$$

$$C_{3,t+1} = R_{t+1} s_t (1 - vN_t) W_t + I_{t+1} + J_{t+1} + N_t Q_{t+1}, \quad (3)$$

$$N_t B_{t+1} = R_{t+1} s_t (1 - vN_t) W_t + I_{t+1}, \quad (4)$$

where β, γ and α denote the discount factors on the utilities derived from her/his retirement-period consumption, children's human capital and parent's retirement-period consumption, respectively. Since there is a limit to each individual's altruism, without losing generality, it is logical to assume that $0 < \alpha < \gamma < \beta < 1$. Each individual's human capital of generation $t + 1$ is

$$h_{t+1} = A E_t^\delta h_t^{1-\delta}, \quad (5)$$

where $\delta \in (0,1)$ is the elasticity of human capital with respect to education expenses, $A > 0$ is the productivity of human capital production. $\tau \in (0,1)$ denotes the individual contribution rate, W_t the income per unit of labor, s_t the saving rate, E_t the education expenses for each child, R_{t+1} the rental rate for physical capital, I_{t+1} the individual account benefits, J_{t+1} the basic benefits, Q_{t+1} the gifts from children, and B_{t+1} the bequests inherited by each child.

Substituting equations (2) - (4) into equation (1) and letting the partial derivatives of it with respect to s_t, N_t, E_t and Q_t be zero gives the first-order conditions for the utility maximization problem (only considering interior solutions):

$$p\beta \frac{R_{t+1}}{C_{3,t+1}} = \frac{1}{C_{2,t}}, \quad (6)$$

$$\frac{\gamma}{N_t} = \frac{E_t + (1 - \tau - s_t)vW_t}{C_{2,t}} + p\beta \frac{R_{t+1} s_t v W_t - Q_{t+1}}{C_{3,t+1}}, \quad (7)$$

$$\frac{\delta \gamma}{E_t} = \frac{N_t}{C_{2,t}}, \quad (8)$$

$$\alpha \frac{N_{t-1}}{C_{3,t}} = \frac{1}{C_{2,t}}. \quad (9)$$

Equation (6) implies that the utility loss from reducing one unit of working-period consumption is equal to the utility gain from increasing R_{t+1} units of retirement-period consumption. Equation (7) implies that the utility loss from reducing labor income and savings with accrued interest and increasing education expenses is equal to the utility gain from raising children's human capital and gifts through increasing a child. Equation (8) implies that the utility loss from reducing working-period consumption is equal to the utility gain from raising child's human capital through increasing a unit of education expenses. Equation (9) implies that the utility loss from reducing working-period consumption is equal to the utility gain from raising parent's retirement-period consumption through increasing a unit of gifs.

2.2. Villages

Villages produce a homogenous commodity in competitive markets. The production is described by Cobb-Douglas function $Y_t = DK_t^\theta (L_t l_t h_t)^{1-\theta}$, where Y_t is the output in period t, K_t the physical capital stock, l_t the amount of labor hired from each peasant of generation t, $\theta \in (0,1)$ the physical capital share of income, $D > 0$ the productivity of physical capital production.

Based on villages' total labor income, villages subsidize the individual contributions at a rate of $\eta \in (0,1)$, and local governments allowance the individual contributions at a rate of $\zeta \in (0,1)$. The central government and local governments together pay rural retirees the basic benefits at a basic benefit rate of $j \in (0,1)$. The village subsidies, local government allowances and basic benefits root in peasants' labor fruit in long term. Thus the product is distributed into capital income, labor income with the subsidies, allowances and basic benefits: $DK_t^\theta (L_t l_t h_t)^{1-\theta} = R_t K_t + (1+\eta+\zeta+j)L_t l_t W_t$. By virtue of Euler's theorem, we have:

$$R_t = \theta D k_t^{\theta-1}, \tag{10}$$

$$W_t = (1-\theta)Dk_t^\theta h_t / (1+\eta+\zeta+j), \tag{11}$$

where $k_t = K_t/(L_t l_t h_t)$ is the physical capital per unit of effective labor.

2.3. The Government

The accumulation in an individual account is used to pay the individual when she/he retires in the next period as funded pension benefits:

$$I_{t+1} = R_{t+1}(\tau+\eta+\zeta)l_t W_t. \tag{12}$$

The central government and local governments together pay retirees the basic benefits: $pL_t J_{t+1} = jL_{t+1} l_{t+1} W_{t+1}$, or

$$J_{t+1} = jN_t l_{t+1} W_{t+1} / p. \qquad (13)$$

2.4. Markets Clearing

Labor market clears when the demand for labor is equal to the supply:

$$l_t = 1 - vN_t \qquad (14)$$

The savings and individual pension contributions, village subsidies and local government allowances in period t generate the capital stock in period $t + 1$:

$$K_{t+1} = L_t (s_t + \tau + \eta + \zeta) l_t W_t. \qquad (15)$$

3. BALANCED GROWTH EQUILIBRIUM

For convenience, we define the following five ratios: $c_2 = \dfrac{C_{2,t}}{l_t W_t}$ is the working-period consumption ratio, $c_3 = \dfrac{C_{3,t+1}}{l_t W_t}$ the retirement-period consumption ratio, $e = \dfrac{E_t}{l_t W_t}$ the education expense ratio, $q = \dfrac{Q_t}{l_t W_t}$ the gift ratio, and $b = \dfrac{B_{t+1}}{l_t W_t}$ the bequest ratio. $n_t = \dfrac{L_{t+1} - L_t}{L_t} = N_t - 1$ is the population growth rate[1]. A balanced growth equilibrium is a competitive equilibrium in which intensive variables such as the saving rate, consumption ratio and population growth rate are constant, whereas extensive variables such as the labor income, human capital, physical capital per unit of labor, consumption grow at the same endogenously determined and constant growth rate, g. The following analysis focuses on the balanced growth equilibrium.

Combining equations (11) and (10) gives $\dfrac{W_{t+1}}{R_{t+1}} = \dfrac{1-\theta}{1+\eta+\zeta+j} \cdot \dfrac{s_t + \tau + \eta + \zeta}{\theta N_t l_{t+1}} l_t W_t$. In the balanced growth equilibrium,

---

[1] The derivatives of n_t with respect to the policy variables are equal to that of N_t.

$$\frac{W_{t+1}}{R} = \frac{1-\theta}{1+\eta+\zeta+j} \cdot \frac{s+\tau+\eta+\zeta}{\theta N} W_t. \qquad (16)$$

Combining equations (6) and (9) and the balanced growth rate gives

$$N(1+g) = \frac{p\beta}{\alpha} R. \qquad (17)$$

Substituting equation (17) into equation (16), rearranging gives

$$s = \frac{p\beta}{\alpha}\varphi - \tau - \eta - \zeta, \qquad (18)$$

where $\varphi = \theta\frac{1+\eta+\zeta+j}{1-\theta}$. Rearranging equation (6) gives $p\beta R c_2 = c_3$. Substituting equations (12), (13), (17), (18) and $Q_{t+1} = (1+g)Q_t$ into equation (3) yields $c_3 = \frac{p\beta R}{\alpha}\left(\varphi + \frac{j}{p} + q\right)$. From equation (2), one can get $c_2 = 1-\tau-s-Ne-pq+(1-p)b/(1+g)$. Combining equations (4), (12) and (18) gives $b = \frac{p\beta R}{N\alpha}\varphi$. Rearranging equation (8) gives $Ne = \delta\gamma c_2$. Hence, $c_2 = \frac{1-\tau-s-pq+(1-p)\varphi}{1+\delta\gamma}$. Combining these equations gives:

$$q = \frac{\alpha(1+\eta+\zeta) - [(1+\delta\gamma) + p(\alpha+\beta) - \alpha]\varphi - (1+\delta\gamma)j/p}{1+\delta\gamma + p\alpha}, \qquad (19)$$

$$c_2 = \frac{\alpha - p\beta\theta}{\theta\alpha(1+\delta\gamma + p\alpha)}\varphi. \qquad (20)$$

$Q > 0$ implies that $\alpha > [(1+\delta\gamma + p\beta)\varphi + (1+\delta\gamma)j/p]/[1+\eta+\zeta+\varphi(1-p)]$.

Substituting equations (6) and (8) into equation (7), rearranging gives $\frac{1-\delta}{\delta}Ne + \frac{p\beta}{\alpha}q = \frac{1-\tau}{1-vN}vN$. Substituting Ne and q into it yields

$$N = \frac{x}{v(1-\tau+x)}, \qquad (21)$$

where

$$x = \frac{[(1-\delta)\gamma\alpha - p\beta\theta(1+\gamma-\alpha+p\alpha+p\beta)]\varphi + \beta\theta[p\alpha(1+\eta+\zeta)-(1+\delta\gamma)j]}{\theta\alpha(1+\delta\gamma+p\alpha)} > 0.$$

$$e = \delta\gamma c_2/N. \qquad (8')$$

Substituting equation (11) into equation (5), rearranging gives

$$\frac{h_{t+1}}{h_t} = A\left(el\frac{1-\theta}{1+\eta+\zeta+j}D\right)^\delta k_t^{\delta\theta}. \qquad (5')$$

Using equations (11), (15) and (18) gives

$$\frac{K_{t+1}/L_{t+1}}{K_t/L_t} = \frac{p\beta\theta}{\alpha N}Dk_t^{\theta-1}. \qquad (15')$$

Balanced growth equilibrium implies $\dfrac{h_{t+1}}{h_t} = \dfrac{K_{t+1}/L_{t+1}}{K_t/L_t} = 1+g$. Combining equations (5') and (15'), rearranging yields

$$g = \left[A^{\frac{1-\theta}{\delta}}D\left(\frac{p\beta\theta}{\alpha}\right)^\theta\left(\frac{\delta\gamma(\alpha-p\beta\theta)}{\alpha(1+\delta\gamma+p\alpha)}(1-vN)\right)^{1-\theta}\frac{1}{N}\right]^{\frac{\delta}{1-\theta+\delta\theta}} - 1. \qquad (22)$$

Combining equations (4), (17) and (18) gives

$$b = (1+g)\varphi. \qquad (23)$$

4. EFFECTS OF EXOGENOUS VARIABLES

Observing the expressions of s, q, c_2, N, e, g and b yields that η and ζ play the same role to the endogenous variables. Hence, it is possible to let the effect of ζ represent that of both η and ζ. Partially differentiating s, q, c_2, N, e, g and b with respect to τ, ζ, j and p gives the effects of the individual contribution rate, local government allowance rate, basic benefit rate and retirement-period survival probability on the saving rate, gift ratio, consumption ratio, population growth rate, education expense ratio, labor income growth rate and bequest ratio. It can be shown that most of the effects depend on the values of relevant parameters. Thus we first calibrate the parameter values, and then examine the effects by simulations.

4.1. Parameter Calibration

Assume the elasticity of human capital with respect to education expenses to be $\delta = 0.25$, and rearing a child requires $v = 0.24$ units of labor. As pointed out by Zhang (1995), for the purpose of this study, A and D can be assumed to be large enough that $g > 0$. What we hope to see here is how the endogenous variables change with the exogenous variables. Hence, we can assume that $A = 4$ and $D = 2$. The physical capital share of income in rural China is low, hence we assume it to be $\theta = 0.16$.

A period length in this model is assumed to be 26 years. The National Bureau of Statistics of China (2010) indicates that the life expectancy of Chinese people in 2000 is 71.4 years old. The span from birth to the end of working period is 52 years, and that from birth to the end of retirement period 78 years. In accordance with the concept of life expectancy, we get $(1-p) \times 52 + p \times 78 = 71.4$, which gives $p \approx 74.6\%$.

According to the *State Council Guidelines on New-Type Rural Public Pension Trials* (Chinese State Council Document 32 in 2009) and the National Bureau of Statistics of China (2011), the individual contribution rate is estimated as $\tau \approx 5\%$, the village subsidy rate $\eta \approx 1\%$, and the local government allowance rate $\zeta \approx 2\%$. A rural resident has 0.95 children. By virtue of equation (13), the basic benefit rate is estimated as $j \approx 10\%$.[2]

The discount factor on utility derived from retirement-period consumption is assumed to be $\beta = 0.980^{26}$. Analogously, the discount factor on utility derived from children's human capital is $\gamma = 0.975^{26}$. α is assumed to be 0.500 because $[(1+\delta\gamma + p\beta)\varphi + (1+\delta\gamma)j/p]/[1+\eta+\zeta+\varphi(1-p)] < \alpha < \gamma$. The above values are benchmark values of the parameters.

4.2. Simulations

Utilizing the benchmark parameter values but raising p gradually from 66% to 75%, we simulate the effect of life expectancy on g, N, c_2, b, s, q and e, which is shown in Figure 1. Since the values of g, N, c_2 and b are far more than that of s, q and e, they are displayed in different panels. A rise in life expectancy increases the labor income growth rate, saving rate and bequest ratio, whereas decreases the population growth rate, consumption ratio, education expense ratio and gift ratio.

Simulating with the benchmark parameter values but τ rising gradually from 1.5% to 6.0% gives the effect of individual contribution rate shown in Figure 2. Raising the individual contribution rate decreases the labor income growth rate, saving rate, education expense ratio and bequest ratio, whereas increases the population growth rate, but has no effect on the gift ratio and consumption ratio.

---

[2] There is some arbitrariness for the parameters in the paragraph since lack of authorized data.

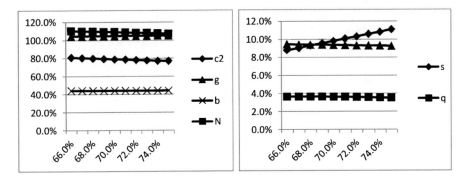

Figure 1. Effect of p on g, N, c_2, b and s, q, e.

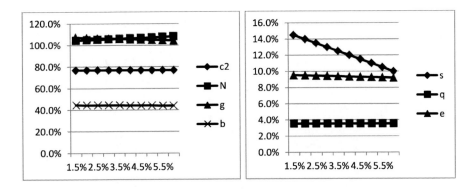

Figure 2. Effect of τ on g, N, c_2, b and s, q, e.

Simulating with the benchmark parameter values but ζ rising gradually from 0.5% to 5.0% gives the effect of local government allowance rate shown in Figure 3. Raising the local government allowance rate decreases the labor income growth rate, saving rate and education expense ratio, whereas increases the population growth rate, consumption ratio, gift ratio and bequest ratio. Raising the village subsidy rate has the same effects.

Simulating with the benchmark parameter values but j rising gradually from 8.0% to 12.5% gives the effect of basic benefit rate shown in Figure 4. Raising the basic benefit rate increases the labor income growth rate, consumption ratio, saving rate, education expense ratio and bequest ratio, whereas decreases the population growth rate and gift ratio.

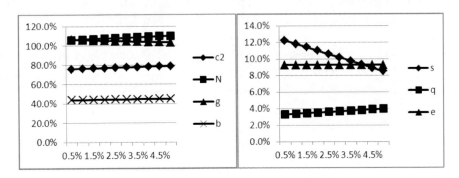

Figure 3. Effect of ζ on g, N, c_2, b and s, q, e.

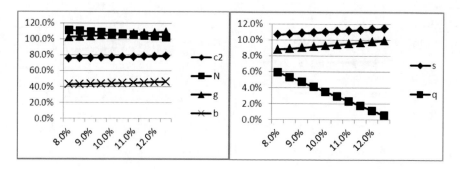

Figure 4. Effect of j on g, N, c_2, b and s, q, e.

Table 1. Elasticity of endogenous variables with respect to exogenous variables

	p	τ	ζ	j
g	6.43%	-2.06%	-1.75%	13.06%
N	-21.96%	2.90%	2.43%	-18.30%
s	180.42%	-30.63%	-22.07%	15.61%
c_2	-39.18%	0.00%	2.42%	9.05%
e	-17.23%	-2.90%	-0.01%	27.33%
q	-32.74%	0.00%	11.34%	-378.81%
b	3.29%	-1.06%	1.53%	15.75%

The arc elasticity of each endogenous variable with respect to each exogenous variable is shown in Table 1. The absolute vales of the elasticity reflect the effect intensities. The effect of basic benefit rate on the labor income growth rate is 2 times as strong as that of life expectancy, which is 3 times as strong as that of individual contribution rate and local government allowance rate. The effect of basic benefit rate on the population growth rate is almost same as that of life expectancy, which is 7 times as strong as that of local government allowance rate and individual contribution rate. The effect of life expectancy on the saving rate is 6, 8 and 11 times as strong as that of individual contribution rate, local government allowance rate and basic benefit rate, respectively. The effect of life expectancy on the consumption ratio is 16 and 4 times as strong as that of local government allowance rate and basic benefit rate, respectively. The effect of basic benefit rate on the education expense ratio is 1.5 and 9 times as strong as that of life expectancy and individual contribution rate, respectively. The effect of basic benefit rate on the gift ratio is 11 and 33 times as strong as that of life expectancy and local government allowance rate, respectively. The effect of basic benefit rate on the bequest ratio is 5, 15 and 10 times as strong as that of life expectancy, individual contribution rate and local government allowance rate, respectively.

CONCLUSION

Employing the endogenous growth OLG model with uncertain lifetime and altruism, this chapter investigates the rural public pension system in China. We examine the effects of life expectancy, individual contribution rate, local government allowance rate, village subsidy rate and basic benefit rate on the labor income growth rate, population growth rate, saving rate, consumption ratio, education expense ratio, gift ratio and bequest ratio. According to the situations in rural China, we simulate the effects and their intensities. Instead of PAYG or fully funded public pension systems in the literature, this chapter studies a partially funded public pension system. Participants, villages and local governments make pension contributions instead of only individuals do in the literature. Each individual derives part of utility from the human capital of her/his children instead of the number of children. The effects are summarized in Figures 1-4, and the effect intensities in Table 1.

The results have important implications. The GDP growth rate of China in 2012 and 2013 is 7.7%, which has fallen evidently relative to the previous decade. China needs to keep a rationally rapid economic growth rate. According to the actuality in rural China, there is an urgency to increase the labor income, control the rural population size, raise the investment and consumption, reduce the education expense ratio and unintentional bequests, and maintain moderate material support within family. These are the development goals of Chinese rural economy and society in a rather long historical period. According to the effects of the exogenous variables and their intensities, it will do more good than harm to adopt the following measures: raise the basic benefit rate, local government allowance rate and village subsidy rate, reduce the individual contribution rate, and improve the living and medical conditions.

The roles of the measures are as follows: Raising the basic benefit rate can increase the labor income growth rate, saving rate and consumption ratio, and decrease the population growth rate; its negative effects are to increase the education expense ratio and bequest ratio and decrease the gift ratio. Raising the local government allowance rate and village subsidy rate can increase consumption and net transfers of wealth in family from children to parents, and decrease the education expense ratio; its negative effects are to decrease the labor income growth rate and increase the population growth rate. Reducing the individual contribution rate can increase the labor income growth rate and saving rate and decrease the population growth rate; its negative effects are to increase the education expense ratio and bequest ratio. Improving the living and medical conditions can increase the labor income growth rate and saving rate, and decrease the population growth rate and education expense ratio; its negative effects are to decrease the consumption ratio and gift ratio and increase the bequest ratio.

The negative effects of the measures can be offset partially or totally by them one another. For example, the negative effects of raising the local government allowance rate and village subsidy rate on the labor income growth rate and population growth rate can be dominated by any one of the two measures: raising the basic benefit rate or improving the living and medical conditions. The negative effect of raising the basic benefit rate on education expense ratio can be offset by improving the living and medical conditions, reducing the individual contribution rate, and raising the local government allowance rate and village subsidy rate. Consequently, the above measures can increase the labor income growth rate and saving rate, and decrease the population growth rate and gift ratio. It is possible to decrease the consumption ratio and increase the education expense ratio and bequest ratio, such kind of negative effects can be further offset by adjust the extent of the measures. As a whole, the measures mentioned above will do more good than harm, after all it is more important to increase the labor income, control the rural population size and promote the economic growth than the other goals.

VI. EXTENSIVE DISCUSSIONS ON PUBLIC PENSION IN CHINA

Chapter 13

URBAN PUBLIC PENSION WITH CAPITAL TAXATION

ABSTRACT

Public pension system is one of the most important common issues in present world. Many countries are trying to reform their public pension systems. Applying an overlapping generations model, this chapter analyzes a partially funded pension system financed by wage tax and capital income tax, and compare it with a pay-as-you-go pension system and a fully funded pension system. It is shown that adjusting the policy variables can make the capital-labor ratio approach to the modified golden rule level from either undercapitalized or overcapitalized to improve social welfare under the partially funded pension system. Comparing it with a fully funded pension system and a pay-as-you-go pension system gives that the partially funded pension system can be regarded as a way to reform the public pension systems.

Keywords: urban public pension; capital income tax; wage tax

1. INTRODUCTION

Public pension system is a common issue for the world, and many countries are discussing how to reform their public pension systems. As well known, there are two typical public pension systems. One is fully funded pension system, in which individual saves compulsorily during working period and enjoys her/his own accumulated savings with accrued interest during retirement period. Another one is pay-as-you-go (PAYG) pension system, in which current workers' pension contributions are transferred to pay for current retirees' pension benefits.

Public pension system has two basic functions: ensuring a minimum living level in retirement period through income redistribution, and preventing individuals' myopia or not to provide adequately material for their retirement. A fully funded pension system can prevent individuals' myopia, but cannot guarantee a minimum living level if the wage of an individual was very low when he/she was young. Furthermore, fully funded pension system has no effect on capital accumulation. A PAYG pension system holds the two basic functions, but introducing a PAYG pension system into an economy will reduce the capital-labor ratio of the economy (see, e.g., Blanchard and Fischer, 1989, pp. 111-113).

It is also well known that social welfare is maximized when the capital-labor ratio is at the modified golden rule level (see, e.g., Blanchard and Fischer, 1989, p. 100 and p. 104). Thus, fully funded pension system cannot improve social welfare by affect the capital-labor ratio. Introduction of PAYG pension system can only improve social welfare by decreasing the capital-labor ratio just when the economy is overcapitalized, i.e., when the capital-labor ratio is higher than the modified golden rule level. But when the economy is undercapitalized or the capital-labor ratio is lower than the modified golden rule level, introduction of PAYG pension system decreases the capital-labor ratio and social welfare. Is there any way to adjust the capital-labor ratio when an economy is either overcapitalized or undercapitalized to approach to the modified golden rule level to improve social welfare?

This chapter explores such a way by analyzing a partially funded pension system and comparing it with a PAYG pension system. China began the transition for workers in state-owned enterprises from a PAYG system to a partially funded system in 1990s (see Feldstein, 1999). According to the *State Council* Decis*ion on Establishing a Unified Basic Pension System for Enterprise Employees* (Chinese State Council Document 26 in 1997)[1], the government establishes an individual account for each employee and a social pool for all employees and retirees. Each employee contributes 8% of her wage to her individual account. Each firm contributes 20% of its payroll, in which less part are credited to individual accounts and main part goes to the social pool account. The accumulation in an individual account is used to pay the individual herself when she retires as fully funded pension benefits. The social pool fund is used to pay current retirees as PAYG pension benefits. Each retiree receives funded pension benefits from her individual account and PAYG pension benefits from the social pool account.

The partially funded public pension system is financed by wage tax and payroll tax, namely, it is financed by labor income tax. Most of the literature dealing with public pensions analyze pension systems financed only by labor income tax, avoiding capital income tax (see, e.g., Samuelson, 1958; Barro, 1974; Feldstein, 1987, 1990; Blanchard and Fischer, 1989; Nishimura and Zhang, 1995; Wigger, 1999; Fuster, 2000; Zhang and Zhang, 2001; Pecchenino and Pollard, 2002; Groezen et al., 2003; etc.). But pension tax levied on capital income does exist (see Kaganovich and Zilcha, 1999, p. 294). Even if there is no partially funded pension system financed by wage tax and capital income tax, it is valuable to explore such a hypothetic system to discuss a way to adjust capital-labor ratio from both sides to approach the modified golden rule level and look for a way of public pension system reform.

It is reported that the capital share of income in China is very high. Chow and Li (2002) estimated with data from 1952 to 1998 in China that the capital share of income to be 0.6. Kan and Wang (2013) estimated it to be around 0.67. Due to the capital share of income in China is very high, perhaps it is better for China to carry out a policy: transform firm pension contributions from payroll tax to capital income tax. In other words, the social pool account balance of the public pension system for urban enterprise employees comes from firms' capital income tax, not from payroll tax.

---

[1] It is the document that this chapter is based on. Analogous research can be done based on the Chinese State Council Document 38 in 2005.

Based on theoretical analyses, this chapter shows that under such a partially funded pension system, raising the capital income tax rate may increase or maintain or decrease the capital-labor ratio; raising the funded-tax share, the share of capital income tax going to the individual account, will increase the capital-labor ratio; the wage tax has no effect on the capital accumulation. The effect of capital income tax on the capital-labor ratio depends on the magnitudes of relevant parameters as well as the elasticity of marginal utility with respect to consumption. It is possible to make the capital-labor ratio to approach the modified golden rule level by adjusting the capital income tax rate and funded-tax share to improve the social welfare. The partially funded pension system also has the two basic functions of pension system. However, introducing a PAYG pension system into an economy must reduce the capital-labor ratio and decrease the social welfare if the economy is undercapitalized. Obviously, the partially funded pension system financed by wage tax and payroll tax can be looked upon a choice for the world to reform the public pension systems.

2. THE MODEL FOR PARTIALLY FUNDED PENSION

2.1. Individuals

At the beginning of period t, N_t identical individuals of generation t enter the work force. Population grows at rate $n = N_{t+1}/N_t - 1$. Individuals live for two periods: working period and retirement period. In working period, each individual supplies inelastically one unit of labor to the market, earns wage, pays pension tax at rate $\tau \in (0,1)$ based on the wage, consumes part of the income, and saves the remainder. In the retirement period, she/he consumes the savings with accrued interest, funded pension benefits and PAYG pension benefits.

Each individual derives utility from her/his working-period consumption, c_{1t} and retirement-period consumption, c_{2t+1}. The utility is described by an additively separable general function. Each individual of generation t solves the following maximization problem:

$$\max_{\{s_t\}} U_t = u(c_{1t}) + \theta u(c_{2t+1}), \qquad (1)$$

s.t.
$$c_{1t} = (1-\tau)w_t - s_t, \qquad (2)$$

$$c_{2t+1} = (1+r_{t+1})s_t + (1+r_{t+1})G_t + B_{t+1}, \qquad (3)$$

where $\theta \in (0,1)$ is the discount factor, w_t the wage, s_t the savings, r_{t+1} the interest rate, G_t the individual account principal, and B_{t+1} the social pool benefits. $u(\cdot)$ is an increasing and strictly concave function: $u'(\cdot) > 0$, $u''(\cdot) < 0$.

Substituting equations (2) and (3) into equation (1), and letting the partial derivative of it with respect to s_t be zero gives the first-order condition:

$$-u'(c_{1t})+\theta(1+r_{t+1})u'(c_{2t+1})=0. \tag{4}$$

Equation (4) means that the utility loss from reducing one unit of working-period consumption is equal to the utility gain from increasing $(1+r_{t+1})$ units of retirement-period consumption.

2.2. Firms

Firms produce a homogenous commodity in competitive markets. The production function is homogeneous of degree one: $F(K_t, N_t) = N_t f(k_t)$, where $k_t = K_t/N_t$ is the capital-labor ratio, $f(k_t)$ the output-labor ratio. $f'(k_t) > 0$, $f''(k_t) < 0$. $\lim_{k \to 0} f'(k) = \infty$, $\lim_{k \to \infty} f'(k) = 0$.

Each firm is levied pension tax on its capital income at rate $\varepsilon \in (0,1)$. That means the rate of return to capital is reduced. Product distribution gives $F(K_t, N_t) = w_t N_t + (1+\varepsilon)r_t K_t$. By virtue of Euler's theorem, we have

$$w_t = f(k_t) - k_t f'(k_t), \tag{5}$$

and $(1+\varepsilon)r_t = f'(k_t)$. Thus the rate of return to capital is

$$r_t = \frac{f'(k_t)}{1+\varepsilon}. \tag{6}$$

2.3. The Government

The government divides the capital income tax into the individual account fund $\mu \varepsilon r_t K_t$ and the social pool fund $(1-\mu)\varepsilon r_t K_t$, where $\mu \in (0,1)$ is the share going to the individual accounts, which is called funded-tax share for simplicity. Individual's wage tax and individual account fund are used to pay the individual when she/he retires in next period as funded pension benefits:

$$G_t = \tau w_t + \mu \varepsilon r_t k_t. \tag{7}$$

The social pool fund is used to pay retirees in current period as PAYG pension benefits: $N_{t-1} B_t = (1-\mu)\varepsilon r_t K_t$, or

$$B_t = (1+n)(1-\mu)\varepsilon r_t k_t.\tag{8}$$

2.4. The Capital Market

The savings and individual account fund in period t generate the capital stock in period $t+1$: $N_t(s_t + G_t) = K_{t+1}$, or

$$s_t + G_t = (1+n)k_{t+1}.\tag{9}$$

3. EQUILIBRIUM ANALYSES

Substituting (2) - (3) and (5) - (9) into (4) gives a dynamic equilibrium system:

$$-u'\left([f(k_t) - k_t f'(k_t)] + \mu\frac{\varepsilon}{1+\varepsilon}k_t f'(k_t) - (1+n)k_{t+1}\right)$$
$$+ \theta\left[1 + \frac{f'(k_{t+1})}{1+\varepsilon}\right]\cdot u'\left((1+n)k_{t+1}\left[1 + \left(1 - \frac{\mu\varepsilon}{1+\varepsilon}\right)f'(k_{t+1})\right]\right) = 0 \tag{10}$$

Assume that there is unique, stable and nonoscillatory steady state equilibrium. Differentiating the dynamic equilibrium system with respect to k_{t+1}, k_t gives

$$idk_{t+1} + jdk_t = 0, \tag{11}$$

where $i = (1+n)u_1'' + \theta u_2' \dfrac{f''}{1+\varepsilon} + \theta\left(1 + \dfrac{f'}{1+\varepsilon}\right)(1+n)\left[1 + \left(1 - \dfrac{\mu\varepsilon}{1+\varepsilon}\right)(f' + kf'')\right]u_2''$,

$j = -u_1''\left[\dfrac{\mu\varepsilon}{1+\varepsilon}f' + \left(\dfrac{\mu\varepsilon}{1+\varepsilon} - 1\right)kf''\right] > 0$.

Therefore the stability condition is $0 < -\dfrac{j}{i} < 1$, or $i + j < 0$.

The wage tax rate does not appear in the dynamic equilibrium system because the wage tax is compulsory savings, which crowd out the voluntary savings by one-for-one. Hence, the wage tax has no effect on the capital stock. Totally differentiating the dynamic equilibrium system in the steady state with respect to k, ε, μ gives

$$(i+j)dk + md\varepsilon + ld\mu = 0,\qquad(12)$$

where $m = \dfrac{kf'}{(1+\varepsilon)^2}\left\{-\mu\left[u_1'' + \theta\left(1+\dfrac{f'}{1+\varepsilon}\right)(1+n)u_2''\right] - \dfrac{\theta}{k}u_2'\right\}$,

$l = -\dfrac{\varepsilon k f'}{1+\varepsilon}\left[u_1'' + \theta\left(1+\dfrac{f'}{1+\varepsilon}\right)(1+n)u_2''\right] > 0$.

Therefore,

$$\frac{\partial k}{\partial \tau} = 0,$$

$$\frac{\partial k}{\partial \varepsilon} = -\frac{m}{i+j},$$

$$\frac{\partial k}{\partial \mu} = -\frac{l}{i+j} > 0.$$

Raising the capital income tax rate may increase or maintain or decrease the capital-labor ratio. The effect of the capital income tax rate on the capital-labor ratio depends on magnitudes of the discount factor, population growth rate, capital income tax rate and funded-tax share as well as the elasticity of marginal utility with respect to consumption. The reasons are as follows. First, an increase in the capital income tax rate raises the individual account fund and furthermore the capital-labor ratio. Second, raising the capital income tax rate reduces the interest rate and raises the individual account principal and the social pool benefits. But the effect of the former is greater than the later, so the retirement-period consumption falls. In order to maximize the utility, it is necessary to increase the savings. Thus the capital-labor ratio rises. Third, raising the capital income tax rate decreases the interest rate, which increases the price of retirement-period consumption, leading to the decrease in the saving and furthermore the capital-labor ratio. The three incidences determine that the effect of capital income tax rate on the capital-labor ratio is ambiguous.

Raising the funded-tax share increases the capital-labor ratio. An increase in the funded-tax share leads to the increase in the individual account principal. The increase in the funded-tax share also reduces the PAYG pension benefits and furthermore the retirement-period consumption. In order to maximize the utility, it is necessary to increase the savings. Both effects increase the capital-labor ratio.

4. THE MODEL FOR PAYG PENSION

This section compares the partially funded pension system with a PAYG pension system financed by the same taxes, wage tax and capital income tax.

Under the PAYG pension system, each worker is levied a pension tax on wage. Each retiree gets only PAYG pension benefits. Each individual solves the following utility maximization problem: maximize equation (1) subject to equation (2) and

$$C_{2t+1} = (1+r_{t+1})s_t + B_{t+1}. \tag{13}$$

The first-order condition is also equation (4).

Each firm is levied pension tax on its capital income at rate ε, too. Product distribution gives $F(K_t, N_t) = w_t N_t + (1+\varepsilon)r_t K_t$. The wage and interest rate are: $w_t = f(k_t) - k_t f'(k_t)$ and $r_t = \dfrac{f'(k_t)}{1+\varepsilon}$, which are the same as equations (5) and (6).

According to PAYG public pension system, all of the wage tax and capital income tax are used to pay current retirees as PAYG pension benefits: $B_t N_{t-1} = \tau w_t N_t + \varepsilon r_t K_t$, or

$$B_t = (1+n)(\tau w_t + \varepsilon r_t k_t). \tag{14}$$

The savings in period t generate the capital stock in period $t+1$: $N_t s_t = K_{t+1}$, or

$$s_t = (1+n)k_{t+1}. \tag{15}$$

Substituting equations (2), (13), (5), (6), (14) and (15) into equation (4) gives a dynamic equilibrium system described by the following difference equation:

$$\begin{aligned}&-u'((1-\tau)[f(k_t) - k_t f'(k_t)] - (1+n)k_{t+1}) \\ &+ \theta\left[1 + \dfrac{f'(k_{t+1})}{1+\varepsilon}\right] \cdot u'((1+n)\{k_{t+1}[1+f'(k_{t+1})] + \tau[f(k_{t+1}) - k_{t+1}f'(k_{t+1})]\}) = 0\end{aligned} \tag{16}$$

Assume that there is unique, stable and nonoscillatory steady state equilibrium. Differentiating the dynamic equilibrium system with respect to k_{t+1} and k_t gives

$$bdk_{t+1} + edk_t = 0, \tag{17}$$

where, $b = (1+n)u_1'' + \theta u_2' \dfrac{f''}{1+\varepsilon} + \theta\left(1 + \dfrac{f'}{1+\varepsilon}\right)(1+n)[1 + f' + (1-\tau)kf'']u_2''$,

$e = (1-\tau)kf''u_1'' > 0$.

The stability condition is $0 < -\dfrac{e}{b} < 1$, or $b + e < 0$.

Differentiating the dynamic equilibrium system in the steady state with respect to k, τ, ε yields

$$(b+e)dk + gd\tau + hd\varepsilon = 0, \qquad (18)$$

where, $g = (f - kf')\left[u_1'' + \theta\left(1 + \dfrac{f'}{1+\varepsilon}\right)(1+n)u_2''\right] < 0$, $h = -\dfrac{\theta f' u_2'}{(1+\varepsilon)^2} < 0$.

Thus,

$$\frac{\partial k}{\partial \tau} = -\frac{g}{b+e} < 0,$$

$$\frac{\partial k}{\partial \varepsilon} = -\frac{h}{b+e} < 0.$$

Under the PAYG pension system, raising the wage tax rate decreases the capital-labor ratio. This result is the same as the well known one (see, e.g., Blanchard and Fischer, 1989, p. 113). Raising the capital income tax rate also decreases the capital-labor ratio. That is to say, when the capital-labor ratio in an economy without public pension system is lower than the modified golden rule level, introducing the PAYG pension system financed by wage tax and capital income tax into the economy will make the capital-labor ratio further lower than the modified golden rule level and reduce the social welfare. On the contrary, when the capital-labor ratio in an economy without public pension system is higher than the modified golden rule level, introducing the PAYG pension system into the economy will make the capital-labor ratio approach to the modified golden rule level and raise the social welfare.

CONCLUSION

Corresponding to public pension system reform, this chapter applies the OLG model to examine a partially funded pension system financed by wage tax and capital income tax, and compare it with a fully funded pension system and PAYG pension system. Under the partially funded pension system, raising the capital income tax rate can increase or maintain or decrease the capital-labor ratio; raising the funded-tax share increases the capital-labor ratio; the wage tax has no effect on the capital-labor ratio. The effect of capital income tax rate on the capital-labor ratio depends on the magnitudes of the individual discount factor, population growth rate, capital income tax rate and funded-tax share as well as the elasticity of marginal utility with respect to consumption. Choosing the capital income tax rate and funded-tax share can adjust the capital-labor ratio to approach to the modified golden rule level to improve social welfare.

Introducing the PAYG pension system financed by wage tax and capital income tax into an economy must reduce the capital-labor ratio. But introducing the partially funded pension system financed by wage tax and capital income tax can increase or decrease the capital-labor ratio, which can be controlled by choosing the magnitudes of the capital income tax rate and the funded-tax share. If the capital-labor ratio is lower than the modified golden rule level, to improve the social welfare, a social planner can introduce the partially funded pension system into the economy. If the capital-labor ratio is higher than the modified golden rule level, to improve the social welfare, the social planner can introduce either the partially funded pension system or the PAYG pension system into the economy. In both situations, the social planner can actively use the partially funded pension system. Hence, the partially funded pension system has relative advantage to the PAYG pension system in the field of improving social welfare.

Comparing with a fully funded pension system and a PAYG pension system, the partially funded pension system financed by wage tax and capital income tax has the following relative advantages. First, adjusting the policy variables, the capital income tax rate and funded-tax share, can make the capital-labor ratio approach to the modified golden rule level from both sides of the modified golden rule level to improve social welfare. Second, the partially funded pension system can reflect both equality and efficiency in public pension because individual's pension benefits are partially related to individual's wage tax for pension. Third, the partially funded pension system holds the basic functions of public pension system. Therefore, the partially funded pension system financed by wage tax and capital income tax can be regarded as a direction to reform public pension systems.

Chapter 14

URBAN PUBLIC PENSION, VAT AND ENDOGENOUS GROWTH

ABSTRACT

Employing the framework of an OLG model with two-sided altruism and endogenous growth, this chapter examines the effect of a partially funded public pension financed by individual wage tax and firm's value added tax (VAT) on the population, economic growth and net intergenerational transfers. It is shown that raising the VAT rate decreases the number of children and the net intergenerational transfer ratio, while increases the growth rate of output per worker. The wage tax rate has no effect on the three variables. We find the optimal or sub-optimal interval of VAT rate under different situations. Only in view of the effect on the population, economic growth and net intergenerational transfers, the hypothetic VAT firm contribution scheme is available to the public pension system for urban enterprise employees in China.

Keywords: public pension; value added tax; endogenous growth

1. INTRODUCTION

China began a partially funded public pension system for urban enterprise employees in 1997, regulated by the *State Council Decision on Establishing a Unified Basic Pension System for Enterprise Employees* (Chinese State Council Document 26 in 1997)[1]: Both employer and employee make pension contributions. Firm contributions are a proportion of the firm's payroll, and employee contributions are a proportion of the employee's wage. The government establishes an individual account for each employee and a social pool account for all employees and retirees. Entire of the employee contributions and less part of the firm contributions are credited to the employee's individual account. Main part of the firm contributions goes to the social pool account. Each retiree receives individual account benefits (funded benefits) and social pool benefits (pay-as-you-go benefits).

---

[1] This chapter is based on the public pension system regulated by the Chinese State Council Document 26 in 1997. But the analysis method can be used to investigate the system regulated by the Chinese State Council Document 38 in 2005.

In practice, the social pool account is short of paying the current retirees. Most of the contributions to individual accounts are also used to pay current retirees as social pool benefits. As Feldstein (1999, 2003) pointed out, the reason is that employers and employees either refuse to participate or, more commonly, understate their full income. Feldstein (2003) suggested that the tax based on individual earnings should be used only to finance the contributions to individual accounts, and value added tax (VAT) is the appropriate source of revenue for the social pool benefits.

Before the suggestions become real policies, it is necessary to examine the impact of them on China's economy and society. It is well known that China is a developing country with more than 1.3 billion population and low per capita GDP. It is necessary for China to keep a comparatively high economic growth and rationally control population size. The population ageing in China is very rapid because of longevity and low population growth rate. The Chinese government is confronted with very heavy burden to pay public pension benefits. Hence, the government advocates maintaining certain level of family old-age security, which means that children provide necessary material support to their retired parents within family.

There are many studies on the relationship between economic growth, fertility and pay-as-you-go (PAYG) public pension. Some of the literature with endogenous growth model treated children as consumption goods. People decide to have children simply because they directly enter the number of children into their utility functions like any other consumption goods (see, e.g., Zhang et al., 2001; Zhang and Zhang, 2003; Groezen et al., 2003; among others). Some of the literature treated children as capital goods, which provide material support when individuals retire, called old-age security. PAYG pension diminishes the importance of children as old-age security good and henceforth decreases fertility (see, e.g., Raut, 1992; Cigno, 1993; Zhang and Nishimura, 1993; Zhang and Zhang, 1995; among others). Some of the literature treated children as both consumption goods and capital goods. Zhang and Zhang (1998) analyzed the effects of social security in a model with alternative motives of having children. It is shown that social security increases per capita income growth when the social security tax is not too high. Wigger (1999a) showed that small sized public pensions stimulate per capita income growth, but further increases in public pensions reduce it. A rise in public pensions reduces fertility if they are either small or large, and stimulates fertility if they are medium sized. Zhang and Zhang (2001) analyzed how bequest motives affect fertility, savings, growth, and the effects of PAYG-social security.

Under the framework of an OLG model with two-sided altruism and endogenous growth, this chapter examines the effect of a hypothetic partially funded pension financed by individual wage tax and firm's VAT on the population, economic growth and net intergenerational transfers. It is shown that raising the VAT rate decreases the number of children and the net intergenerational transfer ratio, while increases the growth rate of output per worker. The wage tax rate has no effect on the number of children, the growth rate of output per worker and the net intergenerational transfer ratio. The optimal or sub-optimal interval of VAT rate is found under different situations. Solely in view of the influence on the population, economic growth and net intergenerational transfers, the hypothetic VAT firm contribution scheme is available to the public pension system for enterprise employees in China.

This chapter extends the models of Zhang and Zhang (1998, 2001) and Wigger (1999a) by introducing China's partially funded pension system and a Chinese culture tradition, *respecting the old and loving the young.* That is, the young present gifts to their parents when they earn labor income and the old leave bequests to their children when they pass away. The tradition determines that there always is operative two-sided altruism, which is different from the probability of operative and inoperative altruism, and from one-sided intergenerational transfers in the literature. Individuals are satisfied with both having children and getting old-age security. Thus children are treated as consumption goods and capital goods. Following Saint-Paul (1992), Zhang and Zhang (1995, 1998, 2001), Wigger (1999a, 1999b), etc., this chapter adopts an endogenous growth model with Romer's (1986) type of capital externality. It is tractable to analyze the effects of the pension contribution rates on the number of children, the rates of intergenerational transfers and economic growth.

2. THE MODEL

A closed economy is composed of numerous individuals and firms and a government. The generation born at the beginning of period t is called generation t, the population size of which is N_t. Each individual has one parent and n_t children (see Abel, 1987a for details). Hence, the population size of generation $t + 1$ is $N_{t+1} = N_t n_t$.

2.1. Individuals

Individuals are identical. Each individual lives for two periods: working period and retirement period. Each individual earns wage by supplying inelastically one unit of labor, makes pension contributions by paying wage tax, receives bequests from her parent, consumes part of her income, rears her children, presents gifts to her parent, and saves the remainder of the income during working period. In the retirement period, she consumes part of her savings with accrued interest, gifts from her children, individual account pension benefits and social pool pension benefits, and leaves the remainder as bequests to her children.

Each individual derives utility from her working-period consumption C_{1t}, retirement-period consumption C_{2t+1}, number of children, the utility of each child V_{t+1} and the utility of her parent V_{t-1}. The utility is described by an additively separable logarithmic function. Each individual maximizes her utility by choosing the number of children, saving rate, gift ratio and bequest ratio:

$$Max_{\{s_t, q_t, n_t, b_{t+1}\}} V_t = \ln C_{1t} + \theta \ln C_{2t+1} + \rho \ln n_t + \beta V_{t+1} + \gamma V_{t-1}, \quad (1)$$

s.t. $$C_{1t} = (1 - \tau + b_t - h_t - q_t - s_t)W_t, \quad (2)$$

$$C_{2t+1} = (1 + r_{t+1})s_t W_t + n_t q_{t+1} W_{t+1} + (1 + r_{t+1})I_t + P_{t+1} - n_t b_{t+1} W_{t+1}, \quad (3)$$

where $\theta \in (0,1)$ denotes the discount factor, and $\rho, \beta, \gamma > 0$ the weights for number of children, utility of each child and utility of her parent. $\beta > \rho$ since individual cares the utility of her each child more than the number of children. τ denotes the wage tax rate, b_t the bequest ratio, q_t the gift ratio, s_t the saving rate. The child-rearing cost ratio is assumed to be (see, e.g., Nishimura and Zhang, 1992; Zhang and Zhang, 1998)

$$h_t = \delta n_t^d, \qquad (4)$$

where $\delta > 0$, $d > 1$. W_t denotes the wage, r_{t+1} the interest rate, I_t the individual account principal, and P_{t+1} the social pool benefits. $q_t, b_{t+1} > 0$ for all t because of the Chinese culture tradition, *respecting the old and loving the young*. $n_t > 0$ is the condition for population to last forever. Assume $s_t > 0$ for all t throughout this chapter to focus on interior solution.

Substituting equations (2) - (4) into equation (1), letting partial derivatives of it with respect to s_t, q_t, n_t, b_{t+1} be zero gives the first-order conditions for the utility maximization:

$$1/C_{1t} = (1 + r_{t+1})\theta / C_{2t+1}, \qquad (5)$$

$$1/C_{1t} = \gamma \theta n_{t-1} / C_{2t}, \qquad (6)$$

$$(dh_t W_t / n_t)(1/C_{1t}) = (q_{t+1} - b_{t+1})W_{t+1}\theta / C_{2t+1} + \rho / n_t, \qquad (7)$$

$$n_t \theta / C_{2t+1} = \beta / C_{1t+1}. \qquad (8)$$

Equations (5) - (8) bear standard tradeoffs between marginal utilities. For example, equation (5) stands for tradeoff between the marginal utility of working-period consumption and that of retirement-period consumption through savings.

2.2. Firms

Firms produce a homogenous commodity in competitive markets. The production function $F(K_t, A_t N_t) = A_t N_t f(k_t)$ is homogeneous of degree one, where $F(K_t, A_t N_t)$ denotes the output, K_t the capital stock in period t, A_t the labor productivity, $k_t = K_t / (A_t N_t)$ the capital per unit of effective labor.

Firms make pension contributions by paying value added tax at rate $\varepsilon \in (0,1)$. The contributions are in fact VAT with consumption base (see, e.g., Atkinson and Stiglitz, 1980;

Feldstein, 2003). According to product distribution, one can get that $F(K_t, A_t N_t) = (r_t K_t + w_t A_t N_t)(1+\varepsilon)$. By virtue of Euler's theorem, we have

$$r_t = f'(k_t)/(1+\varepsilon), \qquad (9)$$

$$w_t = W_t / A_t = [f(k_t) - k_t f'(k_t)]/(1+\varepsilon), \qquad (10)$$

where w_t is the wage rate per unit of effective labor.

In order to ensure existence of a balanced growth path for the economy, the following particular form of A_t is adopted (see, e.g., Saint-Paul, 1992; Zhang and Zhang, 1995, 1998; Wigger, 1999a, 1999b; among others):

$$A_t = K_t / (a N_t), \qquad (11)$$

where a is a positive technological parameter. Therefore, $k_t = a$, and

$$r_t = f'(a)/(1+\varepsilon) = r, \; w_t = [f(a) - a f'(a)]/(1+\varepsilon) = w \text{ for all } t. \qquad (12)$$

2.3. The Government

The individual contributions go to the individual account, the accumulation in which is used to pay the individual when she retires in next period as the individual account benefits:

$$I_t = \tau W_t. \qquad (13)$$

The firm contributions go to the social pool, which is used to pay current retirees as the social pool benefits: $P_t N_{t-1} = (r_t K_t + w_t A_t N_t)\varepsilon$. Using equations (10) - (12) and the definition of k_t gives

$$P_t = n_{t-1} \varepsilon [ar/w + 1] W_t. \qquad (14)$$

2.4. The Goods Market

The savings and individual account principal of the workers in period t generate the capital stock in period $t + 1$.

$$s_t W_t N_t + \tau W_t N_t = K_{t+1}. \qquad (15)$$

3. EQUILIBRIUM ANALYSIS

Combining equations (10), (11), (12), (15) and the work force $N_{t+1} = n_t N_t$ yields the growth rate of capital per worker:

$$1 + g_t = (K_{t+1}/N_{t+1})/(K_t/N_t) = (s_t + \tau)w/(an_t). \quad (16)$$

Analogously, the growth rates of wage and output per worker are also $1 + g_t$.

A balanced growth equilibrium is a competitive equilibrium in which intensive variables such as the gift ratio, bequest ratio and so on are constant, while extensive variables such as the wage, working-period consumption and so on grow at the same endogenously determined and constant growth rate of capital per worker. The following analysis focuses on the balanced growth equilibrium.

3.1. Effect on Number of Children

Equating equations (5) and (6), and using the wage growth rate gives

$$n(1 + g) = (1 + r)/\gamma. \quad (17)$$

Substituting equations (17) and (12) into equation (16), rearranging yields

$$s = (1 + f'(a) + \varepsilon)z/\gamma - \tau, \quad (18)$$

where $z = a/[f(a) - af'(a)]$.

Substituting equation (5) into equation (7), and using the wage growth rate gives

$$\theta(\gamma dh - T) = \rho[\gamma(s + \tau) + T + \varepsilon D], \quad (19)$$

where $T = q - b$ is the net intergenerational transfer ratio, and $D = ar/w + 1 = zf'(a) + 1$.

Substituting equations (2) and (3) into equation (8), rearranging yields

$$\theta(1 - h - T - s - \tau) = \beta[\gamma(s + \tau) + T + \varepsilon D]. \quad (20)$$

Combining equations (19) and (20), rearranging gives

$$h = \frac{(\rho - \beta)[z(1 + f'(a) + \varepsilon) + \varepsilon D] + (\theta + \rho)[1 - (z/\gamma)(1 + f'(a) + \varepsilon)]}{\theta + \rho + (\theta + \beta)\gamma d}, \quad (21)$$

$$T = \frac{\theta\gamma d[1-(z/\gamma)(1+f'(a)+\varepsilon)]-(\beta\gamma d+\rho)[z(1+f'(a)+\varepsilon)+\varepsilon D]}{\theta+\rho+(\theta+\beta)\gamma d}. \quad (22)$$

Differentiating h with respect to ε gives

$$\partial h/\partial\varepsilon < 0. \quad (23)$$

Using equation (4) yields

$$\partial n/\partial\varepsilon < 0. \quad (24)$$

A rise in the VAT rate reduces the number of children. Raising the VAT rate decreases the wage. Workers decrease the child-rearing cost ratio by reducing the number of children. In addition, a rise in the VAT rate leads to higher social pool benefits, which renders children as a means of securing old age income less important and tends to reduce the number of children.

3.2. Effect on Growth Rate of Output Per Worker

Applying equation (17) and the effect on the number of children gives

$$\partial g/\partial\varepsilon > 0. \quad (25)$$

An increase in the VAT rate raises the growth rate of output per worker. This is because there is a negative correlation between the growth rate of output per worker and the number of children, and raising the VAT rate reduces the number of children.

3.3. EFFECT ON NET INTERGENERATIONAL TRANSFER RATE

Differentiating T in equation (22) with respect to ε yields

$$\partial T/\partial\varepsilon < 0. \quad (26)$$

A rise in the VAT rate reduces the net intergenerational transfer ratio. On the one hand, a rise in the VAT rate induces the decrease in the wage, which makes the young give less gifts to their parents. On the other hand, the rise in the VAT rate leads to the increase in the social pool benefits, which enables the old to leave more bequests to their children. The wage tax rate has no effect on the number of children, the growth rate of output per worker and the net intergenerational transfer ratio because the mandatory savings (individual contributions) crowd out the private voluntary savings by one-for-one. Summarizing the above results yields the following proposition.

Proposition 1: Raising the VAT rate decreases the number of children and the net intergenerational transfer ratio, while increases the growth rate of output per worker. The wage tax rate has no effect on the number of children, the net intergenerational transfer ratio and the growth rate of output per worker.

4. OPTIMAL VAT RATE

4.1. Economic Goals

As a developing country with over-population and low per capita GDP, China needs a comparatively high economic growth and rational control on the population size. The government hopes maintain certain family old-age security, i.e., material support from the young to the old within family, to lighten too heavy pension burden. Because higher VAT rate induces higher economic growth and less population, it is necessary for China to seek the optimal VAT rate. If the contribution rate is too low, the economic growth rate will become too low. If it is too high, the population will decrease sharply.

The optimal VAT rate depends on economic goals. On the one hand, the population should be reduced or maintained at the original level, namely, $n \leq 1$. Substituting $n \leq 1$ into equation (21) and rearranging gives

$$\varepsilon \geq \frac{(\theta+\rho)(1-z(1+f'(a))/\gamma)-(\beta-\rho)z(1+f'(a))-\delta[\theta+\rho+(\theta+\beta)\gamma d]}{(\beta-\rho)(z+D)+(\theta+\rho)z/\gamma} = \underline{\varepsilon}. \qquad (27)$$

On the other hand, the population cannot be reduced unboundedly. Substituting the condition for the population to last forever, $n > 0$ into equation (21) and rearranging yields

$$\varepsilon < \frac{(\theta+\rho)(1-z(1+f'(a))/\gamma)-(\beta-\rho)z(1+f'(a))}{(\beta-\rho)(z+D)+(\theta+\rho)z/\gamma} = \overline{\varepsilon}. \qquad (28)$$

Therefore, the corresponding relationship between the intervals of ε and n is $\underline{\varepsilon} \leq \varepsilon < \overline{\varepsilon}$ for $0 < n \leq 1$. The sign of $\underline{\varepsilon}$ depends on the magnitude of relevant parameters. By virtue of equation (27), the condition for $\underline{\varepsilon}$ to be positive is

$$\delta < \frac{(\theta+\rho)(1-z(1+f'(a))/\gamma)-(\beta-\rho)z(1+f'(a))}{\theta+\rho+(\theta+\beta)\gamma d}. \qquad (29)$$

Material support during retirement-period is one of the motives for having children. Can it ensure the net intergenerational transfers run from the young to the old if the VAT rate is in the interval of $\varepsilon \in [\underline{\varepsilon}, \overline{\varepsilon})$? Let us check it. The old-age material support means $T > 0$, i.e., the gifts from child to parent should be more than the bequests from parent to child. Substituting $T > 0$ into equation (22) and rearranging gives

$$\varepsilon < \frac{\theta\gamma d - z(1+f'(a))[(\theta+\beta\gamma)d+\rho]}{(\beta\gamma d+\rho)(z+D)+\theta dz} = \hat{\varepsilon} . \tag{30}$$

If $\varepsilon = \hat{\varepsilon}$, then $T = 0$, i.e., there is no net intergenerational transfers, namely, the gifts from child to parent are exactly equal to the bequests from parent to child.

If $\varepsilon > \hat{\varepsilon}$, then $T < 0$, i.e., there are net intergenerational transfers from the old to the young, namely, the gifts from child to parent are less than the bequests from parent to child.

By virtue of equation (30), the condition for $\hat{\varepsilon}$ to be positive is

$$\theta > \frac{z(1+f'(a))(\beta\gamma d+\rho)}{d[\gamma - z(1+f'(a))]}, \tag{31}$$

where $0 < s+\tau = (1+f'(a)+\varepsilon)z/\gamma < 1$ has been used.

4.2. Choosing VAT Rate

Comparing $\overline{\varepsilon}$ with $\hat{\varepsilon}$ gives $\overline{\varepsilon} > \hat{\varepsilon}$. However, it is hard to compare $\hat{\varepsilon}$ and $\underline{\varepsilon}$. Thus it is necessary to distinguish two cases, $\hat{\varepsilon} > \underline{\varepsilon}$ and $\hat{\varepsilon} < \underline{\varepsilon}$ to examine.

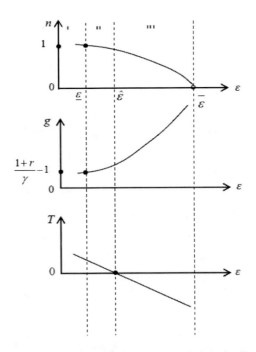

Figure 1. The relationship between n, g, T and ε in Case 1.

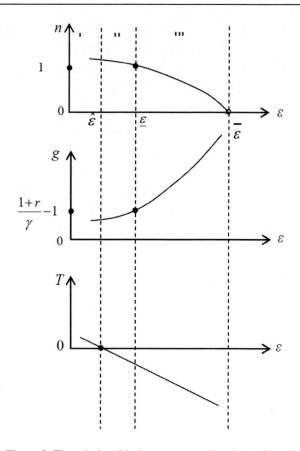

Figure 2. The relationship between n, g, T and ε in Case 2.

Case 1: $\underline{\varepsilon} < \hat{\varepsilon} < \overline{\varepsilon}$. As shown in Figure 1, in Region I, $\varepsilon < \underline{\varepsilon}$, the population increases, the economic growth rate is very low, and the net intergenerational transfers are positive. If $\varepsilon = \underline{\varepsilon}$, the population maintains at the original level and the growth rate of output per worker is $(1+r)/\gamma - 1$. In Region II, $\underline{\varepsilon} < \varepsilon < \hat{\varepsilon}$, the population is reduced in medium size, the economic growth rate is high but not too high, and the net intergenerational transfers are positive. This region is desirable because it satisfies the three economic goals. The net intergenerational transfers become zero if $\varepsilon = \hat{\varepsilon}$. In Region III, $\hat{\varepsilon} < \varepsilon < \overline{\varepsilon}$, the population is reduced largely, the economic growth rate is very high and the net intergenerational transfers are negative.

Case 2: $\hat{\varepsilon} < \underline{\varepsilon} < \overline{\varepsilon}$. Analogously, the relationship between n, g, T and ε is shown in Figure 2. It is impossible to find any region that satisfies the three economic goals. Obviously, if the VAT rate is larger than $\underline{\varepsilon}$ and near to it, the population is reduced in medium size, the economic growth rate is rational high, but the net intergenerational transfers are negative. These results can be summarized in the following proposition.

Proposition 2: (a) The interval for the VAT rate to be larger than and near to $\underline{\varepsilon}$ is the optimal interval in the case of $\underline{\varepsilon} < \hat{\varepsilon} < \overline{\varepsilon}$, and the sub-optimal interval in the case of $\hat{\varepsilon} < \underline{\varepsilon} < \overline{\varepsilon}$.

(b) Taking the VAT rate as $\underline{\varepsilon}$ can maintain the original population size and economic growth rate.

CONCLUSION

Employing the overlapping generations model with endogenous growth, this chapter examines the effect of the partially funded pension financed by individual wage tax and firm's value added tax on the population, economic growth and net intergenerational transfers. In such a pension system, the firm contributions are VAT with consumption base. Individual contributions are accumulated in the individual's account, while firm contributions are collected into the social pool. This chapter also introduces the Chinese culture tradition, *respecting the old and loving the young* into the model to consider two-sided altruism, which differs from one-sided altruism with operative and inoperative probability. Individuals and firms make pension contributions in this model instead of only individuals do in the literature.

This chapter shows that a rise in the VAT rate decreases the number of children and the net intergenerational transfer ratio, while increases the growth rate of output per worker. The wage tax rate has no effect on the number of children, the growth rate of output per worker and the net intergenerational transfer ratio because the compulsory savings crowd out the voluntary savings by one-for-one. This chapter also finds the optimal or sub-optimal VAT rates under different situations. Only in view of the effect on the population size, economic growth and net intergenerational transfers, the hypothetic VAT firm contribution scheme is available to the public pension system for enterprise employees in China.

Since China is a developing country with over-population, rapid ageing and low per capita GDP, it is necessary to choose the optimal or sub-optimal interval of VAT rate under different situations. The wage tax rate should be set on the level at which worker can bear, and when she/he retire, the sum of the accumulation in individual account and the social pool benefits can maintain subsistence.

Chapter 15

FERTILITY LINKED PENSION SYSTEMS AND ENDOGENOUS GROWTH[1]

ABSTRACT

Within the framework of an overlapping generations model with two-sided altruism and endogenous growth, this chapter calculates the rates of fertility, output growth, child-rearing costs, savings, consumption, net intertemporal transfers, bequests and gifts, and compares the equilibrium solutions under different public pension systems. It proves that the fully-fertility-linked public pension system (FFLPPS) is equivalent to the system without public pension (WPPS), and the partly-fertility-linked public pension system (PFLPPS) is equivalent to the conventional public pension system (CPPS). The CPPS is beneficial to developing countries in promoting economic growth and reducing population size. It is necessary for developed countries to weigh gains and losses carefully if they hope to transform their CPPS (or PFLPPS) to the FFLPPS.

Keywords: fertility linked pension; two-sided altruism; endogenous growth

1. INTRODUCTION

Some developing countries are suffering from low economic growth and over-population, while developed countries are suffering from low fertility and population aging. It is argued that there is an interrelation between the population problem and public pension system, and economic growth is also impacted by public pension system.

Nishimura and Zhang (1995) used an exogenous model to compare a system without public pension, a totally fertility-dependent public pension system, and a conventional or partly fertility-dependent public pension system. Adopting the conclusion of Nishimura and Zhang (1992), the optimal allocation with public pension is not sustainable when fertility is endogenous, Nishimura and Zhang (1995) assumed that individuals take the public pension level set by the government as given to maximize their utility. Assuming that altruism runs from children to parents, Nishimura and Zhang calculated fertility, gifts, savings, working-

---

[1] This chapter is revised from the paper, Pay-As-You-Go Public Pension Systems: Two-Sided Altruism and Endogenous Growth, published in Asia-Pacific Journal of Risk and Insurance, 2005. Vol. 1 (1): 33 - 44.

period consumption and utility. One of the results, introduction of the totally fertility-dependent public pension system[2] reduces fertility rate, seems doubtful intuitively. It is also theoretically contradictory to the result of Groezen et al. (2003).

Zhang and Zhang (1995) extended the model of Nishimura and Zhang (1995), and used an endogenous growth model to compare a system without public pension, a fully fertility-related public pension system, and a conventional public pension system. Assuming that altruism runs from children to parents, Zhang and Zhang examined the effects of different public pension systems on the rates of fertility and output growth.

This chapter uses an endogenous growth model to compare a system without public pension (WPPS), a conventional public pension system (CPPS), a fully-fertility-linked public pension system (FFLPPS) and a partly-fertility-linked public pension system (PFLPPS) by extending the models of Nishimura and Zhang (1995) and Zhang and Zhang (1995). Assuming that altruism is two-sided, i.e., children give gifts to their parents and parents leave bequests to their children, we calculate not only the rates of fertility, gifts, savings, consumption, but also the rates of output growth, bequests, net intertemporal transfers and child-rearing costs.

Bequests are sizeable wealth in real life. Kotlikoff and Summers (1981) reported that 80% of U.S. household wealth is inherited wealth. Abel and Warshawsky (1988) and Zhang and Zhang (2001) classified bequest motives into altruistic, exchange, joy-of-giving and accidental motives. In fact, it is hard for most people to distinguish bequest motives clearly when they leave bequests to their children. Abel and Warshawsky (1988) analyzed a joy-of-giving bequest motive in which the utility obtained from leaving bequests depends only on the size of the bequests, and exploited the fact that this formulation can be interpreted as a reduced form of altruistic motive for most purposes. Zhang and Zhang (2001) proved that altruistic and exchange motives yield equivalent outcomes if discount factors are set the same. Analogous to Sheshinski and Weiss (1981), this chapter takes bequests as a determinant of individual's utility function. Following Saint-Paul (1992), Zhang and Zhang (1995, 1998, 2001), Wigger (1999a, 1999b) and so on, this chapter adopts an endogenous growth model with Romer's (1986) type of capital externality. It is tractable to compare the balanced growth equilibrium solutions of the WPPS, CPPS, FFLPPS and PFLPPS.

Within the framework of an OLG model with two-sided altruism and endogenous growth, this chapter obtains some interesting results that have not appeared in the literature. It proves that the rates of fertility, output growth, child-rearing costs, savings, consumption, net intertemporal transfers, bequests and gifts under the FFLPPS are the same as that under the WPPS. The rates of fertility, output growth, child-rearing costs, savings, consumption, net intertemporal transfers, bequests and gifts under the PFLPPS are the same as that under the CPPS. The FFLPPS is equivalent to the WPPS, and the PFLPPS is equivalent to the CPPS. The rates of fertility and child-rearing costs under the CPPS (or PFLPPS) are smaller than that under the FFLPPS (or WPPS). The rates of output growth, consumption, net intertemporal transfers, bequests and gifts under the CPPS (or PFLPPS) are greater than that under the FFLPPS (or WPPS).

---

[2] The pension benefits are strictly linear increasing with individual's children number. See Nishimura and Zhang (1995) for details.

2. THE BASIC MODEL: SYSTEM WITHOUT PUBLIC PENSION (WPPS)

2.1. Individuals

Individuals live for two periods. The generation born at the beginning of period t is called generation t. Let L_t denote the population size of generation t. Each individual earns wage by supplying inelastically one unit of labor, receives bequests from his/her parent, consumes part of the income, rears his/her children, gives his/her parent gifts, and saves the remainder of income in his/her working period or first period. In the retirement period or second period, he/she distributes his/her savings with accrued interest and gifts from his/her children into his/her own consumption and bequests to the children.

Each individual derives utility from his/her working-period consumption C_t^t, retirement-period consumption C_{t+1}^t, bequests left to each of his/her children B_{t+1} and the retirement-period consumption of his/her parent C_t^{t-1}. Each individual maximizes his/her utility by choosing the saving rate, gift rate and fertility rate in working-period and the bequest rate in retirement period:

$$Max_{\{s_t,g_t,n_t,b_{t+1}\}} U(C_t^t, C_{t+1}^t, C_t^{t-1}, B_{t+1}) = \alpha \ln C_t^t + \beta \ln C_{t+1}^t + \gamma \ln C_t^{t-1} + \sigma \ln B_{t+1}, \qquad (1)$$

s.t.
$$C_t^t = W_t + b_t W_t - (s_t + g_t + h_t)W_t, \qquad (2)$$

$$C_{t+1}^t + (1+n_t)b_{t+1}W_{t+1} = (1+r_{t+1})s_t W_t + (1+n_t)g_{t+1}W_{t+1}, \qquad (3)$$

where W_t denotes the wage, s_t the saving rate, g_t the gift rate, and r_{t+1} the interest rate.

$$B_{t+1} = b_{t+1}W_{t+1}, \qquad (4)$$

where b_{t+1} denotes the ratio of bequests to wage per worker[3], which is called the bequest rate for simplicity. The child-rearing cost rate is assumed to be

$$h_t = q(1+n_t)^d, \qquad (5)$$

where n_t is the fertility rate, $q > 0$ and $d \geq 1$ such that the costs of rearing children are either linear or convex. Let $C_t^t = c_{1t}W_t$, where c_{1t} denotes the rate of working-period consumption. Assume that $s_t, g_t, n_t, b_{t+1} > 0$ for all t throughout this chapter to focus on interior solution.

---

[3] Following Veall (1986) and Nishimura and Zhang (1995), this chapter only considers Nash equilibrium. That is, each individual takes the decisions of future generations as given.

The weights in the utility function are assumed as such that $\alpha > \beta > \gamma > \sigma > 0$, $\alpha + \beta + \gamma + \sigma = 1$.

2.2. Firms

Firms produce a single commodity in competitive markets. The production function $Y_t = F(K_t, A_t L_t) = A_t L_t \cdot f(k_t)$ is homogeneous of degree one, where Y_t denotes the output in period t, K_t the capital stock, A_t the labor productivity, $k_t = K_t/(A_t L_t)$ the capital per unit of effective labor. By virtue of Euler's theorem, one can get

$$r_t = f'(k_t), \tag{6}$$

$$w_t = W_t / A_t = f(k_t) - k_t f'(k_t), \tag{7}$$

where w_t is the wage rate per unit of effective labor. In order to ensure existence of a balanced growth path for the economy, the following particular form of A_t is adopted (see, e.g., Saint-Paul, 1992; Zhang and Zhang, 1995, 1998; Wigger, 1999a, 1999b; etc.):

$$A_t = K_t / (a L_t), \tag{8}$$

where a is a positive technological parameter.

Therefore $k_t = a$, and

$$r_t = f'(a) = r, \; w_t = f(a) - a f'(a) = w \text{ for all } t. \tag{9}$$

2.3. The Goods Market

The goods market equilibrium requires that the demand for goods in each period be equal to the supply.

$$K_{t+1} = s_t W_t L_t. \tag{10}$$

2.4. The Equilibrium Solutions

Combining equations (7), (8), (9), (10) and the work force $L_{t+1} = (1 + n_t) L_t$ yields the growth rate of capital per worker:

$$1+\theta_t = (K_{t+1}/L_{t+1})/(K_t/L_t) = s_t w/[a(1+n_t)]. \tag{11}$$

Substituting equation (8) into the production function and using $k_t = a$ gives that the growth rate of output per worker is equal to the growth rate of capital per worker. From equations (7) and (9), one can get the growth rate of wage:

$$W_{t+1}/W_t = 1+\theta_t \tag{12}$$

A balanced growth equilibrium is a competitive equilibrium in which the saving rate, gift rate, fertility rate, etc., are constant, but the wage, working-period consumption C_t^t, retirement-period consumption C_{t+1}^t, etc., grow at the same endogenously determined and constant growth rate of capital per worker.

Lagging equation (3) and substituting equations (2) - (5) into equation (1), and letting the partial derivatives of equation (1) with respect to s_t, g_t, n_t, b_{t+1} be zero gives the first-order conditions for the maximization problem of equations (1) - (3):

$$\alpha/C_t^t = (1+r)\beta/C_{t+1}^t, \tag{13}$$

$$\alpha/C_t^t = (1+n_{t-1})\gamma/C_t^{t-1}, \tag{14}$$

$$(dh_t W_t/(1+n_t))(\alpha/C_t^t) = (g_{t+1} - b_{t+1})W_{t+1}\beta/C_{t+1}^t, \tag{15}$$

$$(1+n_t)\beta/C_{t+1}^t = \sigma/B_{t+1}. \tag{16}$$

Equation (13) means the tradeoff between the marginal utility of working-period consumption and that of retirement-period consumption through savings. Equation (14) means the tradeoff between the marginal utility derived from working-period consumption and that from his parent's retirement-period consumption through gifts. Equation (15) means the tradeoff between the marginal utility derived from child-rearing costs and that from net transfers from children to parent. Equation (16) means the tradeoff between the marginal utility derived from retirement-period consumption and that from bequests left to children.

Equating equations (13) and (14), inserting equation (3) and using equation (12) yields

$$(1+\bar{n})(1+\bar{\theta}) = (1+r)\beta/\gamma. \tag{17}$$

Dividing equation (15) by equation (13) yields

$$\bar{\tau} = d\bar{h}\gamma/\beta, \tag{18}$$

where $\bar{\tau} = \bar{g} - \bar{b}$ is the rate of net intertemporal transfers in equilibrium.

Substituting equation (17) into equation (11) yields

$$\bar{s} = \beta e / \gamma, \tag{19}$$

where $e = a(1+r)/w$.

Substituting equations (2) and (3) into equation (13) yields

$$\bar{h} = [1 - e(\alpha + \beta)/\gamma]/[1 + d(\alpha + \gamma)/\beta]. \tag{20}$$

Substituting equations (18), (19) and (20) into equation (2) yields

$$\bar{c}_1 = 1 - \beta e / \gamma - (1 + d\gamma / \beta)\bar{h}. \tag{21}$$

Substituting equation (3) into equation (16), and using equation (12) yields

$$\bar{b} = \sigma(e + d\bar{h}\gamma / \beta)/\beta, \tag{22}$$

$$\bar{g} = d\bar{h}\gamma / \beta + \bar{b}. \tag{23}$$

3. STATIONARY OPTIMAL ALLOCATION

The government maximizes the balanced growth welfare[4] by choosing the stationary optimal rates of savings, gifts, fertility and bequests, and sets a rational pension level according to the optimal rate of net intertemporal transfers. Therefore the government solves the following maximization problem:

$$Max_{\{s,g,n,b\}} U_t = \alpha \ln C_t^t + \beta \ln C_{t+1}^t + \gamma \ln C_t^{t-1} + \sigma \ln(bW_{t+1}), \tag{24}$$

s.t.
$$C_t^t = (1 + b - s - g - h)W_t, \tag{25}$$

$$C_{t+1}^t = (1+r)sW_t + (1+n)(g-b)W_{t+1}. \tag{26}$$

Manipulation analogous to section 2 gives the optimal solutions:

$$(1 + n_p)(1 + \theta_p) = 1 + r, \tag{27}$$

---

[4] This utility function can be considered as a social welfare function. See Nishimura and Zhang (1995, fn.10) and Zhang and Zhang (1995, p.444) for details.

$$\tau_p = dh_p,\tag{28}$$

$$s_p = e,\tag{29}$$

$$h_p = [1 - e(\alpha + \beta + \gamma)/(\beta + \gamma)]/[1 + d(\alpha + \beta + \gamma)/(\beta + \gamma)],\tag{30}$$

$$c_p = 1 - e - (1+d)h_p.\tag{31}$$

Therefore the government sets the PAYG public pension tax rate as τ_p.

4. CONVENTIONAL PUBLIC PENSION SYSTEM (CPPS)

Under the pay-as-you-go (PAYG) public pension system, the government levies pension tax $\tau_p W_t$ from each worker in period t, and pays pension benefits to each retiree in the same period.

The pension benefits are related to the average social fertility rate under the CPPS. Taking the public pension level as given, each individual may give extra gifts to his parent, leave extra bequests to his children and choose the other variables deviating from the optimal allocation. Each individual maximizes his utility by choosing the rates of savings, gifts, fertility and bequests. Thus each individual solves the following maximization problem: max (1) subject to

$$C_t^t = W_t + b_t W_t - [s_t + \tau_p + g_t + h_t]W_t,\tag{32}$$

$$C_{t+1}^t + (1+n_t)b_{t+1}W_{t+1} = (1+r_{t+1})s_t W_t + (1+n_{at})\tau_p W_{t+1} + (1+n_t)g_{t+1}W_{t+1},\tag{33}$$

where n_{at} is the average social fertility rate, and is equal to n_t in equilibrium.

Manipulation analogous to section 2 gives the equilibrium solutions,

$$(1+\tilde{n})(1+\tilde{\theta}) = (1+r)\beta/\gamma,\tag{34}$$

$$\tilde{s} = \beta e/\gamma,\tag{35}$$

$$\tilde{h} = [1 - e(\alpha + \beta)/\gamma - dh_p(\alpha + \gamma)/\gamma]/[1 + d(\alpha + \gamma)/\beta],\tag{36}$$

$$\tilde{c}_1 = 1 - \beta e/\gamma - dh_p - (1 + d\gamma/\beta)\tilde{h},\tag{37}$$

$$\tilde{\tau} = d\tilde{h}\gamma/\beta,\tag{38}$$

$$\tilde{b} = \sigma[e + dh_p + d\tilde{h}\gamma/\beta)]/\beta, \qquad (39)$$

$$\tilde{g} = d\tilde{h}\gamma/\beta + \tilde{b}, \qquad (40)$$

where $\tilde{\tau}$ is the rate of net intertemporal transfers excess of τ_p, or the rate of net intertemporal transfers outside the CPPS. The total rate of net intertemporal transfers in the equilibrium of the CPPS is $\tau_p + \tilde{\tau}$. And $\tau_p + \tilde{g}$ is equivalent to the total gift rate in the equilibrium of the CPPS.

5. FULLY-FERTILITY-LINKED PUBLIC PENSION SYSTEM (FFLPPS)

The public pension benefits are completely dependent on individual fertility rate under the FFLPPS. Taking the public pension level as given, each individual additionally gives his parent gifts during his working-period and leaves bequests to his children during the retirement period. The net intertemporal transfers outside the FFLPPS depend on the following computation instead of discussions such as Nishimura and Zhang (1995) and Zhang and Zhang (1995). Each individual maximizes his utility by choosing the rates of savings, gifts, fertility and bequests, hence solves the following maximization problem: max (1) subject to

$$C_t^t = W_t + b_t W_t - [s_t + \tau_p + g_t + h_t]W_t, \qquad (41)$$

$$C_{t+1}^t + (1+n_t)b_{t+1}W_{t+1} = (1+r_{t+1})s_t W_t + (1+n_t)\tau_p W_{t+1} + (1+n_t)g_{t+1}W_{t+1}. \qquad (42)$$

The equilibrium solutions are

$$(1+\hat{n})(1+\hat{\theta}) = (1+r)\beta/\gamma, \qquad (43)$$

$$\hat{s} = \beta e/\gamma, \qquad (44)$$

$$\hat{h} = [1 - e(\alpha + \beta)/\gamma]/[1 + d(\alpha + \gamma)/\beta], \qquad (45)$$

$$\hat{c}_1 = 1 - \beta e/\gamma - (1 + d\gamma/\beta)\hat{h}, \qquad (46)$$

$$\hat{\tau} = d(\hat{h}\gamma/\beta - h_p), \qquad (47)$$

$$\hat{b} = \sigma(e + d\hat{h}\gamma/\beta)/\beta, \qquad (48)$$

$$\hat{g} = d(\hat{h}\gamma/\beta - h_p) + \hat{b}, \tag{49}$$

where $\hat{\tau}$ is the rate of net intertemporal transfers excess of τ_p, or the rate of net intertemporal transfers outside the FFLPPS. The total rate of net intertemporal transfers in the equilibrium of the FFLPPS is $\tau_p + \hat{\tau}$, which is equivalent to the total gift rate in the equilibrium of the FFLPPS.

6. PARTLY-FERTILITY-LINKED PUBLIC PENSION SYSTEM (PFLPPS)

Under the PFLPPS, the pension benefits include two parts: one is related to the average social fertility rate; another one is dependent on the individual fertility rate. Taking the public pension level as given, each individual additionally gives his parent gifts and leaves bequests to his children. The net intertemporal transfers outside the PFLPPS depend on the following computation instead of discussions such as Nishimura and Zhang (1995) and Zhang and Zhang (1995). Each individual maximizes his utility by choosing the rates of savings, gifts, fertility and bequests, hence solves the following maximization problem: max (1) subject to

$$C_t^l = W_t + b_t W_t - [s_t + \tau_p + \tilde{\tau} + g_t + h_t]W_t, \tag{50}$$

$$C_{t+1}^l + (1+n_t)b_{t+1}W_{t+1} = (1+r_{t+1})s_t W_t + (1+n_{at})\tau_p W_{t+1} + (1+n_t)\tilde{\tau}W_{t+1} + (1+n_t)g_{t+1}W_{t+1}. \tag{51}$$

The equilibrium solutions are

$$(1+n)(1+\theta) = (1+r)\beta/\gamma, \tag{52}$$

$$s = \beta e/\gamma, \tag{53}$$

$$h = [1 - e(\alpha+\beta)/\gamma - dh_p(\alpha+\gamma)/\gamma]/[1 + d(\alpha+\gamma)/\beta], \tag{54}$$

$$c_1 = 1 - \beta e/\gamma - dh_p - (1 + d\gamma/\beta)h, \tag{55}$$

$$\tau = d\gamma(h - \tilde{h})/\beta, \tag{56}$$

$$b = \sigma(e + dh_p + dh\gamma/\beta)/\beta, \tag{57}$$

$$g = d\gamma(h - \tilde{h})/\beta + b, \tag{58}$$

where τ is the rate of net intertemporal transfers excess of $\tau_p + \tilde{\tau}$, or the rate of net intertemporal transfers outside the PFLPPS. The total rate of net intertemporal transfers in the equilibrium of the PFLPPS is $\tau_p + \tilde{\tau} + \tau$, which is equivalent to the total gift rate in the equilibrium of the PFLPPS.

7. COMPARISON OF DIFFERENT EQUILIBRIUMS

Comparing the above equilibrium solutions gives

$$\bar{n} = \hat{n} > \tilde{n} = n, \tag{59}$$

$$\bar{\theta} = \hat{\theta} < \tilde{\theta} = \theta, \tag{60}$$

$$\bar{h} = \hat{h} > \tilde{h} = h, \tag{61}$$

$$\bar{s} = \tilde{s} = \hat{s} = s, \tag{62}$$

$$\bar{c}_1 = \hat{c}_1 < \tilde{c}_1 = c_1, \tag{63}$$

$$\bar{\tau} = \tau_p + \hat{\tau} < \tau_p + \tilde{\tau} = \tau_p + \tilde{\tau} + \tau, \tag{64}$$

$$\bar{b} = \hat{b} < \tilde{b} = b, \tag{65}$$

$$\bar{g} = \tau_p + \hat{g} < \tau_p + \tilde{g} = \tau_p + \tilde{\tau} + g, \tag{66}$$

$$\tau = 0, \tag{67}$$

$$\hat{\tau} < 0, \tag{68}$$

$$\bar{\tau} > \tilde{\tau} > \tau > \hat{\tau}, \tag{69}$$

$$\bar{g} > \tilde{g} > g > \hat{g}, \tag{70}$$

$$\tau_p > \bar{\tau}, \; s_p < \hat{s}, \tag{71}$$

$$h_p > \hat{h}, \; n_p > \hat{n}, \; \theta_p < \hat{\theta}, \text{ if } \beta \leq \sqrt{\alpha\gamma + \gamma^2} \tag{72}$$

$$c_p < \hat{c}_1, \text{ if } \alpha > (1-\beta^2)/\beta \tag{73}$$

In the above maximization problems, the first-order condition $\alpha/C_t^t = (1+r)\beta/C_{t+1}^t$ holds for the WPPS, CPPS, FFLPPS and PFLPPS. If $c_{2t} = C_{t+1}^t/W_t$ is defined as the rate of retirement-period consumption, and $c_t = (C_t^t + C_{t+1}^t)/W_t$ as the lifetime consumption rate, then $c_{2t} = c_{1t}(1+r)\beta/\alpha$ and $c_t = c_{1t}[1+(1+r)\beta/\alpha]$ holds for the four systems. Thus the behavior of working-period consumption rate can represent that of the retirement-period consumption rate and that of the lifetime consumption rate in the four systems. Of course, this result holds in equilibrium.

Equations (59) - (66) give the following result.

Result 1. The rates of fertility, output growth, child-rearing costs, savings, consumption, net intertemporal transfers, bequests and gifts under the FFLPPS are the same as that under the WPPS. The rates of fertility, output growth, child-rearing costs, savings, consumption, net intertemporal transfers, bequests and gifts under the PFLPPS are the same as that under the CPPS.

This result means that the fully-fertility-linked public pension system is equivalent to the system without public pension, and the partly-fertility-linked public pension system is equivalent to the conventional public pension system.

Equations (59) and (61) yield the following result.

Result 2. The rates of fertility and child-rearing costs under the CPPS (or PFLPPS) are smaller than that under the FFLPPS (or WPPS).

Some developed countries are suffering from low fertility. It seems that the FFLPPS may be useful to the developed countries. Zhang and Zhang (1995) had made such a suggestion. However, it is necessary for this chapter to explore further.

Equations (60), (63), (64), (65) and (66) give the following result.

Result 3. The rates of output growth, consumption, net intertemporal transfers, bequests and gifts under the CPPS (or PFLPPS) are greater than that under the FFLPPS (or WPPS).

Equations (69), (67) and (68) give the following result.

Result 4. The rate of net intertemporal transfers under the WPPS is larger than the rate of net intertemporal transfers outside the CPPS, both of them are positive. However, the rate of net intertemporal transfers outside the PFLPPS is zero, and the rate of net intertemporal transfers outside the FFLPPS is negative.

Equation (67) means that the gifts outside the PFLPPS are exactly equal to the bequests outside the PFLPPS. Equation (68) implies that the gifts outside the FFLPPS are less than the bequests outside the FFLPPS.

Equation (70) gives the following result.

Result 5. The gift rate under the WPPS is the largest. The gift rate outside the public pension system under the CPPS is larger than that under the PFLPPS, which in turn is larger than that under the FFLPPS.

Equations (71), (72) and (73) give the following result.

Result 6. Comparing with the WPPS, CPPS, FFLPPS and PFLPPS, the optimal allocation has the highest rate of net intertemporal transfers and the lowest saving rate; the highest rates of child-rearing costs and fertility and the lowest rate of output growth if $\beta \leq \sqrt{\alpha\gamma + \gamma^2}$; the lowest rate of working-period consumption if $\alpha > (1-\beta^2)/\beta$.

Some results of this chapter are different from Nishimura and Zhang (1995) because their model is an exogenous model with one-sided altruism. Among the limited comparable results, the main differences are as follows:

Difference 1. In Nishimura and Zhang (1995), the fertility rate under WPPS is equal to that under CPPS, which is larger than that under FFLPPS. However, in this chapter, the fertility rate under FFLPPS (or WPPS) is larger than that under CPPS.

Difference 2. In Nishimura and Zhang (1995), the rate of net intertemporal transfers under FFLPPS is larger than that under CPPS and that under WPPS. However, in this chapter, the rate of net intertemporal transfers under FFLPPS (or WPPS) is smaller than that under CPPS (or PFLPPS).

Difference 3. In Nishimura and Zhang (1995), the saving rate under FFLPPS is larger than that under WPPS, which in turn is larger than that under CPPS. However, in this chapter, they are identical.

Difference 4. In Nishimura and Zhang (1995), the working-period consumption rate under FFLPPS is larger than that under WPPS. However, in this chapter, they are equal to each other.

Some results in this chapter are also different from Zhang and Zhang (1995) because the altruism is one-sided and the PFLPPS is not considered in their model. Among the limited comparable results, the main differences are as follows:

Difference 1. In Zhang and Zhang (1995), the fertility rate under WPPS is higher than that under FFLPPS if $\gamma < \beta \leq \sqrt{\alpha\gamma + \gamma^2}$. However, in this chapter, they are the same.

Difference 2. In Zhang and Zhang (1995), the growth rate under FFLPPS is higher than that under WPPS if $\beta > \gamma$. However, they are the same in this chapter.

Difference 3. In Zhang and Zhang (1995), the optimal allocation has a higher growth rate than WPPS if $\beta > \gamma$. However, in this chapter, it is just the contrary if $\beta \leq \sqrt{\alpha\gamma + \gamma^2}$.

CONCLUSION

Under the OLG model with two-sided altruism and endogenous growth, this chapter compares the equilibrium solutions of the system without public pension (WPPS), conventional public pension system (CPPS), fully-fertility-linked public pension system

(FFLPPS) and partly-fertility-linked public pension system (PFLPPS). It proves that the fully-fertility-linked public pension system is equivalent to the system without public pension, and the partly-fertility-linked public pension system is equivalent to the conventional public pension system. This is an interesting finding that has not been revealed in the literature.

This chapter shows that the rates of fertility and child-rearing costs under the CPPS (or PFLPPS) are smaller than that under the FFLPPS (or WPPS). Zhang and Zhang (1995) also obtained that the fertility rate under CPPS is lower than that under WPPS. The result, the fertility rate under CPPS is lower than that under FFLPPS, is different from that of Nishimura and Zhang (1995). The rates of output growth, consumption, net intertemporal transfers, bequests and gifts under the CPPS (or PFLPPS) are greater than that under the FFLPPS (or WPPS). Some comparison results concerning these rates are different from those in Nishimura and Zhang (1995) and Zhang and Zhang (1995). The differences have been shown in the last section.

The above main results have valuable policy implications. The CPPS has a relative advantage to the PFLPPS based on the equivalence of the two systems. The compulsory public pension tax rate under the CPPS is lower than that under the PFLPPS. Therefore the CPPS is easier to carry out than the PFLPPS, especially for developing countries. The FFLPPS has a relative advantage to the WPPS based on the equivalence of the two systems. One of the basic functions of a public pension system is to prevent individual myopia. The FFLPPS has the function, while the WPPS has not. It is almost impossible for any country that has established a public pension system to abolish it.

It is better for developing countries that have not established public pension systems to introduce the CPPS because it can promote economic growth, restrain population explosion, reduce child-rearing cost rate, and increase consumption rate. Zhang and Zhang (1995) had made the same suggestion based on the rates of fertility and output growth.

It is necessary for developed countries to weigh gains and losses carefully if they hope to transform their CPPS or PFLPPS[5] to the FFLPPS. Although the FFLPPS can increase fertility rate, it may decrease economic growth rate, increase child-rearing cost rate, reduce consumption rate, etc. Hence, it is better for a developed country to transform its CPPS (or PFLPPS) to the FFLPPS if it cares more about the problem of population ageing and low fertility than the others. Otherwise it is suitable to maintain the CPPS (or PFLPPS). This is different from Zhang and Zhang (1995).

---

[5] Nishimura and Zhang (1995, p.187) report that some developed countries have the PFLPPS.

REFERENCES

[1] Abel, A. B. (1987a). "Aggregate savings in the presence of private and social insurance". In R. Dornbusch et al. (eds.), Macroeconomics and Finance: Essays in Honor of Franco Modigliani. Cambridge: MIT Press.
[2] Abel, A. B. (1987b). "Operative gift and bequest motives", *American Economic Review*, 77, 1037-1047.
[3] Abel, A. B. (1989). "Birth, death and taxes", *Journal of Public Economics*, 39, 1-15.
[4] Abel, A. B. & Warshawsky, M. (1988). "Specification of the joy of giving: insights from altruism", *Review of Economics and Statistics*, 70, 145-149.
[5] Altig, D. & Davis, S. J. (1993). "Borrowing constraints and two-sided altruism with an application to social security", *Journal of Economic Dynamics and Control*, 17, 476-494.
[6] Atkinson A. B. & Stiglitz, J. E. (1980). *Lectures on Public Economics*, McGRAW-HILL, England.
[7] Auerbach, A. J. & Kotlikoff, L. J. (1987). Dynamic Fiscal Policy, Cambridge: Cambridge University Press.
[8] Babu, P. G., KaviKumar, K. S. & Murthy, N. S. (1997). "An overlapping generations model with exhaustible resources and stock pollution", *Ecological Economics*, 21, 35-43.
[9] Barro R. J. (1974). "Are government bonds net wealth?" *Journal of Political Economy*, 82, 1095-1117.
[10] Barro, R. J. & Sala-I-Martin, X. (2004). Economic Growth, Cambridge: MIT Press.
[11] Blanchard, O. J. & Fischer, S. (1989). Lectures on Macroeconomics, London: MIT Press.
[12] Chinese State Council. (1991). "State Council Decision on Reform of Pension System for Enterprise Employees" (Chinese State Council Document 33 in 1991). Available at http://www.360doc.com/content/ 10/0623/ 20/1677993_34841625.shtml.
[13] Chinese State Council. (1995). "State Council Circular on Deepening the Reform of Pension System for Enterprise Employees" (Chinese State Council Document 6 in 1995). Available at http://www.chinalawedu. com/falvfagui/fg23051/4429.shtml.
[14] Chinese State Council. (1997). "State Council Decision on Establishing a Unified Basic Pension System for Enterprise Employees" (Chinese State Council Document 26 in 1997). Available at http://trs.molss.gov. cn/was40/detail?record=150&channelid=8457.

[15] Chinese State Council. (2005). "State Council Decision on Improving the Basic Pension System for Enterprise Employees" (Chinese State Council Document 38 in 2005). Available at http://trs.molss.gov.cn/ was40/ detail?record=13&channelid=8457.
[16] Chinese State Council. (2009). "State Council Guidelines on New-Type Rural Public Pension Trials" (Chinese State Council Document 32 in 2009). Available at http://www.gov.cn/gongbao/content/2009/content_ 1417926. htm.
[17] Chinese State Council. (2011). "State Council Guidelines on Developing Public Pension for Non-Employed Urban Residents Trials" (Chinese State Council Document 18 in 2011). Available at http://www.gov.cn/zwgk /2011-06/13/content_1882801.htm#.
[18] Chinese State Council. (2014). "State Council Opinions on Establishing Unified Basic Pension System for Urban and Rural Residents" (Chinese State Council Document 8 in 2014). Available at http://www.gov.cn/ zwgk/2014-02/26/content_2621907.htm.
[19] Chow, G. & Li, K. (2002). "China's economic growth: 1952–2010". *Economic Development and Cultural Change*, 51, 247–256.
[20] Cigno, A. (1993). "Intergenerational Transfers without Altruism, Family, Market and State", *European Journal of Political Economy*, 9, 505-518.
[21] Diamond, P. A. (1965). "National debt in a neoclassical growth model", *American Economic Review*, 55, 1126-1150.
[22] Feldstein, M. (1974). "Social security, induced retirement, and aggregate capital accumulation", *Journal of Political Economy*, 82, 905-926.
[23] Feldstein, M. (1987). "Should Social Security Benefits Be Means Tested?"*Journal of Political Economy*, 95, 468-484.
[24] Feldstein, M. (1990). "Imperfect Annuity Markets, Uninteneded Bequests, and the Optimal Age Structure of Social Security Benefits", *Journal of Public Economics*, 41, 31-43.
[25] Feldstein, M. (1999). "Social security pension reform in China", *China Economic Review*, 10, 99-107.
[26] Feldstein, M. (2003). "Banking, Budgets, and Pensions: Some Priorities for Chinese Policy", Available athttp://www.nber.org/feldstein/ chinaforum5.pdf.
[27] Fuster, L. (2000). "Capital Accumulation in an Economy with Dynasties and Uncertain Lifetimes", *Review of Economic Dynamics*, 3,650-674.
[28] Gao, F. (2013). "The Basic Information of the New-type Rural and Urban resident Public Pension", Urban and Rural Resident Social Public Pension Seminar proceedings: 1-10.
[29] Groezen, B., Leers, T. & Meijdam, L. (2003). "Social security and endogenous fertility: pensions and child allowances as siamese twins", *Journal of Public Economics*, 87, 233-251.
[30] Kaganovich, M. & Zilcha, I. (1999). "Education, social security, and growth", *Journal of Public Economics*, 71, 289-309.
[31] Kan, K. & Wang, Y. (2013). "Comparing China and India: A factor accumulation perspective", *Journal of Comparative Economics*, 41, 879-894.
[32] Kang, C. (2012). "Raising Contribution Rate or Postponing Retirement Age?" *Statistical Research*, 12, 59-68.
[33] Kotlikoff, L. J. & Summers, L. H. (1981). "The Role of Intergenerational Transfers in Aggregate Transfers", *Journal of Political Economy*, 90, 706-732.

[34] National Bureau of Statistics of China, Various years, China Statistical Yearbook, Beijing: China Statistics Press.
[35] National People's Representatives Congress. (2010). "Social Insurance Law". Available at http://www.gov.cn/flfg/2010-10/28/content_ 1732964.htm.
[36] National Population and Family Planning Commission of China. (2007). "Different population policies for different regions, town and countryside and nationalities", IOP Publishing PhysicsWeb. http://www. chinapop.gov.cn/zcfg/zcjd/200707/t20070710_ 50004.html. Accessed 15 March 2010.
[37] Nishimura K. & Zhang, J. (1992). "Pay-as-you-go public pensions with endogenous fertility", *Journal of Public Economics*, *48*, 239-258.
[38] Nishimura, K. & Zhang, J. (1995). "Sustainable Plans of Social Security with Endogenous Fertility", *Oxford Economic Papers*, *47*, 182-194.
[39] Pecchenino, R. & Pollard, P. (1997). "The effects of annuities, bequests, and aging in an overlapping generations model of endogenous growth", *The Economic Journal, 107*, 26-46.
[40] Pecchenino, R. & Utendorf, K. (1999). "Social security, social welfare and the aging population", *Journal of Population Economics, 12*, 607-623.
[41] Pecchenino, R. & Pollard, P. (2002). "Dependent children and aged parents: funding education and social security in an aging economy", *Journal of Macroeconomics, 24*, 145-169.
[42] Raut, L. K. (1992). "Capital Accumulation, Income Distribution and Endogenous Fertility in an Overlapping Generations Equilibrium Model", *Journal of Development Economics, 34*, 123-150.
[43] Reilly, T. (2014). Pensions: Policies, New Reforms and Current Challenges, Washington: Nova Science Publishers.
[44] Romer, P. M. (1986). "Increasing Return and Long-run Output Growth", *Journal of Political Economy, 94*, 1002-1037.
[45] Saint-Paul, G. (1992). "Fiscal Policy in an Endogenous Output Growth Model", *Quarterly Journal of Economics, 106*, 1243-1259.
[46] Samuelson, P. A. (1955). Foundations of Economic Analysis, Cambridge: Harvard University Press.
[47] Samuelson, P. A. (1958). "An exact consumption-loan model of interest with or without the social contrivance of money", *Journal of Political Economy, 66*, 467-482.
[48] Samuelson, P. A. (1975). "Optimum social security in a life-cycle growth model", *International Economic Review, 16*, 539-544.
[49] Sheshinski, E. & Weiss, Y. (1981). "Uncertainty and optimal social security systems", *Quarterly Journal of Economics, 96*, 189-206.
[50] UN Secretariat. (2007). "World Population Prospects: the 2006 Revision". IOP Publishing PhysicsWeb. http://earthtrends.wri.org/text/ population-health/variable-379.html. Accessed 26 March 2010.
[51] Veall, M. R. (1986). "Public Pensions as Optimal Social Contracts", *Journal of Public Economics, 31*, 237-251.
[52] Wang, Y., Xu, D. Wang, Z. & Zhai, F. (2001). "The Implicit Debt, Transition Cost, Reform Forms and the Influence of China's Pension System", *Economic Research Journal*, (5), 3-12.

[53] Wigger, B. U. (1999a). "Pay-as-you-go public pensions in a model of endogenous output growth and fertility", *Journal of Population Economics*, *12*, 625-640.
[54] Wigger, B. U. (1999b). "Public Pensions and Output Growth", *Finanzarchiv*, *56*, S: 241-263.
[55] Yang, Z. (2007). "Partially funded pension, fertility and endogenous growth", *Insurance and Risk Management*, *75*, 1-12.
[56] Yang, Z. (2009a). "Urban public pension, replacement rates and population growth rate in China", *Insurance: Mathematics and Economics*, *45* (2), 230–235.
[57] Yang, Z. (2009b). "Urban public pension, fertility and endogenous growth in China", *Statistical Research*, *26* (5), 77-81.
[58] Yang, Z. (2011a). "A Theoretical and Empirical Study on the Optimal Replacement Rate of Urban Public Pension under Uncertain Lifetime", *Management Review*, *23* (2), 28-32.
[59] Yang, Z. (2011b). "New-style rural old-age insurance and peasant income growth". Peking University China Center for Insurance and Social Security Research Forum 2011 Annual Conference. In: The Twelfth Five-year Plan · New Challenge: Comprehensive Risk Management for Economy and Society. CCISSR eds., Peking University Press: 356-369.
[60] Yang, Z. (2012). "Urban Public Pension and Economic Growth in China", *Asia-Pacific Journal of Risk and Insurance*, 2012, Vol. 6, Iss. 2, Article 4.
[61] Yew, S. L. & Zhang, J. (2009). "Optimal social security in a dynastic model with human capital externalities, fertility and endogenous growth", *Journal of Public Economics*, *93*, 605-619.
[62] Zhang, J. (1995). Social security and endogenous growth. *Journal of Public Economics*, *58*, 185-213.
[63] Zhang, J. (1995). "Does unfounded social security also depress output growth?" *Economics Letters*, *49*, 307-312.
[64] Zhang, J. (2001). Long-run implications of social security taxation for growth and fertility, *Southern Economic Journal*, *67*, 713-724.
[65] Zhang J. & Nishimura, K. (1993). "The Old-Age Security Hypothesis Revisited", *Journal of Development Economics*, *41*, 191-202.
[66] Zhang, J. & Zhang, J. (1995). The effects of social security on population and output growth, *Southern Economic Journal*, *62*, 440-450.
[67] Zhang, J. & Zhang, J. (1998). "Social security, intergenerational transfers, and endogenous growth", *The Canadian Journal of Economics*, *31*, 1225-1241.
[68] Zhang, J. & Zhang, J. (2001). "Bequest motives, social security, and economic growth", *Economic Inquiry*, *39*, 453-466.
[69] Zhang, J. & Zhang, J. (2003). "Long-run effects of unfunded social security with earnings-dependent benefits", *Journal of Economic Dynamics & Control*, *28*, 617-641.
[70] Zhang, J., Zhang, J. & Lee, R. (2001). "Mortality decline and long-run economic growth", *Journal of Public Economics*, *80*, 485-507.
[71] Zhang, J., Zhang, J. & Lee, R. (2003). "Rising longevity, education, savings and growth", *Journal of Development Economics*, *70*, 83-101.

INDEX

A

actuality, 154, 165
age, 112, 113, 121, 127, 128, 136, 141, 180, 181, 186, 208
aging population, 207
agriculture, 121
altruism, 32, 33, 36, 39, 41, 46, 96, 97, 100, 104, 105, 143, 157, 164, 179, 180, 181, 189, 191, 192, 202, 205
altruistic motive, 31, 32, 41, 95, 96, 105, 106, 127, 128, 192
Asia, viii, 45, 191, 208
assets, 3, 4, 16, 29, 41

B

basic benefit rate, 111, 113, 115, 119, 120, 121, 122, 123, 124, 125, 127, 128, 130, 135, 136, 141, 142, 144, 149, 150, 152, 153, 154, 155, 156, 158, 161, 162, 163, 164, 165
basic pension benefit rate, 111, 113, 124, 127, 128, 136
basic pension system for rural residents, 111, 113, 124, 125, 127, 128, 135, 141, 142
Beijing, iii, ix, xi, 207
bequest ratio, 155, 156, 159, 161, 162, 163, 164, 165, 181, 182, 184
bequests, 21, 31-34, 47, 68, 83, 95, 96, 97, 98, 102, 112, 142, 156, 157, 165, 181, 185, 187, 191, 192, 193, 195, 196, 197, 198, 199, 201, 203, 207

C

caliber, 12, 24, 36, 101
capital accumulation, 96, 112, 124, 125, 136, 169, 171, 206

capital goods, 180, 181
capital income tax, viii, 169, 170, 171, 172, 174, 175, 176, 177
Census, 121
childhood, 24, 47, 58, 69, 142, 156
child-rearing cost, 182, 185, 191, 192, 193, 195, 201, 202, 203
Chinese government, 5, 20, 46, 48, 68, 81, 180
Chinese special population policy, viii, 3, 4, 16, 31, 32, 42, 92, 95, 96, 125
closed economy, 5, 20, 33, 47, 58, 69, 82, 97, 114, 128, 142, 156, 181
college students, 32, 82
commodity, 6, 22, 34, 49, 59, 70, 84, 98, 115, 130, 144, 158, 172, 182, 194
competitive markets, 6, 22, 34, 49, 59, 70, 84, 98, 115, 130, 144, 158, 172, 182, 194
computation, 198, 199
Congress, 207
consulting, 128
consumption ratio, 141, 142, 145, 147, 148, 149, 150, 151, 152, 154, 155, 156, 159, 161, 162, 163, 164, 165
conventional public pension system, 191, 192, 201, 202
correlation, 185
cost, 52, 53, 147, 182, 185, 193, 203
culture, 180, 182, 189

D

degradation, 62, 73
derivatives, 17, 24, 27, 34, 36, 39, 40, 48, 50, 59, 70, 97, 119, 129, 135, 143, 145, 157, 159, 182, 195
developed countries, viii, ix, 12, 24, 113, 121, 191, 201, 203
developing country(s), 45, 46, 58, 66, 78, 96, 128, 180, 186, 189, 191, 203

diminishing returns, 46
disclosure, 87
distribution, 6, 22, 34, 49, 60, 84, 98, 144, 172, 175, 183
domestic demand, 112, 124, 127, 136
dynamic system, 7, 23, 35, 42, 85, 86, 106, 116, 117, 131, 135

E

earnings, 68, 180, 208
economic development, 112
economic growth, viii, 3, 4, 19, 20, 29, 46, 55, 57, 58, 62, 63, 64, 65, 66, 68, 78, 82, 96, 105, 112, 113, 124, 128, 136, 141, 142, 154, 155, 165, 179, 180, 181, 186, 188, 189, 191, 203, 206, 208
economic growth rate, 3, 4, 19, 20, 55, 57, 58, 62, 63, 64, 65, 66, 68, 78, 96, 105, 112, 124, 165, 186, 188, 189, 203
education expense rate, 45, 47, 50, 52, 53, 54, 55, 56
education expense ratio, 46, 57, 58, 62, 63, 64, 65, 66, 67, 68, 69, 73, 74, 75, 76, 77, 78, 141, 142, 145, 147, 148, 149, 150, 151, 152, 154, 155, 156, 159, 161, 162, 163, 164, 165
employees, viii, 3, 12, 15, 19, 20, 24, 28, 31, 32, 41, 45, 47, 55, 57, 65, 67, 68, 77, 81, 82, 87, 91, 95, 96, 105, 113, 142, 170, 179, 180, 189
employers, 180
employment, 112
endogenous fertility, 67, 69, 206, 207
endogenous growth model, viii, 43, 45, 46, 47, 57, 67, 68, 113, 139, 141, 142, 155, 156, 180, 181, 192
endogenous variable, 12, 16, 24, 25, 31, 36, 37, 38, 54, 55, 58, 65, 67, 68, 69, 75, 76, 77, 78, 86, 88, 91, 92, 100, 101, 121, 124, 135, 150, 152, 153, 154, 161, 162, 164
England, 205
equality, 177
Exogenous fertility, 57
exogenous model, 1, 79, 109, 191, 202
exogenous variable, viii, 12, 16, 23, 24, 31, 35, 36, 57, 58, 62, 64, 65, 67, 85, 86, 88, 92, 100, 121, 123, 124, 152, 162, 164, 165
externalities, 47, 68, 156, 208

F

families, 32, 46, 48, 67, 95, 127, 128, 136
family income, 46, 47, 58, 66, 68, 78
family members, 31
family planning, 57, 67

family planning policy, 57, 67
fertility, viii, 46, 57, 67, 68, 69, 77, 113, 142, 156, 180, 191, 192, 193, 195, 196, 197, 198, 199, 201, 202, 203, 206, 207, 208
fertility rate, 192, 193, 195, 197, 198, 199, 202, 203
financial, 4, 16, 19, 20, 29, 31, 32, 42, 68, 82, 92, 112, 124, 128, 136
financial crisis, 4, 16, 19, 20, 29, 31, 32, 42, 68, 82, 92, 112, 124, 128, 136
firm contribution rate, 3, 4, 9, 10, 12, 13, 14, 15, 16, 19, 24, 25, 26, 27, 28, 29, 31, 36, 37, 38, 39, 40, 41, 42, 45, 47, 52, 53, 54, 55, 57, 58, 62, 64, 65, 66, 67, 68, 74, 75, 76, 77, 78, 113
fiscal expenditure, 111, 125, 127, 136
fitness, 38
force, 47, 58, 69, 114, 117, 121, 128, 142, 156, 171, 184, 194
fully-fertility-linked public pension system, 191, 192, 201, 202
funding, 207

G

GDP per capita, 58, 66, 78
gift motive, viii, 127, 128, 135, 155
gift ratio, 46, 113, 141, 142, 155, 156, 159, 161, 162, 163, 164, 165, 181, 182, 184
gifts, 31, 32, 33, 34, 95, 96, 97, 98, 102, 127, 128, 129, 135, 136, 156, 157, 158, 181, 185, 187, 191, 192, 193, 195, 196, 197, 198, 199, 201, 203
governments, 4, 20, 112, 113, 115, 121, 124, 125, 128, 130, 136, 142, 144, 156, 158, 165
gross domestic product (GDP), 20, 45, 46, 58, 66, 78, 82, 96, 128, 165, 180, 186, 189
growth models, 46
growth rate of output per worker, 179, 180, 185, 186, 188, 189, 195
guidance, viii

H

health, 207
hiring, 6, 49
housing, 42
human, viii, 46, 47, 48, 50, 53, 58, 59, 60, 62, 64, 66, 68, 69, 70, 75, 78, 141, 142, 143, 144, 145, 150, 155, 156, 157, 158, 159, 162, 165, 208
human capital, viii, 45, 46, 47, 48, 50, 53, 58, 59, 60, 62, 64, 66, 68, 69, 70, 75, 78, 141, 142, 143, 144, 145, 150, 156, 157, 158, 159, 162, 165, 208
husband, 29, 32, 46, 56, 78, 112, 127, 136, 142

I

image, 15, 16
immigration, 24, 36, 87, 101
income tax, viii, 169, 170, 171, 172, 174, 175, 176, 177
India, 206
indirect effect, 75, 119
individual account benefit replacement rate, 81, 82, 84, 86, 87, 91, 92, 95, 96, 99, 100, 101, 105, 106
individual account benefits, 21, 31, 33, 35, 36, 37, 38, 41, 42, 47, 48, 59, 69, 70, 81, 83, 85, 86, 87, 88, 91, 92, 95, 97, 100, 101, 102, 105, 106, 112, 114, 118, 119, 128, 129, 143, 156, 157, 179, 183
individual account principal, 3, 4, 5, 7, 8, 9, 10, 11, 12, 13, 14, 15, 16, 171, 174, 182, 183
individuals, viii, 5, 19, 20, 31, 32, 33, 46, 47, 57, 58, 65, 67, 69, 83, 97, 112, 113, 114, 128, 136, 142, 156, 165, 169, 171, 180, 181, 189, 191
inflation, 3, 4
injury, 42
international financial crisis, 4, 16, 19, 20, 29, 31, 32, 42, 68, 82, 92, 112, 124, 128, 136
investment, 3, 4, 16, 29, 31, 32, 41, 47, 92, 124, 136, 165
issues, 169

L

labor income growth rate, 141, 147, 148, 149, 150, 151, 152, 154, 155, 156, 161, 162, 163, 164, 165
life expectancy, 19, 20, 24, 25, 26, 27, 28, 29, 31, 32, 35, 36, 37, 40, 41, 81, 82, 86, 87, 88, 89, 90, 91, 92, 95, 96, 100, 101, 102, 104, 105, 106, 113, 155, 156, 162, 164, 165
lifetime, viii, 14, 19, 20, 21, 26, 28, 31, 32, 33, 38, 41, 81, 82, 89, 91, 95, 96, 103, 105, 128, 155, 156, 164, 201
lifetime uncertainty, viii, 19, 20, 28, 31, 32, 33, 41, 81, 96, 155, 156
local government, 111, 112, 113, 115, 116, 119, 122, 123, 124, 125, 127, 128, 130, 131, 135, 136, 141, 142, 144, 145, 149, 150, 151, 152, 153, 154, 155, 156, 158, 159, 161, 162, 163, 164, 165
local government allowance rate, 111, 113, 118, 119, 122, 123, 124, 125, 127, 128, 135, 136, 141, 142, 148, 149, 150, 151, 152, 153, 154, 155, 156, 161, 162, 163, 164, 165
longevity, 19, 102, 156, 180, 208

M

magnitude, 11, 53, 186
manipulation, 7, 23, 42, 93, 106, 116, 131
marginal product, 6, 22, 49, 115, 130
marginal utility, 34, 171, 174, 176, 182, 195
market economy, 27, 38, 39, 41, 60, 71, 82, 90, 91, 96, 103, 105
median, 16
medical, 19, 20, 29, 32, 42, 81, 82, 92, 96, 155, 165
Microsoft, 38, 102
military, 32, 82
Ministry of Education, xi
models, viii, ix, 20, 32, 82, 96, 113, 128, 142, 156, 180, 192
modified golden rule level, 4, 14, 20, 27, 28, 38, 39, 41, 82, 89, 90, 91, 96, 103, 105, 169, 170, 171, 176, 177
mortality, 19, 32, 128, 142, 155
multiplier, 17, 39
myopia, 169, 203

N

Nash equilibrium, 193
negative effects, 29, 141, 165
net intergenerational transfer ratio, 179, 180, 184, 185, 186, 189
net intertemporal transfers, 191, 192, 196, 198, 199, 200, 201, 202, 203
new-type rural public pension, vii, viii, 111
number of children, viii, 47, 57, 58, 65, 67, 72, 113, 142, 143, 147, 150, 156, 165, 179, 180, 181, 182, 184, 185, 186, 189

O

old age, 185
opportunity costs, 74, 75
output per worker, 179, 180, 184, 185, 186, 188, 189, 195
overcapitalized, 169, 170
Overlapping generations model, 3
over-population, 45, 46, 78, 186, 189, 191

P

Pacific, viii, 45, 191, 208
parents, 31, 46, 96, 127, 135, 136, 141, 165, 180, 181, 185, 191, 192, 207
Pareto, 32, 82, 102

partially funded public pension system, 4, 5, 15, 32, 45, 67, 68, 82, 113, 165, 170, 179
participants, vii, 111, 112, 121, 124, 125, 128, 142, 156
partly-fertility-linked public pension system, 191, 192, 201, 203
payroll, 3, 5, 6, 20, 22, 34, 42, 45, 47, 49, 60, 68, 70, 84, 96, 98, 170, 171, 179
per capita consumption, 19, 20, 23, 24, 25, 26, 28, 29, 111, 113, 117, 118, 119, 120, 122, 123, 124
per capita GDP, 45, 46, 96, 128, 180, 186, 189
per capita income, 45, 46, 47, 52, 53, 54, 55, 67, 68, 74, 75, 76, 77, 78, 113, 142, 180
policy, viii, 4, 14, 15, 16, 19, 20, 26, 29, 31, 32, 39, 41, 46, 50, 53, 54, 55, 57, 66, 67, 68, 71, 75, 77, 78, 82, 89, 90, 91, 92, 96, 103, 105, 112, 116, 119, 125, 127, 131, 136, 145, 150, 153, 154, 159, 169, 170, 177, 203
policy variables, viii, 16, 50, 53, 54, 55, 75, 77, 78, 119, 136, 145, 150, 153, 154, 159, 169, 177
pollution, 205
population policy announced in 2013, 56, 78, 127, 136
population size, viii, 5, 20, 33, 45, 46, 55, 78, 83, 97, 113, 154, 180, 181, 186, 189, 191, 193
portfolio, 32, 96, 128
probability, 19, 21, 24, 25, 27, 33, 36, 37, 39, 41, 83, 87, 90, 92, 97, 100, 102, 104, 105, 155, 156, 161, 181, 189
production function, 4, 15, 46, 47, 58, 68, 115, 130, 142, 155, 172, 182, 194, 195
profit, 34, 70, 84
proposition, 186, 188
public pension system for rural residents, viii, 111, 112, 113, 124, 125, 127, 128, 135, 141, 142, 153
publishing, 3, 81

R

rate of return, viii, 58, 61, 66, 69, 70, 73, 77, 172
real assets, 4, 20
reality, 82, 113
recognition, viii
recovery, 29, 92
redistribution, 169
reform, vii, 4, 16, 29, 31, 32, 42, 46, 82, 96, 101, 113, 169, 170, 171, 176, 177, 205, 206, 207
reform and opening door policy, 4, 16, 29, 31, 32, 42, 46
regulations, vii, 15, 27, 40, 90, 104
replacement rate, viii, 81, 82, 84, 86, 87, 89, 90, 91, 92, 95, 96, 98, 99, 100, 101, 102, 104, 105, 106, 113, 208

researchers, viii
resources, 125, 205
retirement age, 113
returns to scale, 130
revenue, viii, 4, 20, 180
risk, 124, 136
root, 115, 130, 158
rural areas, viii, 24, 36, 87, 101, 112, 124, 128, 150, 154, 155
rural population, 112, 125, 165
rural poverty, 112, 128, 155

S

security, 4, 20, 32, 42, 46, 47, 68, 82, 96, 113, 128, 142, 180, 181, 186, 206, 207, 208
sensitivity, 55
signs, 27, 40, 123
simulation(s), 12, 13, 14, 75, 104, 105, 121, 123, 142, 150, 156, 161
smoothing, 74
social development, 78, 155
social pool benefit replacement rate, 81, 82, 84, 86, 87, 89, 90, 91, 92, 95, 96, 98, 99, 100, 101, 102, 104, 105, 106
social pool benefits, 3, 4, 9, 10, 11, 12, 13, 14, 15, 16, 21, 31, 33, 35, 36, 37, 38, 41, 42, 47, 48, 59, 62, 69, 70, 74, 81, 83, 85, 86, 87, 88, 89, 91, 92, 95, 97, 101, 102, 104, 105, 171, 174, 179, 180, 182, 183, 185, 189
social resources, 4, 20, 32, 82, 96
social security, 4, 20, 32, 46, 68, 82, 96, 112, 128, 142, 156, 180, 205, 206, 207, 208
social welfare, 4, 14, 15, 16, 20, 26, 27, 32, 38, 39, 40, 82, 89, 90, 96, 103, 104, 169, 170, 171, 176, 177, 196, 207
society, 165, 180
solution, 32, 58, 66, 69, 77, 182, 193
specifications, 46, 113, 142
stability, 7, 8, 23, 35, 42, 85, 93, 99, 106, 107, 112, 116, 117, 118, 119, 120, 131, 132, 173, 175
state, ix, 7, 8, 13, 14, 17, 23, 27, 32, 35, 37, 39, 42, 85, 86, 90, 93, 99, 100, 101, 103, 106, 113, 116, 117, 128, 131, 132, 133, 170, 173, 175
State Council, vii, 3, 4, 15, 19, 24, 27, 31, 36, 53, 64, 68, 75, 81, 111, 112, 113, 121, 128, 150, 155, 162, 170, 179, 205, 206
State Council Document 38 of 2005, 3, 15, 27, 31, 36
state-owned enterprises, 170
statistics, 12, 24
stock, 7, 22, 35, 50, 59, 60, 70, 71, 85, 99, 112, 113, 116, 131, 145, 159, 173, 175, 182, 183, 205

structure, 111, 125, 127, 136
style, 208
subsidy, 111, 112, 113, 118, 122, 123, 124, 125, 127, 128, 135, 136, 141, 142, 148, 149, 150, 151, 152, 153, 154, 155, 156, 162, 163, 165
subsistence, 189
survival, 24, 25, 27, 36, 37, 39, 40, 41, 83, 87, 88, 90, 92, 100, 102, 104, 105, 161
sustainability, 113
sustainable development, 124, 136
sustainable economic growth, 29, 45, 46, 55, 68, 78, 92, 127
system without public pension, 191, 192, 193, 201, 202

T

target, 81, 82, 90, 92, 96, 104, 106
tax base, 180
taxation, viii, 5, 20, 47, 121, 142, 208
taxes, 4, 20, 46, 47, 82, 96, 113, 174, 205
technological progress, 4, 12, 121
technology, 46
twins, 206
two-sided altruism, 96, 179, 180, 181, 189, 191, 192, 202, 205

U

UN, 36, 37, 40, 100, 102, 207
uncertain lifetime, viii, 19, 32, 81, 82, 91, 95, 96, 105, 128, 155, 164
undercapitalized, 169, 170, 171
urban, vii, viii, 3, 4, 12, 15, 19, 20, 24, 25, 28, 31, 32, 38, 41, 45, 46, 47, 55, 57, 64, 65, 67, 68, 77, 81, 82, 87, 88, 91, 95, 96, 102, 105, 111, 112, 113, 128, 142, 155, 170, 179
urban areas, 32, 82

urban population, 15, 25, 38, 88, 102
Urban public pension, 3, 19, 45, 57, 67, 81, 95, 169, 179, 208
urbanization, 32, 82

V

value added tax, viii, 179, 180, 182, 189
variables, 12, 14, 15, 16, 24, 25, 27, 31, 36, 37, 38, 39, 50, 54, 55, 58, 62, 64, 65, 69, 73, 75, 77, 78, 86, 88, 90, 91, 92, 95, 100, 101, 103, 113, 121, 123, 124, 135, 145, 150, 152, 153, 154, 159, 161, 162, 164, 165, 179, 184, 197
VAT, vi, 179, 180, 182, 185, 186, 187, 188, 189
VAT tax rate, 179, 180, 185, 186, 189
village subsidy rate, 111, 113, 118, 122, 123, 124, 125, 127, 128, 135, 136, 141, 142, 148, 149, 150, 151, 152, 153, 154, 155, 156, 162, 163, 165

W

wage rate, 183, 194
wage tax, 4, 20, 47, 169, 170, 171, 172, 173, 174, 175, 176, 177, 179, 180, 181, 182, 185, 186, 189
wage tax rate, 173, 176, 179, 180, 182, 185, 186, 189
Washington, 207
wealth, 32, 127, 128, 141, 165, 192, 205
welfare, 4, 14, 15, 16, 20, 26, 27, 32, 38, 39, 40, 47, 68, 82, 89, 90, 96, 103, 104, 169, 170, 171, 176, 177, 196, 207
workers, 7, 16, 42, 55, 106, 135, 169, 170, 183

Y

yield, 25, 88, 192, 201